DOGFIGHT!

I levelled off at 19,000 feet and scanned the sky around me in search of enemy planes. My heart skipped a beat when I saw that Phil Leeds had been unable to cling to my tail through the tortuous turns of the last minute or two.

At just that moment, Phil passed me. A Zero was on his tail, pumping .30 caliber bullets into his Corsair.

I pulled a very tight turn to the right to join the parade. At the same time, I two-blocked the throttle—pushed it to the firewall and then eased back to keep my engine from burning out—and immediately squeezed off a trailing burst. I had little hope of hitting the Zero, but I wanted to shake the enemy pilot's concentration.

The Japanese pilot saw my tracer just as I was able to pull my bullets in to strike his tail. Chunks of metal were streaming off the Zero's tail when the Japanese pilot used his best evasion tactic...

ACE!

A Marine Night-Fighter Pilot in World War II

COLONEL R. BRUCE PORTER
WITH ERIC HAMMEL

Introduction by "Pappy" Boyington

J

JOVE BOOKS, NEW YORK

This Jove book contains the complete
text of the original hardcover edition.

ACE! A MARINE NIGHT-FIGHTER PILOT IN WORLD WAR II

A Jove Book / published by arrangement with
the authors

PRINTING HISTORY
Pacifica Press edition published 1985
Jove edition / September 1987

ISBN: 0-515-09159-6

Jove Books are published by The Berkley Publishing Group,
200 Madison Avenue, New York, New York 10016.
The name "JOVE" and the "J" logo
are trademarks belonging to Jove Publications, Inc.

For My Family—
Pat and Wendy,
Patrick, Christopher, and Amy

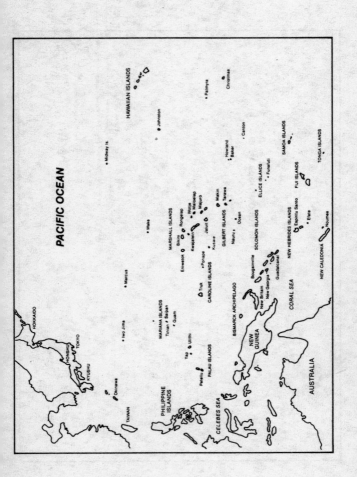

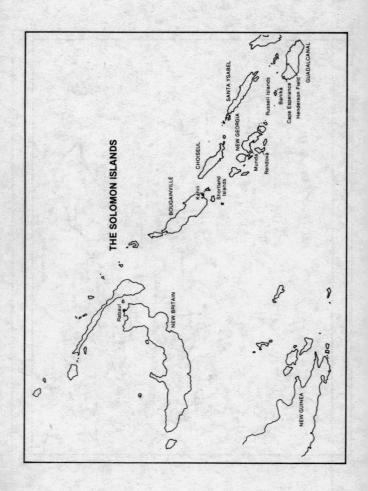

THE SOLOMON ISLANDS

BOUGAINVILLE

Kahili

Shortland
Islands

CHOISEUL

SANTA YSABEL

NEW GEORGIA

Munda

Rendova

Russell Islands

Banika

Cape Esperance

Henderson Field

GUADALCANAL

Rabaul

NEW BRITAIN

NEW GUINEA

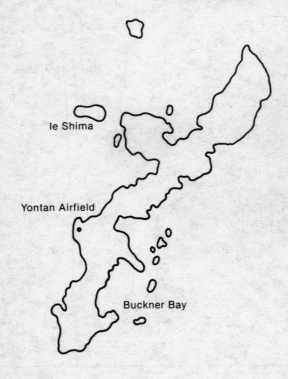

OKINAWA

Ie Shima

Yontan Airfield

Buckner Bay

INTRODUCTION

I first met Bruce Porter at the airbase at Turtle Bay, in the New Hebrides, in very early June, 1943. I and my fighter squadron had just returned from a pretty wild leave in Sydney, Australia. A few days after I met Bruce, I was called on the carpet and relieved of my command by a superior officer who did not approve of some of the ways I and my pilots had chosen to unwind.

Immediately following my relief and transfer to a staff job—that very afternoon—I ran into Bruce Porter, who was with two young lieutenants from my former command, Marine Fighting Squadron 122. The three pilots were leaving the base skeet range, where they had been honing their hand-eye gunnery skills. As I was stalking past the skeet range looking for a way to vent my fury and frustration at the unfair turn my life had taken, I literally collided with the three of them.

I needed to tell my tale of woe to someone, so I joined up with then-Captain Porter and the two lieutenants, who had served with Bruce in Samoa earlier in the war. They were on their way to the Officers' Club to kill the rest of the afternoon, and I was invited to tag along. I realized that I outranked all of them and could have had them listen to my entire life story if I chose to, but I saw that the three pilots were intently interested in my story. When I had said all that was on my mind, they gave me encouragement.

At length, Bruce offered to drive me over to the quarters of my old flying comrade, Brigadier General James "Nuts" Moore. He and his companions had made me believe that the general would get me out of the jam I was in.

Bruce was right: I *was* given back my squadron. But my celebration later that evening got a little out of hand and I broke my leg. My squadron returned to combat without me.

When I returned to Turtle Bay from the hospital in New Zealand, I was given command of what was to become the infamous Black Sheep Squadron. When I put in an immediate request to have Bruce and the two lieutenants transferred to my command, I was stunned to learn that both lieutenants had been killed and that Bruce had been shipped back to the United States at the conclusion of nearly 20 months' duty in the war zone.

I did not see Bruce Porter again until after the war. I was shot down late in my combat tour, and I spent the rest of Pacific War as a Prisoner of War. I did run into Bruce at various times after the war. I never forgot the kindness he afforded me on the afternoon we first met. I am happy to report that we have been neighbors, golfing partners, and friends for many years.

★

Bruce Porter's wartime experiences in many, many ways echo the Pacific War experiences of so many Marine combat fighter pilots. Like Bruce, most of us were trained as naval aviation cadets, nearly all of us flew Corsair fighters, and most of us faced first combat in the Solomon Islands. That alone makes Bruce's story worth telling. His story is our story.

Of considerable added interest is the story of Bruce Porter's transition to night fighters. I do not think the Marine Corps placed as many as two hundred of its 10,000 wartime pilots in night combat in World War II. Bruce is unique among that tiny fraternity in several regards: he commanded one of the few night-fighter squadrons to see combat, he is the only night-fighter squadron commander to score multiple kills on a single mission, and one of only six Marines to accomplish that feat.

To date, there has been very little written about night-fighter pilots during World War II. They made a valuable contribution to our aviation arsenal, which was developed to its fullest in the latter stages of the war.

I highly recommend Bruce Porter's story to you. It tells of training, flying, and fighting the way I remember it.

Pappy Boyington

Gregory ("Pappy") Boyington
Colonel
U.S. Marine Corps (Ret)

PART I

Wings of Gold

1

My flying career began on a rainy Southern California Saturday morning in December, 1939.

I was nineteen years old and a member of the University of Southern California Class of 1942. I had only a vague idea of what I wanted to do with my life; perhaps I would become an engineer, like my father, or a lawyer. The world was wide open to me, and the future seemed bright, for all its haziness.

Roy Margrave, who had been my closest friend during our years at Los Angeles High School, called me that morning at the Sigma Alpha Epsilon Fraternity House and asked if I was doing anything special. Roy was attending Santa Monica Junior College, so I had not seen him for a while.

"No, I'm just sitting around."

"Well, it sure is a miserable day, Bruce. How about a movie? There's a good one at the Forum; Robert Taylor in *Flight Command*."

Airplanes had never particularly fascinated me, though I had built my share of models during my teen years. I could not have cared less about a movie about planes, but it was, as Roy said, a miserable day, and I wanted to spend some time with my friend. I agreed to meet him at the Forum to see the matinee.

The movie, which was about United States Navy pilots flying the modern F3F fighter plane from aircraft carriers, held me in a firm grip from the first reel to the last. I could not then say what was happening, but I knew that something was overtaking me. I knew I wanted to do in real life what those actors were doing in the movie. I began having daydreams about flying right there in the Forum Theater.

Roy was even more taken with the notion of becoming a pilot. Once the movie ended, he would talk of nothing else. I suppose if I had thought about it, I would have realized that he had given it a lot of thought before that Saturday. Only after the movie had ended did I realize that *Flight Command* was his first choice in a city filled with movie theaters. Perhaps Roy's enthusiasm affected me a little, but I was also enthusiastic in my own right. The thrill of seeing the movie touched something deep within me that had never been touched before.

Neither of us knew how to fulfill that sudden onset of purpose, so we went our separate ways that evening and fell back into our long-established routine of attending classes and studying. Despite the grind, however, I was vaguely aware from time to time that something had changed. Whenever I had a spare moment to myself, I thought of flying. And whenever I spoke with Roy, the subject of flying came up.

By odd coincidence, the fraternity hosted a pair of Navy ensigns in January, 1940, about a month after Roy and I had seen *Flight Command*. The two young men were assigned to the Navy recruiting station in Los Angeles, and they were routinely visiting all the college campuses in the area to recruit officer candidates for the Naval Aviation Cadet Program. When I heard the news, I called Roy, who agreed to attend the luncheon at which the two naval officers would be speaking.

The two ensigns delivered the usual pitch about career opportunities and seeing the world, and then both flatly stated that they had joined the Navy right out of college so that they could get in on the ground floor of the action that was heating up in Europe. Both ensigns were wearing Wings of Gold on the left breasts of their tunics—the insignia of the naval aviator. As soon as the formalities had run their course, Roy and I cornered one of the fliers and asked him detailed questions about the aviation cadet program. I knew that he was only a few years older than Roy and I, but he seemed so much more wordly-wise. I was impressed with his self-confidence, and I projected my own personality forward to a time when I might be like him. I was impressed with the uniform and, more than anything, with the level of excellence represented by those gleaming Wings of Gold.

One of the inducements the Navy was offering was of particular interest. In exchange for signing up for four years' service in the U.S. Navy Reserve, I would be receiving a bonus of $500 per year, payable on separation from active duty. As was the case with many young men of my generation, attending college posed a severe financial burden on my family. My father was an engineer, and he had made a good, steady income through most of the Great Depression, but the $2,000 I would accumulate from my years in the service would go a long way toward paying for the second half of my college education. Besides, I would be receiving a good base salary and, if I passed flight training, a flight allotment as well. It seemed like a good financial deal all the way around.

During the talk, the two pilots had referred to the pilots' elimination program, a sort of preliminary flight school at which the Navy and prospective pilots could look one another over. I had no idea whether I had any aptitude for flying; I was simply dazzled with the notion of commanding a fighter airplane. The elimination course seemed the way to go, for I would have an opportunity to fly an airplane and, if I got that far, to do so on my own, to solo. The nearest "E" base was just down the road, in Long Beach, and that was where Roy and I would have to go to sign up for the Naval Aviation Cadet Program.

★

The very next Saturday, Roy and I drove to Long Beach in his father's car and asked our way to the Navy recruiting office. I was impressed by the recruiting poster right outside the door of our destination: "Cadets for Naval Aviation. Take that something extra, and you got it. Apply nearest U.S. Navy Recruiting Station."

Roy and I crossed the threshold. There, an old Navy chief—the first of the breed I had ever encountered—asked us some questions about our health and academic standings, then oversaw the completion of lengthy forms and a contract with the United States Navy. He told us that we would be called back for a thorough physical in a few weeks and, if we passed that, to E-base training in a few months.

I felt wonderful, like I had somehow taken control of my life and given it direction. I knew I had nothing to lose (the thought of dying in a training accident never remotely occurred to me) and that at the least I would come away with a powerful sense of adventure.

As Roy and I stepped out of the recruiting office, I happened to see another sign, which read, "Join Marine Aviation." Beneath the headline was a photo of the same F3F fighter plane that had captivated me when I had seen *The Hell Divers*. Wow, I thought, that's what I want to fly! I looked at Roy, and Roy looked at me. Had we made a mistake? Had we joined the wrong service?

"Damn it," I muttered, "I didn't know the Marines had airplanes!" Until the notion of flying had entered my head, I had always thought of becoming a Marine infantry officer if the United States was drawn into a war.

Just then, a dashing Marine captain dressed in a blue tunic crossed by a leather Sam Browne belt and shod in high leather boots stuck his head through the doorway and said, "Hey, boys, come on in. I want to talk to you."

We followed him into the tiny office, which was filled with a desk and two side chairs. "Are you interested in getting away to Florida for a few months? Would you like to be aviators?"

I saw then that the captain was wearing Wings of Gold on the left breast of his exquisitely tailored high-collared blue tunic.

"Um, er, uh," I sputtered.

"We, uh, just signed up with the Navy," Roy admitted.

"Is that right?" the captain thundered.

Without another look at his two red-faced guests, the Marine turned in his chair and knocked on the thin wall partition behind his back. The chief petty officer Roy and I had been talking to only minutes before slid open the window panel. "Yes, Sir?"

"Chief, give me the papers you have on these two." Back to us, "What're your names?"

"Porter."

"Margrave."

"Right, Chief, give me the papers on Porter and Margrave."

"Aye, aye, Sir." And he handed over all the papers, including our contracts.

The captain slid the frosted window closed, turned back to his desk, and tore the whole pile of papers right down the middle. As he dumped them into a wastebasket beneath the desk with one hand, he pulled another stack of forms from a drawer with the other and placed half in front of me and half in front of Roy. Then he looked us both straight in the eyes and said in his booming voice, "Boys, you look like Marine material to me."

He then explained that the Marine Corps program was identical to and interchangeable with the Navy's, except that all Marine aviators received advanced training as fighter pilots and would eventually have to qualify for aircraft carriers. If we were accepted, and if we passed the elimination program, we would be sent to Florida, where we and other Marine cadets would be trained right alongside young men bound for the Navy; other than the end stages of training, our course would be identical to the one for which we had signed up next door. "The difference," the captain told us, "Is that you'll be Marines." He said it with such an air of confidence and superiority that I never doubted my decision to go for it. By the time I left that cramped office, I *felt* like a Marine!

★

The rigorous physical did not faze me in the least. I was in top condition from having been on my high school and college swim and water polo teams for years. My grades were good, too, so there was no worry about not qualifying from that standpoint. By the time I would receive my orders for elimination training that summer, I would have completed the required two years of college.

My final semester at USC went by in a whirlwind of mixed emotions. I was not sure when I would have to report for elimination training, but I knew that I would have time to complete the year and that I stood a good chance of missing the first weeks of my junior year in the event I was indeed eliminated. As a special hedge against failure, I put even more work than usual into keeping my grades high.

But the thought of flying had captivated me. It was all I really cared about, all I really talked about. By the time I passed my physical, I had learned a great deal about the program from fellow students who had looked into it and signed up. I was even surprised to learn that Lee Sparrow, a friend who had graduated from Los Angeles High School a few years before me, had already passed E-base at Alameda, California, and was then a Marine cadet attending flight school in Corpus Christi, Texas. I wrote to Chirp, as we called him, and received an effusive response welcoming me to the club.

School ended with neither Roy nor I having received our orders. In fact, neither of us heard a word from the Marine Corps about anything. We knew that the program was growing but still limited because the facilities could accommodate relatively few new bodies at a time, but we continually fretted, for the war in Europe was spreading, and it seemed increasingly probable that the United States would become involved. There was no way to release all the excitement that was building up. By the time my twentieth birthday rolled around in mid August, our circle of friends had shrunk to the two of us; by then we had nothing to say to any of the lesser beings with whom we had associated until that spring of far horizons.

Our orders arrived in mid July. We were to report to Long Beach on September 16 for elimination training.

The final two months of waiting nearly killed us, for there was nothing worth starting except some summer romances, and even those seemed to be of questionable value. Roy and I just hung around managing our egos and overlooking our inner fears. By then, however, neither of us doubted that we would get all the way through the rigorous training and earn our Wings of Gold.

2

Right at the outset, Elimination Base expanded my world view, for I met young men from all over the country—from the endless plains of the Midwest, the smoky factory cities of the Northeast, high in the majestic Rockies, the arid Southwest, and the foggy Pacific Northwest. I had never been outside Utah, where I was born and lived for my first six years, or California, where I was raised, or Nevada, where I worked my teen summers for some of my father's engineer cronies. I had acquired a sense of America, but I had never confronted its staggering variety until those September and October weeks in 1940.

We all had two things in common: We were all in topnotch physical condition, and we all wanted to become naval aviators. I detected other traits that we shared as well—a sense of adventure and a belief that war was just over the horizon.

But I also thrilled to our differences. That elimination class was filled with nearly every type of American, at least every type that could send its sons to college. I rubbed elbows with the sons of wealthy bankers and brokers, doctors, college professors, school teachers, and attorneys, and miners' sons, and ranchers' sons, and the scions of merchant families great and small. Most of us had Anglo-Saxon surnames, and there was a sprinkling of Hispanics, mainly from old California families; a fair percentage were from families that had come from all over Europe; some had even been born overseas. We had among us Jews and Catholics and members of nearly every Protestant denomination as well as doubters and unbelievers. What we did not have was non-Caucasians, not in the America of 1940. I was among the youngest of the hopefuls; most of my classmates were up to five years older and had already earned their degrees. Some had even tasted the rigors and pleasures of the business or professional worlds.

We all knew why we were there and, for those who forgot, it was hammered in time and again: the Navy wanted to know if we had the right stuff to become military aviators. If we did, we would pass through E-base and be discharged to await orders to flight school at Corpus Christi, Texas, or Pensacola or Jacksonville, Florida, where further trials and tests awaited us. If we did not, we would be handed our papers and just sent home, our hopes of wearing Wings of Gold shattered forever. The objective of ground school and early flight training at Long Beach was to move us to the ultimate moment of truth, the solo. If we mastered that to our instructor's satisfaction, we would be able to travel to Florida. The future even at that point was fairly bleak, we were told, for the Navy and Marine Corps were acquiring far more cadets than they could easily absorb. Most cadets, we were told, washed out of flight school—or died in training accidents. No one ever talked about the inevitable possibility of our common purpose, which was fighting America's enemies: death in battle. All we talked about was the glory and challenge of it all.

★

The first thing they had to do at E-base was instill military attitudes, to provide us with a nodding acquaintance with the arcane ways of the United States Naval Service. Since the Marine candidates were all nominal privates and the Navy people were seaman recruits (we all made private first class or seaman apprentice on the second day), the first thing they taught us was to salute any officer we encountered outdoors—but not indoors, and never without a hat—or "cover" as the Marines called it—on our heads. We learned that "having a duty" meant "working" and that even on land a "bulkhead" is a "wall," a "deck" is a "floor," an "overhead" is a "ceiling," a "hatchway" is a "door," and, most important, a "head" is a "rest room." We also learned how to clean, which is to say scrub, all those things "the Navy way."

On duty or off, whenever we could, we gaped at all the service-type airplanes in the base hangars, and we all constantly wondered aloud and to ourselves if they were actually going to let us fly them.

Once we had the rudiments of ground school out of the way, we got right into elimination flight training, which has everything to do with flying an airplane. Each of us was assigned to an instructor, usually a Navy ensign or lieutenant junior grade (jay-gee) or a Marine lieutenant with a few years of flying under their belts. I yearned to wear a glamorous uniform like theirs, complete with my own Wings of Gold.

Our trainer was the N3N, a rather small all-fabric biplane universally known as the "Yellow Peril," partly because it was painted a bright yellow (to warn real fliers away, I suppose). This was a *real* airplane, an open-cockpit model in which the student flies in the rear seat and the instructor flies up front. It was always cold in those Yellow Perils, for there was only a windscreen to ward off the chilly air one finds at altitude. We bulked up for each flight in a heavy flight suit, gloves, leather helmet, and goggles. There was nothing to protect us from the sharp, heady smells of gasoline from the engines, carbon from the exhaust stacks, and shellac and dope from the fabric wings and fuselage. The N3N and other trainers of the period were perfectly suited for their work. They were reliable, responsive, and highly forgiving of heavy-handedness. They were actually reputed to be able to fly themselves! The rush of air past the student's ears gave a real sense of flight and started us on the road to being able to fly by the seats of our pants, to *feel* flight. The plane was small and basic; we could immediately see and feel the results of our various pressures on the throttle, joystick, rudder pedals, and trim tab, and that allowed us to correct ourselves and modify our sense of feel to the point where even we could see that the act of flying might one day be automatic, a natural extension of our unconscious minds, much like driving a car had already become for most of us.

The N3N's instrumentation was basic and universal. There were gauges to show manifold pressure, engine heat, and oil pressure—not much more than a familiar automobile dashboard. To monitor direction and attitude, we had a compass and needle-ball indicator. In its way, the last is the most important. A needle-gauge going back and forth showed the attitude of the plane's wings relative to the ground and a little ball bouncing up and down showed how far up or down its nose was pointing; if the plane was climbing, the ball dropped, and if it was diving, the ball rose relative to a "horizon" line in the center of the gauge. Readings from this instrument combined with those from the airspeed indicator are critical because a climb at too low a speed will lead to a stall, which can be deadly, and because it becomes increasingly difficult to recover from a dive at too fast a speed. "Needle-ball airspeed" is what pilots check most often.

The philosophy of E-base was to discover if a young man had the aptitude and coordination required to fly a military airplane. If he did not, then the extremely high cost to the Navy of training him at flight school would be sidestepped. *Elimination* base was just that. I had never been in an airplane, much less airborne, before my arrival at Long Beach, so I was initially surprised at the number of candidates who had mastered flying at civilian schools; some came to us with many hundreds of hours in trainer, private, and even commercial airplanes. I was also surprised to see that a fair percentage of these washed out of E-base. (I later understood that they had picked up bad habits and could not be trained to fly "the Navy way.")

My first time at the controls of the N3N was a nightmare of jerky, uncoordinated movements, overcorrections, needless exertions and red-faced certainty that I did not, in fact, have the right stuff. The instructor calmly got me—and himself—out of trouble and never uttered a sound of dismay. Until we were safely on the ground. Then he looked at me—a wet rag, sweating fear and embarrassment into my bulky flight suit—and said just the thing to make my day: "Porter, you will *never* solo. You are the *dumbest* cadet I have ever laid eyes on." Each word was a body blow to my hard-earned reputation for being a natural athlete, a death knell for my dream of soaring off to a heroic future on Wings of Gold.

It never dawned on me—would not dawn on me for years—that my performance that first time at the controls was well within the norms for utter novices like me and that the instructor's words were part of a prescription aimed at seeing how another in a long line of All-American golden boys would react to earned criticism. All I knew was that I was halfway to having to return home in disgrace. As much as I thought I had been paying attention up to that point, it was nothing compared with how I strained from then on to comprehend every nuance of every command that was hurled my way.

Each new day and each hour at the controls demonstrated that I indeed had some promise. I began to acquire a feel for flying, though I was not remotely a "natural." Each advance took hard work and hard thinking. I got better at it, and my instructor let me know how pleased he was becoming by increasingly speaking his encouragement through the gosport, the flexible rubber tube that connected the instructor's mouthpiece with the special helmet we cadets wore in flight. This was our only means of communication over the unmuffled sound of the noisy radial engine.

The ultimate expression of my instructor's pleasure came just after we landed one day in the middle of the second week of October, when I had completed all of about ten hours of flight instruction. I had taxied to the dispersal area and was about to shut down when the instructor climbed onto the wing from his cockpit, motioned a thumb's-up, and leaned over to shout in my ear, "Porter, you're on your own. Take 'er up yourself." He patted me on the shoulder, jumped to the ground, and simply walked away.

★

The morning was made for soaring like an eagle. It was crisp and cool even on the ground, and the sky was a huge, clear canopy of blue with only a border of lacy blue clouds over the wide Pacific horizon.

My thoughts went immediately to my stomach, which was doing heaving flip-flops beneath my flight suit; I could almost see it jumping around down there. I had known that this moment might come—had dreamed about it for weeks—but I was unprepared for the suddenness of the challenge. I had not realized until that moment how much I had come to rely on just seeing the top of my instructor's leather-helmeted head in the front cockpit, on hearing his pointers and words of encouragement, on knowing that his steady hands were hovering just above his own set of controls, and on the subtle pressures I was sure he exerted to keep me from killing us both.

I found myself whispering the familiar litanies that had been poured into my head since I had first taken to the air; I conjured up my instructor's calm voice as he ran me through each new checklist on the way to acquiring each new skill.

I held the stick loosely in my right hand and reached over to the throttle lever with my left. My feet were firmly on the brakes as I sneaked a peek at the trim tab to see if it was still there. All the gauges indicated that I was ready for flight, so I moved my feet from the brakes to the rudder pedals and finally got around to advancing the throttle to the correct setting for taxiing. Then I concentrated on directing the suddenly huge Yellow Peril to the end of the runway. My vision narrowed to that line of concrete and beyond, to Signal Hill and its cluster of oil wells, which would provide me with a suitable aiming point — for the N3N, like all Navy single-engine airplanes, taxied nose-high because of its low tail-wheel.

Slowly—too slowly at first—I advanced the throttle toward full power and tentatively lifted my feet from the brakes. The yellow two-seater surged forward. I was committed to flight or an ignoble abort, which was really out of the question. As I gathered speed, I directed my feet as I had been taught, to lightly tap first one and then the other rudder pedal, which nudged me from left to right in an approximation of a straight-line take-off. As I gathered yet more speed, the tiny voice inside my head and a by-then-familiar feeling in my belly directed me to pull the joystick steadily but smartly toward the pit of my stomach.

I suddenly had the never to be forgotten, always thrilling sense of being airborne, committed to flight or death at my own hand. I kept my attention rooted on the rapidly approaching oil wells and saw that I would clear them with ease.

I was soaring!

I was a bundle of super-activated senses, aware only of the endless sky above, the singing of the struts holding the top wing to the bottom, the rush of cold air past my ears, and the salty tang of the sea in my nostrils.

I tooled around over the ocean and the Long Beach area for fifteen or twenty minutes, alone with my thoughts and feelings, but ever mindful of my tyro status as a pilot. I tried a few simple maneuvers but did not feel inclined to test myself or the airplane. I was content with the mixed feelings of accomplishment and ever-present danger that had become my flying companion and sanity test. I lazily circled this way and that, rolled on my side to see what there was to see, then recovered and executed a gentle dive and then a gentle climb and then a few lazy-eights.

The empty sky was mine and I intentionally lost myself in its vastness and among the siren swells of the singing struts. I might have been shouting, "Whee," so great was the elation.

Then I came back to reality. I was safe in the air as long as my engine functioned and I did not run out of fuel or try to reach any limits of talent or training. But I had to land the biplane for the first time without my instructor being on hand to correct me if I came in too steeply or simply panicked. There is something about novices and landings that can spell doom.

My first task was finding the base, for I had been paying absolutely no attention to my whereabouts.

I saw that I was over the ocean and that nothing but more of the same was ahead, so I swung wide to the left—the normal direction of flight for approaching an airfield—and peered at the shoreline and hills beyond to see if I could detect any familiar sights. I had no sense of being lost, but I did not know where I was either.

It was time to monitor my instruments. I glanced at my wristwatch to see how long I had been aloft, which is a good rule-of-thumb method for gauging fuel consumption. Then I scanned the instruments to see how the airplane was doing. There was still plenty of fuel and the engine was okay. My needle-ball and airspeed indicators told me I was flying straight at a normal speed of 87 knots.

I was struck then by how calmly I was reacting. The thrill was still there, but I had the sense of being in control. It was a fragile sense, I knew, but it was definitely there. If the Marine Corps was looking for solid, confident aviation cadets, I felt they had one in me. All I had to do was find the runway and survive the upcoming landing. Then I could tell them.

As I neared the coast, I was able to pick out familiar landmarks and thus reorient myself. I found Signal Hill, with its oil wells, and saw the runway right behind it. Another Yellow Peril was in the traffic pattern, and I had to wait for him to land before beginning my approach. The other airplane's wobbly landing convinced me that it was also being flown by a novice on his first solo. His safe arrival on the ground renewed my flagging confidence as I lined myself up on the runway, which looked narrower and shorter than I remembered.

At first, I floated a little, not quite getting the wheels on the runway, then I cut my throttle back a hair too much or too soon and bounced the sturdy N3N on the hard surface. My instincts took over at that point, which is the best way to land, and I instantly found the groove. My feet alternated between tapping the brakes and the rudder pedals; and I kept the nose pointed straight down the runway as the N3N lost momentum. By the time I realized I was safely down, it was time to pull off onto the taxiway and roll into the dispersal area, where I cut my engine.

My instructor came out of the dispersal hut as my feet touched Mother Earth. I tried to stiffen my buckling knees as he held out his hand and boomed, "Congratulations, Porter! You got an 'up!' " I would be going to flight school in Florida.

3

Roy Margrave also received an "up" that day, following his solo, so we prepared to return home.

The next day, October 12, after receiving our discharge papers (so the Marine Corps would not have to pay us while we sat at home awaiting orders to flight school), we cleared out of the old boarding house in which we had been billeted, piled our belongings into my 1932 blue Ford coupe and drove north to Los Angeles over the broad boulevards that then served as the primary arteries around and through the Los Angeles basin. Naturally, all the conversation had to do with airplanes, flying, and traveling to Florida to attend flight school. We were extremely happy and proud young men.

The next three months were nearly as painful for Roy and me as the summer months had been. We just sat and waited for our orders. Though we knew that our names were moving up on the list of candidates as new classes were formed, we could not understand why it was taking so long, nor could we stand being away from the recently acquired thrill of flying. When we heard in late November that one of our E-base classmates had been called up, we phoned Captain Hugh Brewster, the officer who had stolen us from the Navy, and asked him to see if our names had been inadvertently dropped from the list; we just knew they had. He told us to sit tight; no one seemed to know who would be called when or why some received orders before others.

Roy came up with a good idea for combatting the intellectual vacuum in which we found ourselves. One boring afternoon, he asked, "Do you know Morse Code, Bruce?"

"I don't know my ass from a hot rock about that." (But I clearly had learned how to speak like a serviceman!)

He explained that he had heard at E-base that the radio telegraphy course at flight school was a killer and that untold numbers of otherwise fit cadets washed out because they could not learn Morse Code at the required pace. "They have a night course at L.A. City College. We ought to go down and sign up. We'll need the advantage."

So we went to school to learn Morse Code and kill time in what we imagined was a productive enterprise. We also had the assurance of beating the system in one small way. I had no other means for employing my brain or my time, so I really applied myself. Eventually, I was able to transcribe a respectable thirty words a minute in code.

★

Roy and I were ordered to report at the Naval Air Station, Pensacola, to begin flight school on February 21. Train tickets arrived from the Navy Department in time for us to leave Los Angeles on February 18, a Tuesday. Aside from the excitement of finally going to flight school, I was filled with the realization that this was to be my first trip outside my home region. My appetite for exploration had been whetted at E-base, where I had met so many different new kinds of Americans, so I was literally aglow at the thought of all the new prospects that lay before me.

The afternoon of our departure was cold, windy, and rainy, just like the Saturday in 1939—only a year before?—on which I had been hooked on the idea of flying. My parents and I climbed into the family's gray 1936 Ford and drove to Union Station, where we met the Margrave family for all the last good-byes. After tears had flowed and embraces had been exchanged all around, Mother silently handed me a little box she had been saving for the last moment; I knew it was filled with a large batch of home-made fudge, my favorite.

I felt lonelier than I had ever felt in my life as I boarded that sleeping car, carrying only the tiny valise my orders had stipulated for the journey. I was homesick the moment the train lurched to a start. The reality of being on my own did not quite measure up to the notions that I had built up over most of the past year of embarking on a great adventure. Nevertheless, one part of my mind was devoted to terror-filled images of a slightly older me returning to Union Station in disgrace after washing out of Pensacola. That was a future I could not bear to imagine.

★

The first part of the trip was over more-or-less familiar terrain, the great desert that began just over the line of hills that hemmed metropolitan Los Angeles against the Pacific. Roy and I had used up our exuberance and left one another alone with his thoughts. I just stared out the window at the passing empty landscape and infrequent small towns, thinking more of the past than of the future as the sun set behind me.

Noon found us approaching Dallas, which had to be on another planet, so different was it from Southern California. The layover between trains was long enough to allow Roy and me to sit down to a meal.

Immediately, my glance fell on a sign, the likes of which I had never seen or believed existed in my America: "No Niggers Allowed." Wow! I was in someone else's nightmare. Roy let his breath out in a great gust and said in my ear, "I don't believe what I'm seeing, Bruce." I felt like I had been slapped across my face.

I had never given race a thought in all my life. I had not known many blacks, but I had always gotten along with them, taken them for granted as fellow athletes and classmates, and had casual social contacts with them for as long as I had lived in California. I know I had heard of segregation in the South, but, until confronted with it in its crudest public form in that Dallas train station, I had never experienced its obnoxious reality.

The farther we hurtled across the South, the worse the fleeting images became. The shanty towns that had grown up beside the train tracks rudely awakened us two California kids to yet newer realities. I did not see many white faces around the many tumbled-down railside shanties all the rest of the way across Texas, Louisiana, Mississippi, Alabama, and Florida. I saw black men riding horses and mules and, in a few places, black women and children walking along railside roads with bare feet despite the blustery winter rains and winds. I saw what might have been poor whites, too, but I was incensed with them, and I dismissed *their* poverty as being somehow less threatening and more genteel than the pockets of black misery that seemed to dominate that green yet bleak landscape. I also saw neat little towns of brick and board, and signs of rural prosperity among the overwhelming sights of poverty that seemed to dominate our journey through the Deep South. Each stop along the way brought new images: segregated restrooms, segregated dining facilities, segregated waiting rooms, segregated water fountains, even segregated railroad cars. The shock of it reverberated through my soul.

It never occurred to either of us to strike up conversations with our fellow passengers. We were the only aviation cadets on the train, so we had no obvious connection with anyone else. But I am sure our reticence stemmed mainly from the shock of seeing segregation at work all around us; I did not particularly want to associate with southern whites, and I was physically afraid to put my best instincts to work and spend time with the blacks on the train.

★

Pensacola provided us with a few new shocks as soon as we alighted from the train. The first and most important was that, despite our expectations, no one met us.

We had no idea where the base was or how we were supposed to get there. I am sure the railroad worker from whom we begged directions was smirking at us and thought we were just another pair of wet-behind-the-ears hopefuls, bound for better lives as officers, gentlemen, and naval aviators or, more likely, soon to be returning home in defeat.

We pooled nearly the last of our cash to pay for a cab to the air station's main gate, where we presented our orders to the Marine sentry. Roy and I were allowed to pass through, but the cab was not. The guard shack seemed to be in the middle of nowhere. It was getting late, and anywhere we might be heading looked too far away to walk to. One of the Marine sentries grunted something about a bus that would be by before dark, then clammed up in the way I eventually learned only Regular Marines can when their space is being polluted by lesser beings, which is to say everyone who is not a Regular Marine or a member of a Regular Marine's immediate family.

The gray-painted Navy bus arrived in due course, and we were driven toward the center of the sprawling complex that would be our new home—or the Waterloo of our dearly held dreams of flight. Typically, we never thought of dying there.

I only dimly perceived it, but I was beginning the process of crossing the threshold between boyhood and manhood.

The Great Adventure had begun.

4

As soon as Roy Margrave and I reported at the Pensacola Naval Air Station Receiving Barracks on February 21, 1941, we were assigned to Class 162-C, a mixed group of 105 Navy and Marine cadets. These were to be my comrades—those of them who were not washed out or killed or injured in training accidents—for the next six months, assuming *I* completed the course.

One of the first things I learned after reporting and meeting some of my classmates was that most of us were college students and graduates from all around the country but that there were also a dozen or so Navy enlisted men who had been selected from the Fleet to receive flight training. While the rest of us would be commissioned in the Navy or Marine Corps upon completion of flight training, the enlisted men would return to the Fleet as Naval Aviation Pilots, NAPs. I also learned that an officer candidate who washed out would be discharged from the service, whereas an NAP cadet would return to the Fleet at his former rate. Most of the NAP cadets had not attended college, but I found them to be among the best and brightest cadets, at least as highly motivated as any of us college types.

After spending the night in my spartan quarters, which I shared with three other cadets, I was roused at 0500—5 *a.m.*—and rushed through a busy day of forgettable meals, collection of clothing and flight gear, several routine lectures, class meetings, and orientations barked at us by the old-line Navy chiefs who would be our overseers during the first phase of our training. The two weeks of orientation and military indoctrination would include zero hours on aeronautical subjects; all we would learn about was the Navy and its arcane ways.

It was on that first full day at Pensacola that we E-base survivors learned that it would be many weeks before we flew again, and perhaps months before we flew alone. It seemed universally incomprehensible that the Navy Department was not yet ready to acknowledge our status as veteran birdmen.

We were also told that aviation cadets arriving at Pensacola as little as a year before had faced a slower-paced fourteen-month course but that we were expected to master everything they had had to master in only six months. We were admonished that first day, and constantly for the remainder of our time at Pensacola, that our nation might be at war someday soon, possibly even before we earned our Wings of Gold. That brutal possibility loomed over us every moment we were there.

★

Calisthenics was and would remain the first order of our daily business throughout our stay at Pensacola. We were all strong young men in peak physical condition, and the Navy aimed to keep us that way—if we did not first contract pneumonia. It was February, and our expectation of balmy weather was not enough to keep the chill bay winds from moaning across the table-flat training base at 0500, the time at which we mustered for our daily workout every morning clad only in shorts and tee-shirts. The cold alone was sufficient incentive for our partaking of vigorous exercise, for to flag or stop meant pure agony as soon as the wind touched our sweat-soaked skin.

Then it was back to our "compartment" (our "room") to shower and change into our starched officer-type uniforms (the room having been put in perfect order before calisthenics) and march in formation to breakfast, where we usually ate a gray, nondescript, and utterly forgettable meal.

Marching in formation is what we did most and, in time, best. First we learned how to march in formation, then we proceeded to march *everywhere* in formation. The formation marching was itself an early and useful form of indoctrination, for it helped break down our individual inclinations and make us part of the herd. This con-

stant breaking down of individual traits was somewhat at odds with
the need to hone the individual, lone-wolf traits we all would later
need as pilots, but that is always the troubling ambiguity of the
service—the constant need for regimentation for the long years of
peace between the wars, and the instant requirement for individual
initiative during the wars all servicemen wait for. Except for a few
cadets who had attended military school, we were all totally unregi-
mented individualists when we arrived, and most of us acceded only
because we knew we would not fly again if we did not kowtow to the
group ethos.

Indoctrination classes those first two weeks included short
courses in seamanship, Navy command procedures, keeping out of
trouble, Navy courts and boards, fundamentals of the Naval Service, and military drill in abundance. We even had classes in handling small boats and small arms (which is not to say "short arms,"
whose care and handling was discussed in mind-numbing, bone-
chilling detail in an hours-long venereal disease lecture). We all
learned a good deal of Navy and Marine Corps history and the role
of Navy and Marine Corps aviation.

As stridant as those old chiefs were in pounding us senseless
with military jargon, that indoctrination course was not designed to
cause anyone to fail, but merely to get us ready for what lay ahead,
and that was plenty of opportunities to fail.

★

The aviation ground school classes—the real beginning of our
technical training—were taught in a striking new building that was
dedicated only two weeks before my class arrived. It was the first of
many tangible signs to us of the Navy's commitment to massively
building its air service. The main course was divided into three
phases—navigation, power-plant structures, and radio code, all of
which would also be taught in ever more detail throughout the
flight-training phase as well as during our weeks of preflight
ground school

Aviation ground school was the basis of flight training. The
Navy had learned in sorrow that men can fly airplanes even if they
do not understand the physics involved, but men cannot fly airplanes *and survive indefinitely* if they do not understand the physics
involved. The same is true for such arcane subjects as celestial navigation, land navigation, overwater navigation, map-reading, com-

munications, and a whole range of other acquired intellectual
skills.

Quoting the 1941 edition of *The Flight Jacket*, my class year-
book:

> In the navigation course the young airman learns to
> arrive swiftly and accurately at a determination of his
> position by means of celestial sights, or by using a plot-
> ting board, or a combination of both, for there are no
> landmarks over the trackless oceans where he will be
> operating and the stars and his instruments are his only
> friends.
>
> In the study of engines and structures he learns how
> to get the best performance out of his engine on the lim-
> ited fuel supply he will carry, how to load his plane to
> give the best handling qualities for the purpose at hand.
> With a knowledge of radio code he possesses a key which
> will allow him to carry out his mission with the fleet.
>
> Along with these there is a course in meteorology
> designed to give a working knowledge of the weather,
> clouds, and their causes, high and low pressure areas,
> and how to read a weather map. Semaphore and blinker
> [communication] complete the comprehensive course.

Only on occasion did any of us stop to think that aviation had
begun in 1903, well within the lifetime of all of our parents and
only seventeen years before I, one of the youngest members of Class
162-C, was born. And, before five years had passed, most of what we
learned in 1941 was rendered obsolete as a practical means of getting from place to place in an airplane.

The six weeks I spent in aviation ground school were among the
most tedious of my life. I was chomping at the notion of getting
airborne again at the controls of a single-engine airplane, and they
were teaching me *theory*!

All of the information that was drummed between my ears was
new to me, every bit of it. However, I had been an academic achiever
for so long—even with the nine-month hiatus since ending classes at
USC in June, 1940—that I had very little trouble applying myself to
all the new disciplines. I did not excel, but I did pass, sometimes
with the help of friends. In fact, I do not think that any of us passed
without the help of our friends. One of the most grueling aspects of
ground school was Morse Code training. Despite the advantage I

gained from having taken a course with Roy Margrave at Los Angeles City College in the autumn, I was hard pressed to get my twelve words per minute up to the minimum level of twenty words per minute required of all flight cadets. I passed, but barely. If I had not taken the course in L.A., I would have washed out for sure. As it was, some fine potential pilots were sent home as a result of the Morse Code requirement before they even had an opportunity to fly again. (The real irony is that I never once used Morse in all my years of flying, nor did I ever use blinker code, which also nearly bilged me. However, several Navy and Marine pilots in my class owe their lives to one or the other of these communications systems.)

★

On base or off, we wore the same uniforms as Navy officers and were indistinguishable from them in all ways, save our insignias of rank, which were small metallic eagles worn in place of a second lieutenant's or ensign's gold bars. Our pay was less than a second lieutenant's or ensign's pay, and we were ranked below second lieutenants and ensigns. In all noninstructional settings, where enlisted instructors ruled supreme, we were ranked below them. For all practical purposes, we were treated like dirt on base. I don't know of any cadet in my class who abused his nominal rank; most of us were far too sheepish at this point to dare to *feel* like officers.

Even for cadets, prewar service was very much a gentlemen's club during off-duty hours, which for us was from Saturday afternoon to Sunday night.

I am certain that those Saturday liberties kept most of us sane. We returned to quarters the moment the last class was dismissed, changed, packed our bags, and headed for the San Carlos Hotel, which had become the cadets' traditional playground. There, over our favorite drinks—Southern Comfort or rum with Coke were favorites that season—and a hearty meal of buffalo steak or fried chicken, we often compared notes with members of classes ahead of ours, trying to dope out the future to set our information-filled minds at ease. Naturally, the only thing we talked about besides women—and there were enough camp followers to keep us happy—was flight school and flying. These were really the only common denominators for a group of young men from so many diverse backgrounds.

One of the great privileges was being able to associate with *real* Navy and Marine aviators who stopped by the San Carlos for drinks or dinner. Most of them were happy to indulge us with tales of flying or good advice. Most were not much older than the cadets, and a few were even younger. They had a leg up on us, but we knew, if war broke out, that we would be flying together in the then-minuscule Marine and Navy air wings. When there was time for us to go to the base Officers' Club, we rubbed elbows with these same pilots and other Navy and Marine officers based in the area. Their acceptance of us, more than anything else, gave me a sense of belonging.

We Marine cadets naturally gravitated to one another over those long weeks of ground school. Roy Margrave remained my closest friend, but I found myself particularly drawn to several others. Jeff Poindexter, a brash, boisterous, hilarious University of Montana first-string football player, had a special way with women that made him an ever-popular companion. Jack Amende, who had been raised in Seattle, was bright and witty, a real comer. I seemed to spend a lot of time with them and several fellow Marines from California, like Phil Crawford, from Pomona, and Stan Tutton, from Stockton.

I had always been a fairly outgoing young man, very much in the manner of college students of the day, but I had never really felt comfortable beyond my basic natural reserve until I began gaining confidence as a full-fledged member of the elite all-male club one joined simply by surviving each new phase of flight school.

I felt that I was growing in many ways. But the real test lay ahead, in the air.

5

After six weeks of mainly tedious ground school activities filling every work hour, Class 162-C was advanced to Squadron-1, the first of three flight-school phases. The first half of each workday would be spent in the air or on flight instruction, and the other half would be spent on continuing classroom training.

After being awakened by reville at 0400, attending morning muster and calisthenics, cleaning our compartments and eating breakfast, my half of the class was picked up at the barracks by "cattle bus," a sort of tractor-trailer with seats, and an uncomfortable one at that. After up to an hour's ride across the sprawling base, I could be dropped off at Saufley or Corry Fields, the two main runways that with many smaller fields composed Pensacola Naval Air Station. There, I would join my flight instructor for a preflight check and, if scheduled, some time aloft. The other half of the class went to school in the morning and flew in the afternoon.

The first ten-hour phase was spent on basic familiarization with the N3N, the same Yellow Peril I had already flown at E-base in Long Beach. The objective was to give the instructor a good opportunity to see if I really had the right stuff. I was also taught the rigidly enforced course rules, for the air was filled with airplanes more or less under the control of young men endowed with widely varying attention spans and levels of talent and skill.

About one-fourth of the cadets who would be washed out of Class

162-C were sent home during the ten-hour pre solo phase. One of them turned out to be Roy Margrave, whom three instructors felt stood a good chance of being killed while in the air. I was given time for only the briefest of farewells before Roy was rushed off the base to return home. Roy soon fulfilled his dream, however. The Army Air Corps snapped him up, and he flew in the upcoming war.

I soloed again as a matter of course and completed a flight so routine that no details remain in my memory.

It was during the first phase of Squadron-1 that Class 162-C suffered its first fatality. I landed at the end of my routine check hop and felt that "something" was not right with the cadets who had already parked their N3Ns. As I joined the group for the usual postflight bull session, I saw that everyone's face was drawn and grim. Then I was told, "So-and-so got it." I barely knew the dead man, but I knew he could have been me or Roy Margrave or any of my new friends. I and every cadet there knew there would be others, and each of us must have wondered at one moment or another that day if he would be one of the departed.

The next milestone was the dreaded twenty-hour check, in which each cadet had to hit a tiny field with a dead engine, a simulated emergency landing that was as real as the real thing.

The third phase of Squadron-1 was devoted to basic aerobatics: the snap roll, the wingover, the cartwheel, the split-S, the falling leaf, the Immelmann, and other stunts.

Early in this third phase of Squadron-1 flight training, which thankfully involved mainly solo flying, I developed a staggering problem with my equilibrium, which manifested itself in gripping stomach pains and nausea. I was so sick each time I landed that I would immediately vomit my breakfast. After three or four such bouts, I owned up and told my flight instructor of the problem and requested permission to visit the flight surgeon. I fully expected one or the other to wash me out of the school, but I knew I needed help.

I never made it to the flight surgeon.

The instructor was more sympathetic than I had imagined he would be. "Just give it another try, Porter. If you're still sick, then you should quit because of the strain you're putting on your nervous system."

I realized that I was facing the end of my dream, and the thought of following Roy Margrave on that long train ride home was more than I could bear. I bore down on my mind and ordered it to get itself straight.

The next time I flew, I went through the full course of gut-wrenching stunts and felt no nausea whatsoever when I landed. The problem was completely resolved for all time.

Once my mind was at rest, my confidence grew prodigiously. The tiny landing fields began looking larger and the figure-eights I flew around pylons looked more and more like figure-eights. My hand grew steadier and my mind grew clearer. In fact, my flying skills advanced more rapidly than my classroom skills. I was one of the class goats who had to study long into the night, usually under the blankets with the aid of a flashlight after lights-out. I would have failed without the extra tutoring offered up by my roommates.

Everything soon began running together. I had my first taste of night flying in Squadron-1. Here, for safety's sake, the Yellow Peril is taken aloft by the instructor, but I was quickly given the controls and expected to find my way around using ground lights and some basic navigational work. The mixed feeling of exhilaration and fear was agonizing, particularly when I had to land. The moment before the airplane's wheels touched the light-edged runway was the longest in my life; we just hung there, uncommitted, until I summoned the courage to feel my way the last foot or two to earth.

The most changeable element of flight training was the moody Gulf weather. We were trained early to keep a weather eye on the sky and to watch the numerous signal masts for the recall flag, which was hoisted as soon as the weather started moving in. At that point, it always seemed to be a game of "every man for himself" as scores of trainers fled before low clouds and rain toward the nearest runway. Thankfully, ingrained discipline forced us to line up and orbit leftward around the runway—and wait our turns—before landing. There is something special, and sinister, about landing an open-cockpit plane with cold rain driving in your face.

After the least talented, most dangerous cadets had been washed out, we did our first formation work, starting with straight-ahead flying in the basic three-plane V element and working slowly up to echelons and cross-overs. The danger here was overanticipation; I didn't know what my fellow goslings were going to do, and they weren't sure about me. Midair crashes were not unheard of, even in the Fleet. I got through the trauma by thinking about the differences between learning to drive a car on an empty street and finally having get somewhere along busy city boulevards. The addition of vertical space, aerodynamics, wind and other flight variables thankfully never occurred to me.

Toward the end of my time at Squadron-1, the air station community was rocked by news of an instructor who was hedgehopping so close to the ground that he took off a local sharecropper's head with his airplane's wing. The local newspapers ran glaring headlines and followed the court-martial proceedings from start to finish. The court came down very hard on the young officer; I heard that he was ejected from the Navy.

Suddenly, we faced the final check flight, a comprehensive ninety-minute hop in which every maneuver learned in Squadron-1 must be executed to the instructor's exacting specifications. Each of us was given time for several preparatory solo hops to hone our skills and smooth out the rough spots the instructor obligingly identified.

I and most of my classmates received "ups" and were advanced to Squadron-2, where we would begin checking out on more advanced trainers and the heavier service-type airplanes actually being flown in the Fleet. I celebrated my advancement by purchasing a spiffy, brand-new, cherry-red Ford convertible. It did wonders for my social standing.

★

After familiarizing ourselves with the new, heavier aircraft we would be flying in Squadron-2, we went to work on perfecting our formation flying. "Perfect" is the word. All the Navy pilots I had met to that time, no matter if they were flying single-or multi-engine aircraft, prided themselves in being able to fly in *perfect* formations. Teamwork was the core of Navy flying; it made all the difference between life and death.

Formation work, which is how a great portion of active military flying is done, dominated our efforts in Squadron-2. As we gained confidence in ourselves and one another, we were able to edge closer and closer to one another, to obey hand-signals from the flight leader, and to execute group maneuvers with increasing skill.

Our primary Squadron-2 trainer was the SNJ, which the Air Corps also used under the designation AT6. We also used the OS2U, a real operational fleet scout plane that usually flew off battleships and cruisers. For our purposes, the OS2U's standard pontoons had been replaced with wheels.

The first lasting lesson we learned in Squadron-2 is that the varying designs of airplanes affect both their ground-and air-handling characteristics; well-briefed, well-practiced pilots familiar with their airplanes fly better and live longer.

The only single-engine airplanes the Navy would purchase were tail-wheel models with tail-hooks, which can be landed on aircraft carriers. All tail-wheel airplanes taxi nose-high. The only time a pilot can see well straight ahead while on the ground in such an airplane is during the final moments before takeoff, when the tail wheel lifts and the fuselage is more or less parallel with the ground. As I had learned at E-base and throughout Squadron-1, about the best a taxiing pilot can do is approximate a straight line down the runway by tapping the rudder pedals with his feet. Since the torque of the more powerful aircraft engines we encountered in Squadron-2 had a pronounced tendency to pull the airplane to the left, we all had to refine the instincts we had honed in the flimsier, less powerful N3N.

The more powerful airplanes also had vastly different air-handling capabilities and required greater strength, stamina, and coordination to fly than the Yellow Perils. Stick pressure is needed to guide the airplane up and down and side to side and to keep it level. Since the required pressure for the desired maneuver is a factor of speed, which is a factor of engine power, too much or too little pressure in a faster, more powerful airplane can send the machine plunging or spinning out of control. But stick-handling is just one of the many acquired skills that must be *simultaneously* employed to keep an airplane in the air and pointed in the right direction or to guide it safely back to earth. The pilot must keep an eye on and be able to correct propeller pitch, manifold pressure, cylinder-head temperature, fuel mixture, and no end of other details that had been introduced but not necessarily comprehended during boring ground-school lectures.

Reviewing the pilot's checklist, a preflight ritual forevermore, became vital to survival. After seeing a few takeoffs with the prop in high pitch and a few "floater" landings with flaps down, where the pilot is unable to quite get the wheels on the ground, we came to realize that the forgiving nature of the Yellow Peril had been supplanted by the killer instinct of what seemed to us then like willful thoroughbreds.

Our lives were filled with reviews and practice, what modern educators would call behavior modification. We became compulsive in all facets of our lives because our lives depended on our ability to do everything right and in just the right order. We knew that there was some leeway for errors but we never really knew what would get us by and what would not, and none of our dead classmates could tell us at what point they flew beyond the ability of their airplanes to bring them home.

More members of Class 162-C washed out, and more died.

Those of us who got through Squadron-2 were invited to select the sort of duty we wanted upon graduation from flight school, in only a month's time. I and all the other Marines were committed to fighters, but my Navy classmates could choose from among fighters, scout-bombers, scouts, observation, and transports. Several of the latter selections would lead to flying multi-engine aircraft, which was considerably different from the single-engine airplanes with which we would be training all the way through Pensacola. None of the Navy pilots was guaranteed his choice, and there was no guarantee that the Marines would indeed wind up in fighters, for the Marine Corps inventoried just about all the same types of aircraft as the Navy.

★

Squadron-3 was devoted almost exclusively to instrument and blind flying and, in the final phase, celestial navigation. More cadets washed out of Navy flight schools during Squadron-3 than the combined total for Squadrons 1 and 2. More were killed in training accidents, too.

The first few "flight" hours in Squadron-3 were spent in Link Trainers, a mock-up of an airplane cockpit, complete with instrumentation covered by a hood to simulate blind flying conditions. This single training aid probably saved more cadets' lives than all the compulsive habits pounded into our heads over the previous months of training. If a cadet was prone to previously undisclosed panic, vertigo, or claustrophobia, it was better to confront it in the Link Trainer than in the air.

All the emphasis on perfection in the earlier phases crystalized in Squadron-3, for we spent many hours in hooded rear cockpits, our views of the world restricted to the instruments before our eyes. The smallest variations in altitude, for example, would bring a scream of protest from the instructor, who was strapped into the front cockpit, his hands only inches from the stick and throttle lever. The instructors were utterly unforgiving of minor transgressons. They had to be; for the time being, their lives literally hung in the balance.

Upon posting the first death attributed to blind flying in Class 162-C, all of us who thought that anything less than perfection might get us by were rudely awakened to the reality. We could blame any number of earlier deaths on luck or lack of talent, but we were now fairly accomplished pilots only two months away from receiving our Wings of Gold. The only cause of death in Squadron-3 was lack of attention to detail.

One of the scarier talents we had to acquire was riding a radio beam to the ground. This, we learned, is why the Navy required perfect hearing of its cadets (though not its older pilots, who were often nearly deaf after decades of open-cockpit flying). A radio pulse sounding in our earphones told us where we were relative to a radio transmitter, which was our fixed navigation point. Variations to the right or left brought forth variations in the tone ("dah-dit" for right, for example, and "dit-dah" for left); being too far from the transmitter brought a weakened signal, and flying nearer brought an increasingly stronger signal. There was, however, no way to gauge altitude by means of the radio signal; that required precision work with an altimeter, a needle-ball gauge, and an airspeed indicator. All this was done "under the hood," which immeasurably added to anxiety. In time, the instructor would remove the hood so the cadet could see where he actually was. The results were usually surprising.

Too soon, the cadet would be graded on what he had learned under the hood. If he received an "up," he was another step closer to receiving his Wings of Gold. If he received a "down," he was one of only three steps closer to the main gate and a ride home at government expense. A really egregious showing might earn him a government-paid burial.

Simply passing the instrument and blind-flying phases was not insurance of a successful career. There are pilots' graves the world over (many of them empty) to attest to the vertigo, confusion, miscalculation, and panic that stalks every pilot every time he takes to the air or must land under instrument control. Even seasoned pilots with thousands of hours of instrument-flying experience are susceptible to the split-second lapses that can spell doom and sorrow.

All Navy and Marine pilots were taught to use navigational plotting boards, which were located directly beneath the instrument panel of all service models. Directly beneath the plotting board, on which we placed navigation strip charts (a chart of the sector in which we were flying), was a chart for determining altitude and wind speed by how wave caps looked. Such information in turn would help us upgrade our plotting boards and thus find our way around a seemingly featureless ocean. Of course, being able to read the stars at night would yield the airplane's heading and other vital information. And all these skills could be used in place of instruments, which, though coming into service in increasing quantity and quality, were nevertheless prone to failure or damage. They also provided a comforting check of the instruments, particularly in bad weather, where rapidly changing wind conditions could severely affect the altitude, attitude, ground speed, and heading of any airplane, right up to the largest multiengine models.

Upon completion of the celestial navigation phase of Squadron-3 in mid-May, 1941, I and my fellow Marines—including Jeff Poindexter, Jack Amende, Phil Crawford, and Stan Tutton—were assigned with several of our Navy classmates to the fighter school at Opa-Locka, Florida, a suburb of Miami. If I weathered Opa-Locka, I would earn my Wings of Gold and my commission as a second lieutenant of Marines.

6

The entire atmosphere at Opa-Locka was different from what I had lived through at Pensacola.

First, it was balmier on the Atlantic Coast, though the pleasant weather in May soon gave way to summer heat and humidity that bordered on the unbearable. One of the best aspects of our flying schedule was the ability to simply cool off.

Second, we were treated like human beings, starting with the moment Jeff Poindexter and I were saluted by the sentries as I drove my red convertible through the main gate for the first time. We drew liberty every evening from 2115 hours, and all night on Saturdays. On work nights, we usually repaired to the Hollywood Beach Hotel, which functioned as the base officers' club while a new facility was being built on base. The hotel extended all "O-Club" members a twenty-five percent discount on rooms, meals, drinks, and golfing fees. When possible, we headed for nearby Miami, which was then a fairly small city but a fun place to be. I usually drove in with Jeff Poindexter, Jack Amende, and as many other Marines as we could fit into my red Ford convertible. Jeff often returned the favor of car privileges by supplying the women; he certainly had a way with them. Part of the fun of getting off base was being saluted by the many Navy enlisted men who lived and worked throughout the area.

Our progress at Opa-Locka was rated on an individual basis rather than on a class syllabus. Members of my Pensacola class who were assigned to fighter training were joined at Opa-Locka by cadets from the primary flight schools at Jacksonville, Florida, and Corpus Christi, Texas. And there were even full-fledged Navy officers who had qualified for flight training after serving with the Fleet.

Navy line officers or Marine ground officers had to serve in the Fleet or the Fleet Marine Force for two years before attending flight school. The Naval Aviation Cadet Program for which I had qualified dispensed with this rule in the interest of quickly building up the Naval Service's air-war capability; there were not enough officers who wanted to transfer from the Fleet to do the trick, and there was no point in having us serve in the Fleet for two years when we were so desperately needed right then. If not for the NavCad Program, I would not have qualified for any officer-candidate program because I was under 21, a detail that would not be rectified until August, weeks after I was expected to earn my Wings of Gold.

Finally, the pressures of ground school were pretty much lifted. We faced classroom training, to be sure, but most of it was aimed at familiarizing us with fighter tactics or airplane models in advance of practical work in the air. The spectre of washing out of the cadet program at Opa-Locka was almost indiscernable; there were so few active military pilots in 1941 that the farther along we got in our training, the more valuable we became to our nation's war contingency plans. A few of our Navy comrades who did not make it as fighter pilots were shipped off to observation or transport, but only one cadet I know of was actually sent home.

The one exception happened to be my roommate, and his problem arose out of the presence at Opa-Locka of Commander Gene Tunney, the former heavyweight boxing champion-of-the-world. We reported to Tunney every day at 0600 for our morning workout, and the champ really worked us out. After about a week of that, my roommate (we were in two-man rooms) told me one morning, "Hell, I'm not going through those goddamn early drills again. I'm in great shape, and I need the sleep." Thereafter, he got one of his buddies to call "Present!" for him at morning muster, and he remained in bed until I returned to change for breakfast. After about another week, our skipper, a Navy line officer, held a room inspection while we were out with Gene Tunney. My roommate, the only cadet on base who was still in his bunk, left Opa-Locka the very next day.

★

The very first morning of flight training brought home one of the biggest thrills I ever experienced as a pilot, and one of the biggest disappointments. I walked around the hangar to which I had been assigned and turned in to find before me an F3F fighter—the same airplane that had hooked me on becoming a naval aviator when I first saw it in *Flight Command* in 1939.

There it was: a stubby, metal-fuselage, cloth-winged, single-engine, open-cockpit biplane with one .50-caliber machine gun and one .30-caliber machine gun mounted atop the engine cowling and synchronized to fire through the propeller disk. The F3F's .50-caliber was fitted out with only fifty rounds of ammunition, and the .30-caliber could fire up to 200 rounds.

I was all set to take her up, but it turned out that it would be weeks before we would be entrusted with what then amounted to one of the Navy's first-line fighters. The purpose of that morning confrontation with my dreams was a rather deflating "inspirational" lecture on how we would get a crack at the F3F if we earned the privilege through first checking out in two-seaters and lighter airplanes. In no event would any cadet begin fighter-tactics training until the instructors were certain he had the right stuff.

Our early work involved flying one another around in two-seaters and sending and receiving Morse Code in the air, which we found was a lot different in a bumpy cockpit than it had been in ground school. We also had to complete scouting assignments because, we were told, a fighter pilot is a valuable part of the Fleet and has to be prepared to fill in wherever he is needed.

We quickly worked up to the point where we each undertook a series of spins, stalls, and other basic aerobatic maneuvers over one of the huge swamps bordering the station while the instructors watched from the ground. If a cadet's airplane-handling skills met the unstated criteria, he was slated to begin the meat of the course. If not, he did it over and over again until he passed or was sent elsewhere. Unimaginable as it seemed, not everyone continued on.

As soon as I had flown to my instructor's satisfaction, I was finally allowed to take an F3F aloft. This was a far more powerful airplane than anything I had flown to date; I could feel the power of its super-charged 850-horsepower Wright radial engine surging through the controls. This was flying!

Flying the F3F gave me my first taste ever of flying an airplane with retractable landing gear. This was something of a novelty in American service-type airplanes. The mechanism was operated by a hand crank that turned through about thirty revolutions. The gear was activated by a chain that, when fully extended, was held in place by a lock in order to hold the gear securely down. If a landing approach was being made with the landing gear snug against the bulkheads, a buzzer would sound when the throttle was closed.

Within days, we moved on to polishing our skills on the classic fighter tactics, most of which had been developed during World War I by French, British, and German pilots. One of the best of these was the Immelmann, named for its German developer, an ace of aces who, like most of his brothers, died at the controls of his Fokker fighter in France.

In just one week, three cadets failed to recover from Immelmanns and crashed into the vast swamp bordering the base, a particularly horrifying place known to abound in alligators, water moccasins, and other deadly fauna. Rescue parties found all three cadets dead in the cockpits of their F3Fs, with no explanation as to the cause of the crashes.

All the rest of us, and the base staff, were chilled by the mystery. The F3F had been in service for years. As far as anyone knew, all its bugs had been ironed out. Was there a failure in maintenance? That could mean that everyone flying an F3F was at risk. Had there been a common failure on a particular component of the three downed fighters? Had there been a common failure among the three dead cadets in understanding some vital element of instruction? Had the instructors failed to properly brief them . . . and us?

Test pilots faced these questions with new airplanes, and pilots generally faced them when new versions of old-model airplanes were introduced or upon the introduction of modifications to a hitherto reliable model. But these were old-model F3Fs, released from the Fleet for training purposes only upon the introduction of newer fleet versions; these were not the F3Fs that should have been taking pilots to their deaths.

Finally, a fourth pilot went into what should have been a death spin, identical in every way to the fatal spins but for the young man at the controls. He was Wortham Ashcroft, a Texas-raised Marine cadet about my age who had been through Pensacola in Class 163-C, right behind me. Wortham was a big, robust young man who, when his F3F went into an uncontrollable inverted spin, used his incredible strength and calm demeanor to wrestle the controls to a standstill. Once he had stopped spinning, Wortham released his seat harness and dived clear of the airplane at just enough altitude to allow his parachute to deploy before he fell into the swamp. Rescuers got to him before the alligators did, and he was able to tell us what had happened as soon as he regained his power of speech.

It turned out that no one had ever told us how to get out of an inverted spin, which was fairly common when an F3F attained a certain attitude. Since that attitude was guaranteed in the Immelmann maneuver, we could not correct for it. Once into the spin, we had no way of knowing how to pull out—thus the deaths of three cadets and Wortham Ashcroft's near death.

I don't know what, if anything, happened to the man who was responsible for leaving out the vital information, but all F3Fs were grounded for a few days while the instructors reviewed every characteristic and tendency of the airplane along with every known corrective measure. In the case of the inverted spin, we were shown that the corrective was exactly opposite to the method we had been taught for recovering from a normal spin.

★

While learning the basic maneuvers and how to move smoothly from one to another in flight, we spent long hours in the classrooms watching films of aerial dogfights and studying mind-twisting charts showing, for example, how the remaining fuel supply and its disposition in the fuel tanks would affect the maneuverability of the airplane. We learned, as we had been learning for months, that everything in, on, and around the machine affected its flying capabilities and thus our chances of surviving a dogfight. The number of variables became impossible to follow, which was the point. In the end, we were told, surviving combat was in very large part a factor of how well prepared the pilot was to meet the unexpected.

Each flight was a new experience as we undertook our first fighter tactics, our first air-to-air dogfighting, our first aerial gunnery. Everything was aimed at getting us to the point where the airplane fit like an extension of our bodies and nervous systems. Only then could we make the correct life-or-death decisions without taking precious moments to consciously consider them.

One of our top instructors was Lieutenant "Jumpin' Joe" Clifton, whose loud, clear voice rang in our earphones whenever he saw the slightest flaw in our technique. Jumpin' Joe repeated his "two musts" every day we were in his care: In order for a fighter pilot to stay alive, he must have the altitude advantage, and he must constantly search all the airspace around his airplane to find enemy fighters before they can nail him.

To practice what we had learned in individual dogfights, the instructor would designate one F3F as the attacker and the other as the defender. Each would be assigned a particular altitude and heading.

In one of my early dogfights, for example, I was designated the attacker and ordered to fly my F3F toward the defender, but 1,000 to 2,000 feet higher and 4,000 feet to one side. When I came within 2,000 feet of the target, I was to turn toward it and execute a high-side run, initially approaching from the seven o'clock or eight o'clock position (the defender's nose being twelve o'clock and the tail being six o'clock).

On the signal from the instructor, I rolled into a left turn, nose down, and held the target in my field of vision. Ignoring everything else in the sky and my instrument panel was mandatory; all my attention had to remain fixed on that "enemy" F3F. As the airspeed built up to around 250 knots, my F3F approached the target's four o'clock position at the same altitude. I eased back on the throttle until my closing speed was under control, then I added full throttle to catch up. I took care to avoid "pulling G's," which pulls the blood from the pilot's brain and fuel from the fighter's engine as gravitational pressures build up in a turn. I got my airspeed corrected by making minute adjustments to the throttle, so I was set to pass beneath the target's tail with sufficient speed to recover and regain a good attacking position from the other side. In real combat, I would have been firing my two machine guns from less than 300 yards.

This first high-side attack, which I had rehearsed on the ground before ever attempting it aloft, was made against a target that did not defend itself. After my instructors were sure I knew just what I was doing, I had to make a high-side run against a maneuvering fighter, which is something altogether different.

A more elegant attack maneuver is the split-S, which is commonly used when the enemy aircraft is seen approaching at a lower altitude.

On my first split-S attack, I waited until the target was almost directly beneath me, then I rolled into an inverted position and dived straight down on him from above, firing as I came within range, and diving past him and recovering for another attack with virtual impunity. In combat, the split-S could be expected to force the enemy pilot to take strenuous evasive measures—if he was not destroyed or disabled on the first diving pass.

The defender has two basic choices, assuming he sees the attacker in time: He can try to run away, or he can wait until the attacker is committed and then turn into the attacker just before the firing run begins. Since the guns were boresighted to converge on a spot from 200 to 250 yards in front of the propeller, the defender must make his move with split-second precision. Of course, in real combat the variables mount against any individual attacker, and only skill and experience—and luck, of course—can come close to assuring a kill. We were constantly reminded to allow for unknown and bizarre reactions from potential adversaries, who in real combat would be using every trick in and out of the book to save their lives and end ours. We had to be able to react to the unexpected.

If the defending pilot was not killed in the first firing pass, he would naturally try to run or to maneuver onto the attacker's tail, and the attacker would try to maneuver onto the defender's tail. However, the pilot who won that position would soon have his hands full, for no pilot with an attacker on his tail could be expected to sit still. The attacker could expect the defender to roll, spin, dive, pull up, slow his airplane, or speed it up — any evasive maneuver or combination of maneuvers that might set him free. Sometimes, the solution was simple. If, for example, the defender had the heavier or faster airplane, he would probably just put the nose over and dive away.

As we added new maneuvers to our repertoires, we incessantly drilled alone and in pairs. Every known possibility was presented to us and practiced ad nauseum.

In a way, one of the problems we faced was that all the air-to-air dogfighting practice was done in F3Fs. Once we knew the plane well enough, we could maneuver our adversary into making a mistake arising out of its handling capabilities or design quirks. A good example of this was knowing that the fuel system was built in such a way as to cause the engine to quit after a few minutes of inverted flight. Thus, if I could force an adversary into prolonged inverted flight, I could win simply because he would eventually have to climb to get the engine going again. However, the opposing pilot knew the same thing about my F3F, so it became a matter of whose engine quit first, and that was pretty much a matter of luck. What we really thought we needed to know was how our F3Fs would stand up against the modern German fighters of the day, for we fully expected to be at war with Germany within the next year or two.

★

After time out for formation flying, more acrobatics and simulated carrier landings (on wide, unmoving runways), we went back to work on combat skills, beginning with fighter-plane dive-bombing, in which we had to hold the bombsight on a target as we hurtled earthward at awesomely steep angles. We learned to overcome our fears of hanging weightless and to recover from the horrendous gravitational forces exerted on our airplanes and our bodies upon pulling out of a dive-bombing run.

Then we started work on aerial gunnery, the crux of the fighter pilot's trade. At first, we made endless passes in two-seaters, trying to aim camera guns at target sleeves towed behind other airplanes. The sleeve, really a 12-foot cloth banner, was at the end of a 200-foot cable attached to the target aircraft. The objective, once live firing started, was to put as many of a known number of rounds into the sleeve as we could manage in a single pass. The target sleeve was used by numerous cadets, so the points of our ammunition was dipped into paint cans, a different color for each pilot. Once the exercise was over and the sleeve was available on the ground, we would all gather around and count our hits. Our ratio of hits to rounds fired increased—or we might be sent elsewhere. Anyone who missed the sleeve completely took a tremendous amount of ribbing from fellow cadets and some tough talk from the gunnery instructors. (To help improve our shooting eyes, we spent a great deal of time at the skeet-shooting range, working on hand-eye coordination.)

As each pilot's score improved, he was instructed to execute increasingly complex attacks against the target sleeve. Angles of approach and aiming deflections were widely varied. We had to be prepared to execute firing runs—and hit the target—while inverted or sharply turning, from near and from afar. Our F3Fs carried gun cameras, which rolled as soon as we touched the gun-button knobs on our joysticks. In this way, we had a means for discovering our deficiencies and improving on them.

★

There was no set time for graduation, no fixed syllabus for any of us. We each had been advancing at his own pace, more or less in concert with the pack. If we needed more time on one aspect of the training, we were given it, within reasonable bounds. If a cadet could move ahead more quickly, he did so as soon as the instructors knew he was ready.

I knew I was nearing the climax of my formal fighter schooling one day in late July when Jumpin' Joe Clifton sought me out on the flight line and told me to met him at "angels 10" (10,000 feet) over a particular point in the Everglades. "When you see me," he ordered, "Come at me from dead ahead and try to get on my tail. I'll do everything I can to keep you off me."

Great knots grew in my stomach. Lieutenant Clifton was the boss, a well-respected Fleet fighter pilot with many hundreds of hours in the air. I doubted I could beat him in an honest one-on-one, but I also knew he was less interested in my beating him than in how tenaciously I maneuvered against him. Of course, there was always the possibility I might prevail.

Neither pilot has an advantage in a head-on approach, but the one who can fly straight and level the longest has the best chance of getting rounds into his adversary, who nearly always pulls up. My only edge over Joe Clifton was that he knew of cases where overeager cadets had killed themselves and their instructors by bullheadedly remaining on course and causing a head-on collision. I am sure my worthier opponent felt that I would not do that, but there is no telling what a cadet will really do to make an impression until he does it.

We met over the Everglades and hurtled at one another at a combined speed of 300 or 400 miles per hour. As I had hoped, Jumpin' Joe pulled up first—straight up at full power—and dived away while I was still trying to turn my airplane. I pulled all the G's I could, and so did he. We found one another and renewed our attacks, trying to force the other to break off in such a way as to lose all advantage. Round and round we went, twisting, evading, feinting. My mind went on automatic, responding to what my eyes could see before my brain had a chance to think about it. I lost track of where I was in the sky; my only frame of reference was that other F3F, just the way it was supposed to be.

Then I realized that I was on his tail and that I had been able to stay there for some time despite his erratic evasive maneuvers. I almost lost it as a surge of excitement passed through me, but my earphones crackled and I heard my adversary say, "Good enough, Porter. Let's go home."

★

On the morning of July 25, 1941, I was ordered to report to a captain at the Marine Barracks. There, in his office, I was handed a packet of orders directing me to report to the Marine Corps Air Station at Quantico, Virginia, in thirty days.

The captain shook my hand and welcomed me to the Marine Corps. Then he suggested that I go over to the base exchange to purchase my gold second lieutenant's bars and, by the way, my coveted Wings of Gold.

The moment arrived and passed before I quite knew what was going on.

PART II

OFF TO WAR

7

I left the Marine Barracks, bought my wings and gold bars at the base exchange, cleaned out my room, said good-bye to the very few cadets and instructors I could find, jumped in my little red convertible, and headed out the main gate, bound for California. I saw the last of Opa-Locka by noon.

It felt so good to have met the challenge that I put all my energies into driving and thinking about my coming life as a Marine fighter pilot. I barely looked out of the car at the crushing scenes that had so disturbed me on my first trip through the South. Perhaps by then I was used to seeing it, or I might have been influenced in turning a blind eye by my close association with the many southerners I had met during my months of flight training. Whatever the case, I kept my eyes on the road and my interest pinned on getting home to Los Angeles as quickly as possible. I was earthbound, but soaring nonetheless. The sense of freedom I felt was a tonic; I felt better about myself and my decision to fly with the passing of each mile.

I had always dreamed of spending time in New Orleans, and I knew I would be there before nightfall. By the time I arrived, however, my dreams of a libidinous evening had been erased by the lure of home. My aim was simply to drive through town and gas-up the car so that I could get a very early start before dawn. It occurred to me, as the gas was being pumped, that my new Navy training extended beyond my life as a fighter pilot; I was being downright compulsive—"prepared" in Navy vernacular—about my equipment far from the sight of my flight instructors.

Next morning, as I was rolling through some out-of-the-way Louisiana countryside, I came upon a long convoy of gray Army trucks filled with hundreds or even thousands of GIs on their way to take part in maneuvers. Cars were authorized to pass the slow-moving convoy down the left side of the road, and I did exactly that with my newfound fighter pilot's disdain for allowing others be out in front.

I was dressed in civilian clothing, and my bright red convertible drew a lot of attention from the hundreds of men who had been denied access to such a sporty convenience. My seeming freedom from military cares drew a lot of attention, too, for I was clearly of military age. For the next half-hour, at least one dogface in almost every troop-filled truck managed to get off a quick verbal barb as I followed a line of civilian vehicles past them: "Hey, smartass, wait'll you get in the service," or some such. I chuckled to myself and kept driving. They were right; I was better off than any of them. But not in the way they thought. I was, after all, a Marine second lieutenant, and a fighter pilot to boot.

The roads through Louisiana and on into Texas were all narrow two-lanes, all more-or-less typical of the main thoroughfares of the day. The miles passed in a forgettable stream of rest stops and hamburger stands. I drove until I simply could not focus on the road any longer and pulled into a cheap roadside motel.

About the middle of the next day, in Denning, New Mexico, I picked up a hitchhiker, one of a very few I had thus far encountered. The act had no compassion behind it; I was looking for a back-up driver who could take the wheel while I dozed in the passenger seat. Home was beckoning, and its pull was growing stronger with each passing mile.

The rider was a clean-cut kid on his way to California to find work. I asked him right off if he wanted to drive, and he thankfully leaped at the opportunity. I kept a weather eye on him for only a few minutes, then drifted off into a dead sleep, the result of paying too much attention to the road for too long.

Next thing I knew, the car was sliding around a sharp turn at high speed along a rural New Mexico canyon road. My senses instantly alert, I sat up straight and stiff, certain I was being afforded my last look at the world. My left foot sought the nonexistent clutch and my right foot stomped the spot where it thought the brake should have been. The car went clear off the road in a cloud of dust and swung broadside toward the yawning abyss to the left as the hitchhiker fought to get it under control. I am sure my eyes were bulging, and I distinctly felt words I could not quite form struggling from my throat.

As the convertible came to a safe landing and rocked on its springs, I vowed never to place myself in the hands of a co-pilot again; it would be single-seat fighters for me, or nothing.

I wordlessly motioned the hitchhiker to get out and switched places with him as I fought to regain my composure. I drove rather slowly to the next town and dropped the crestfallen young man off at the first crossroads, then put as many miles between myself and my would-be executioner as my shattered nerves and overtired reflexes would allow. I tried to recall just one flight-training incident that had terrified me more than my rude New Mexico awakening, but I could not.

The effects of my afternoon nap had been so dissipated that I stopped early at another roadside motel and fell into an exhausted, not very restful sleep. My only real comfort was in knowing I was well within striking distance of home.

I was on my way well before dawn and drove straight through to Palm Springs, California. This was familiar turf. The long heat of my summer day in New Mexico, Arizona, and the California desert brought on a crazed desire for a cold glass of iced, fresh-squeezed orange juice. I realized that I had been looking for a roadside juice stand, a familiar Southern California fixture, for the entire day. I stopped at the very first one, just outside Palm Springs, and, to the delight of the bored-looking proprietor, downed one tall glass after another until my stomach could literally hold no more.

Home was just down the road. I should have stopped in Palm Springs, but I felt so restored by the massive infusion of iced orange juice that I kept going until I pulled up in front of my parents' home. There, I hugged and kissed my mother, shook hands with my father, refused an offer of dinner, and staggered straight to my room for what I hoped would be limitless hours of comfortable sleep. Except to eat a few quick nibbles of the food Mother set by my bed, I slept straight through for two days.

When I could sleep no more, I sought out my parents and dutifully reported every shareable detail of my new life as a fighter pilot. It took a while before Mother stopped flashing pained expressions at some of the raw vernacular I had picked up in Florida; with a great deal of effort, I was soon able to edit my thoughts before they became words.

I waited to call my girlfriend until my head was clear and my stamina had been restored. I knew that I would be viewing my old life from a different place after the adult rigors of flight school, but I yearned to go to all the old places and see all the old people before I was really committed to the military life.

Some days, and most evenings, I hung out with my friends at McDonald's Drive-In on Wilshire Boulevard—which, I am told, was the flagship of the McDonald's hamburger chain. Many days we drove down to San Onofre, just north of Camp Pendleton (which had been turned into a huge Marine infantry training base only a year before), where I put my big, heavy, wooden surfboard into the water and paddled out in search of the perfect wave. On other days, it was off to Santa Monica with friends for body-surfing and endless rounds of beach parties.

I spent a great deal of time and energy having fun, but I knew that flight school had placed a yawning gap between my past with these old friends and my future in the air. In time, I grew bored with the surfing, bored with the nightlife, bored with my girlfriend. The laughter seemed to ring hollow after a week of running around, and my mind began wandering forward to the wonders I had yet to experience.

After a little inner debate, I called Roy Margrave to see how he was getting on. He was a bit sheepish at first because he had washed out of Pensacola and I had earned my Wings of Gold. He told me he had signed up with the Army Air Corps and was awaiting orders to flight school. The discomfort rapidly dissipated; we had been friends for too many years and had too much in common to let my success and his temporary setback stand in our way. At least he could talk about flying.

I was really on a roll for a while, but in the end I was happy to begin planning my trip back to Quantico, Virginia, where I would be assigned to an active fighter squadron. I decided to take the northern route, through San Francisco, Denver, a lot of Midwest towns, and then through Pittsburgh, Philadelphia and Baltimore. Typically, I left no time for sightseeing, though it had been my dream for as long as I could remember to see all the great eastern cities.

Mother found a dependable rider to help with the driving and share expenses. He was on his way to begin college at Yale and was at least conversant in nonflying subjects I could endure. By the time we crossed the Mississippi, the seat of my pants yearned to be airborne again.

I dropped my rider off at Thirtieth Street Station in Philadelphia and turned south down Route 1.

8

On leaving Opa-Locka, I had been ordered to report to the adjutant of Marine Air Group 11 (MAG-11) at Quantico, Virginia, following my thirty-day leave, and that is what I did on September 1, 1941.

After reading my orders, the captain checked my name on his roster and briskly told me I was assigned to Marine Fighting Squadron 121 (VMF-121), a newly formed squadron commanded by Major Samuel Jack.

I naturally asked for directions to the squadron's operations office; I was all set to get going. However, the group adjutant told me that VMF-121 was involved in maneuvers in New Bern, North Carolina, and was working out of the adjacent Marine Corps Air Station at Cherry Point. I looked on in confusion and was beset by a sinking heart as the news mounted. I had no idea what the deployment of the squadron would mean to me. Would I have to stay at Quantico on nonflying status until it got back? Would I be temporarily assigned to another unit? Would I be given some office duties for which I was unprepared?

"Lieutenant, why don't you find yourself a place to live up here, and I'll see about getting you down to New Bern to join the squadron. You can report back to me when you're settled in."

I was not familiar enough with the Marine Corps to know if I was being fobbed off or shuffled until a better solution presented itself to the adjutant (who was a nonflying officer and could not be expected to know what any sort of a grounding meant to a fighter pilot). I meekly accepted his recommendation of a local rooming house and asked how and where I would be fed.

I quickly found a room in one of the tiny rural Virginia towns near the base, and then I hung around Turner Field, Quantico's airfield, for the next few days, gabbing with pilots from other squadrons but really just killing time and hating to be grounded.

The group adjutant finally sent word that he had my travel papers in hand and that I was to report to him for instructions. As soon as I checked in, the captain gave me road directions to New Bern and told me to report as fast as I could get there.

My last stop was at the group quartermaster shop, where I drew all of my flight gear, which included both winter and summer clothing and flight helmets (fleece-lined leather for the winter and khaki-colored cloth for the summer).

I drove out the main gate of Quantico that afternoon and, after overnighting in Raleigh, was in New Bern the following morning. I finally reported to the squadron adjutant, who asked, "Where the hell have you been, Porter? You were supposed to be here days ago!"

I was soon introduced to Major Sam Jack, a kindly, colorful, highly decorated, 35-year-old veteran of the Banana Wars, in which the Marine Corps had been immersed in Central America almost continually during the two decades following World War I (which, until a few months later, we called the Great War or *the* World War). Jack, who sported one of the most charming, folksy personalities I had (or would) encounter in my military career, set me right at ease as he told me a bit about the squadron and its mission. He also asked me questions in a way that convinced me of his genuine interest. Jack called in the squadron executive officer, Captain John Condon, a dark, extremely handsome man in his late twenties, who welcomed me aboard while administering me a firm handshake. Both Jack and Condon were Annapolis graduates.

After about ten minutes of warm, friendly conversation with the skipper and the exec, I was introduced to 1st Lieutenant Bob Fraser, with whom I would be flying as part of a six-plane fighter division led by Captain Elmer Brackett, a former ground officer with several years in fighters, now the squadron flight officer. Fraser, a mild stutterer, asked me right off if I wanted to room with him in his two-man tent. He seemed friendly enough at first glance, and I was eager to make some new friends. I told him I would be glad to room with him.

"Great, B-bruce. Say, is that your red F-f-ford convertible I saw on the way in? We can r-ride over after we get off d-duty."

My newfound roommate showed me the field and the airplanes and introduced me to pilots and groundcrewmen, Captain Brackett among them. I sensed right away that my division leader was the tough sort of Marine officer I had been warned about during flight school. As we were walking away from the captain, Bob Fraser told me that he was known throughout the Corps as an extremely tough disciplinarian. "It wah-wouldn't b-be so b-bad, B-bruce, but he's also one helluva l-lousy p-pilot!"

I was also tickled to find my old Pensacola classmate Phil Crawford among the squadron's newly absorbed second lieutenants.

Later that afternoon, as I trundled between my car and the tent with all my flight gear, Bob Fraser laughed and told me that the winter stuff might not be needed for quite a while because the F4F Wildcat fighter I would be flying had an enclosed canopy. "B-but," he drawled, "the Marine C-corps says a f-fighter p-pilot shall draw his winter g-gear, and s-so he sh-shall!"

★

The next day was a flying day. Captain Brackett wanted to check me out in the new Grumman F4F-3 Wildcat fighter the Marine Corps had recently acquired.

I had been warned that Brackett was considered something of a martinet. I cannot say that he was pleasant, but he was business-like and very thorough as he patiently explained the F4F's characteristics and drawbacks. He warned me, for example, that the airplane had an awesome tendency to groundloop to the left as a result of its extremely powerful engine torque.

As Brackett looked on from the edge of the field, I rolled through a few long taxis to get a feel for the Grumman's powerful 1,200-horsepower radial engine and its tricky ground-handling characteristics. I noticed right away how relatively quiet the enclosed cockpit was as compared with the many open-cockpit models I had flown until then. It was a pleasure.

When I had completed a series of simple ground maneuvers to my flight leader's satisfaction, I tried a few easy wheels-down take-offs and touch-and-go landings. It was all routine, though I did see where this modern fleet fighter could get away from an unwary tyro.

A number of squadron pilots had already explained that the most troublesome aspect of handling the Wildcat was the manually operated landing gear. Although Grumman had also designed the F3F, which had designed-in retractable landing gear, the same firm's F4F had originally been a fixed-gear plane. The war in Europe had proven that fighters needed more speed than ever before, so Grumman had been ordered to make F4F's gear retractable to cut down on drag. The late addition of the retracting mechanism resulted in an awkward design. (The airplane had also been designed as a biplane! We all would have enjoyed brief, interesting combat careers if we had had to fly it against any German or Japanese fighters that way.)

The trick with the F4F gear was to turn a handle in the cockpit twenty-eight times backward while holding the airplane as steady as possible during the critical climb after lift-off. It sounded easier than it was, for the handle was awkwardly located just behind the pilot's right knee. That meant releasing the throttle lever to pass the joystick to the left hand. Each of the twenty-eight right-handed turns projected motion to the left hand, which meant that the stick simply could not be held motionless. The result was inevitably a wobbly takeoff. Fighter pilots of the day were proven masters of manual agility and coordination, but that landing gear retraction handle was a bit much. Because the landing gear struts were close together and looked a bit bowed from ahead or behind, the F4F in takeoff was said to look like a drunken, knock-kneed bumblebee. I was also warned that deploying or retracting the gear might be dangerous. If the friction-brake was not set just right, the handle could get away and spin out of control against the pilot's right leg. And there was always the danger of cords from the pilot's earphones or throat mike getting fouled in a spinning handle. Broken bones and cracked shins were common enough to be routine gossip.

I ran through a number of sloppy wheels-up takeoffs and wheels-down landings and soon mastered the feat of coordination the unique landing gear required. Like everything else I had thus far encountered as a pilot, it was simply a matter of practice and more practice.

The second flying day was to begin with a check-flight in formation with Fraser and Brackett. As much as familiarizing me with the thoroughbred fighter, Brackett clearly wanted to see if I had what it took to be a Marine fighter pilot. ("Oh b-boy," Bob Fraser moaned as we walked from the ready room to the flight line, "W-watch out, B-bruce!")

I taxied in behind Brackett and Fraser, well aware of my junior pilot status but breathing fire over the excitement of being at the controls of the hottest fighter in the Fleet. I got the gear up passably after lift-off and eased into the number-three position off the flight leader's left wing, just a little behind and below Fraser, who was flying Brackett's right wing. The objective of the exercise was to see if I could instantly and smoothly respond to Brackett's lead. While also scanning the sky, as if in search of enemy aircraft, I had to focus all my attention on the flight leader's slightest movements. The captain repeatedly tried to throw me out of the tight formation as he maneuvered at the outer edge of reasonable expectations. When he succeeded in rattling me a few times, his acerbic voice immediately reverberated in my head, "Close it up, Porter! You're with a combat squadron now!" I was stung, but I looked over at Fraser once in time to catch a furtive thumbs-up.

We were coming into the landing pattern when, without any warning, I saw Brackett's landing gear suddenly drop. I was so intent upon following the captain's lead that I flipped the safety on my gear handle without taking a firm grip. That steel handle spun out of control through all twenty-eight turns and cracked into my shin the first three or four. A faint sound of laughter came over my earphones, and I seriously considered pressing the gun-button knob on my joystick in the vague hope that a few rounds had been left following the airplane's last gunnery hop. I was so angry that tears welled in my eyes as I climbed down from the cockpit after parking in the dispersal area. As I limped away, Brackett flashed a huge, smug smile when he saw me with my eyes aglisten. I nodded at him and he nodded at me, then we wordlessly went our separate ways. Bob Fraser gently guided me by the elbow toward the ready room for a relaxing cup of coffee. "Y-you d-did f-fine, B-bruce. J-just f-f-f-f-fine," he chuckled.

★

I quickly found that Jeff Poindexter, Stan Tutton, and Jack Amende, my flight-school buddies, and Louis Gordon, with whom I had become friendly at Opa-Locka, were flying with VMF-111, the other half of MAG-11's fighter complement. Since they were billeted just across the sandy runway from VMF-121, I managed to spend a good deal of time with them, as well as with my new friends in my own squadron.

The squadron's social life was typical of the prewar service. Despite full working days in the air, young lieutenants were invited to dine with the commanding officer and his wife and to take part in the all-male camaraderie of eating in the squadron messhall. Slowly, we were adopted into the Marine Corps and all its tribal traditions.

Off-duty activities frequently took my fellow lieutenants and me to the beach at Morehead. There was no surfing on this Atlantic Coast, but there were plenty of women as long as the weather remained mild, well into October. I was discovered by a pretty southern belle during one of my early trips off base, and I managed to see quite a lot of her whenever there was time. Things became pretty serious in that quarter as time rolled by.

After a few weeks of living and flying together, Fraser and I decided to rent an apartment in a big southern house overlooking the Neuse River. The rent was well within our budgets, but I would have paid a lot more to get out of our dusty, musty tent, which I was sure had been abandoned by Napoleon in Russia in 1812.

Strangely, we were not permitted to wear our uniforms or flight gear off base. The nation was girding for war, and many thousands of young men were flocking to the colors in anticipation of the great conflagration. But our commanders felt that wearing uniforms in civilian settings was somehow provocative. I sneaked out one day with my combat boots and leather flight jacket on— simply to show off my Wings of Gold, second lieutenant's bars, and fighter-pilot status—and I was soon hauled up before the usually affable Sam Jack, who chewed me up one side and down the other using combinations of sounds that I had never heard from a human mouth before.

★

I nearly did myself in on my second or third solo flight in my Wildcat, when I curved out over the ocean and took her down right on the deck. "Flathatting," as we called it then, was frowned upon by the people who had to conserve airplanes and the men who flew them, but it was a legitimate combat evasion technique and had to be honed. Naturally, my real intent that day was simply to ride the waves and attain the full feeling of power that can only be imparted with the earth hurtling close by at top speed. The objective was to ease on down as low as I could without quite cutting the highest waves with my prop.

I felt wonderful while it lasted. The airplane was smoothly barrelling along at top speed, heading right for a line of low hills I thought were right on the beach. Well, not quite. The next thing I knew, a line of tall trees loomed up in front of the disc of my propeller. I had only a matter of seconds in which to pull up. I felt a tight little jar, but the airplane flew okay, so I simply chopped back on the throttle, levelled off, and flew home, where I made a routine landing. As soon as I had taxied into the dispersal area, I jumped to the ground and raced my plane captain to the propeller. All of the blades were knicked, and bits of wood and a largish branch were in the engine air intake. The plane captain, a pleasant-featured sergeant I barely knew yet, looked at me expectantly as I composed my features.

"Well, sergeant, uh, just be glad you got a plane back." He grinned as he shook his head, "Yes, Sir, I sure am. Ah, I guess we can keep it between you and me."

"Yes, well, I, uh, hoped we could."

★

We took part in training every working hour of every working day, running heavy formation flying, practicing our gunnery techniques against air and ground targets, and generally familiarizing ourselves with the airplane.

While simply becoming better pilots and better able to fly together were the main objectives of our squadron and group work, one very important responsibility we faced was to try to develop new tactics that would employ the F4F's best features and mask its deficiencies. The first two Marine F4F squadrons, VMF-121 and VMF-111, had to blaze a trail for the many squadrons, new and old, that would be equipped with Wildcats by mid 1942. We learned a thing or two from the Navy, which had had the airplane for many months longer than the Marines, but we also had to find new methods on our own. Unlike Navy fighter units, which had to guard the carriers, Marine squadrons were expected to be employed primarily as offensive weapons or in direct or close support of Marine ground units.

I soon learned that I and my fellow new pilots of average talent were sort of guinea pigs in the development of the new tactics. It is true that we all sought to find the outer limits of the F4F's capabilities and to suggest ways in which the basic fighter design could be improved over time, but we also had to learn what was practical and realistic for the slowest learner in the group. Thousands of pilots would have to be trained for the new war, and most of them would be at or near the average. I correctly guessed the commanders thought that if pilots like me could survive, anyone could.

Soon, we were working with Army and Marine ground troops, helping them learn about the possibilities of close air support and learning ourselves how to deliver it in our extremely fast modern fighters.

Finally, our training cycle was interrupted on November 10, 1941, with orders for MAG-11 to participate in the Red-and-Blue Maneuvers, the largest joint-service exercise held to that time in the United States. We would be flying out of Knollwood, North Carolina, which my gentleman squadron mates assured me boasted the finest golf courses on the East Coast.

Our first flight out of the dirt strip was a navigation familiarization hop. Under the leadership of Captain Brackett, most of VMF-121 spent long hours flying from point to point in the area in which the maneuvers would be held. We fixed reference points we could all find and marked our maps with code names and notes of our own. It was a grueling day. One of the problems I encountered in flying over North Carolina was that everything looked the same. It is all flat, featureless terrain with the same-looking towns, the same-looking fields, and the same-looking pine forests. Even the older pilots had trouble picking out landmarks. All of us wound up with headaches from just plain too much looking at the ground.

We returned to base very late and on the last of our fuel. Some of us frankly thought that the squadron flight officer had become temporarily lost, but he said not. As it happened, one of the new lieutenants ran out of fuel and had to belly-land in a cow pasture; he was lucky to survive, much less walk away from the wreck of his F4F, which is what he did. And Staff Sergeant P. C. Cook, one of our experienced enlisted pilots, walked away from his second destroyed F4F in five months after trying to make a powerless ("dead-stick") landing on the field. He had lost his first Wildcat ditching in the Potomac because of a landing gear problem the day after the squadron received the new fighters.

We never got to use any of the Knollwood golf courses during the frenetic weeks of delivering support for Army and Marine ground units and staging mock dogfights against Marine and Air Corps squadrons all over that part of North Carolina. One of the many advantages, besides simply getting in air time, was learning how to control one's emotions during confrontations. Major Jack and other blooded veterans assured the younger pilots that a mock attack was as real as the real thing, and I certainly felt every bit of the mounting tension before, during, and after each sortie.

It was so cold at Knollwood that our groundcrews had constant problems with our Wildcats' usually reliable oil dilution systems. The groundcrewmen had to visit each F4F every evening to dilute the oil, then they had to return to do it again each morning before attempting to start the engines. Often as not, this simple preventative was defeated by the low overnight temperatures, and the planes could not be started by the usual means—blank shotgun shells usually kicked the engines over fast enough to get them going. The only solution then was for the groundcrewmen to attach long elastic "bungee" ropes to the propeller cuffs and run as quickly as they could away from the airplane. This was a sort of a cross between starting a rubberband-driven model airplane and starting an outboard motor. I never saw the bungee-impelled engines kick over the very first time.

The bitter cold also gave rise to a memorable incident involving two of our groundcrew mainstays, Sergeants Wilbur "Bud" Stuckey and Richard Conn. The two were returning to our camp area from the outdoor showers (which we were sure drew water directly from an ice-encrusted creek near our campsite). They had towels around their waists and were carrying their clothing under their arms when they were loudly challenged by an Army major who wanted to know which side they were on. "Blue or Red?" the major roared. Bud Stuckey shouted back, "Blue, Sir! *Very* blue!"

★

Without my really noticing it, I was becoming a competent fighter pilot, as good as any of the fledglings who were beginning to enter the Marine Corps in greater numbers every month. By the end of November, 1941, I was far from being the squadron's junior pilot, so great was the influx.

9

VMF-121 returned to New Bern from Knollwood the last week of November, at the conclusion of the joint exercises, and we resumed our schedule of training, absorbing new second lieutenants, and testing and retesting fighter tactics.

I went into New Bern to play pool with Bob Fraser and several other pilots on the afternoon of Sunday, December 7, 1941. After losing several cut-throat games, I went off to pick up my date, whom I drove back into town to see a movie in the company of my pool-playing buddies and their dates.

The show was about half over when the lights went on and a Marine officer rushed to the stage to say that he thought he had heard on the radio that Pearl Harbor was under attack. We all stood up when we heard that, but there was nothing for us to do. Details were sketchy.

Minutes later, two military policemen rushed in and told us that all military personnel were to report to their headquarters immediately, dressed in uniform. Our dates were left to fend for themselves as Bob and I and the others scattered to get our cars.

We all spent the rest of the day and many hours into the evening listening to the radio and sharing gossip and views in the squadron ready room. Someone dug up an old atlas, and we got to work trying to find Pearl Harbor. All I knew was that it was in the Pacific, and I only knew that because the Pacific Fleet and Japan were being mentioned in the radio bulletins.

Details mounted as we milled around in confusion and anger, but there remained no clear picture. All the senior officers were out of town for the weekend, so we had no clear direction, no official information about anything.

I am sure that every pilot there had to choke down the bile of emotion at one time or another that evening; I know I did. Our nation was at war with Japan, and we were its leading edge of defense. It only remained to be seen if our leaders would take this opportunity to find a way into the war in Europe, which, even I knew, was where our interests more clearly lay.

None of us knew it at the time, but the total operational Marine Corps air establishment consisted of 204 airplanes, including numerous transport and observation models, and several varieties of fighters and dive-bombers. This small force was scattered from the Virgin Islands in the Caribbean to Oahu in Hawaii, and Wake Island in the nether reaches of the Pacific.

Bob Fraser and most of the other unmarried pilots took turns trying to place long-distance calls to their girlfriends, and I tried to call home in response to rumors that the West Coast had come under heavy air bombardment. The nation's phone system was completely overwhelmed by millions of such calls, and no one got through. Bob and I finally gave it up and drove back to our apartment to try to get some rest. We barely slept and went back to the field early the next morning. The place was in utter chaos.

Major Sam Jack called us together after breakfast, at 0700, to tell us that President Roosevelt and the Congress had issued a Declaration of War in response to the unprovoked attack on Pearl Harbor. No mention was made then of the grievous harm inflicted on our Pacific Fleet. Jack let it all sink in for a few moments, then ended in an unusually terse manner: "Get your flight gear and report back in fifteen minutes; we're taking off for Quantico."

As the other pilots dispersed, I rushed up to the major and excitedly shouted in his face, "Hey, skipper, Bob Fraser and I are sharing an apartment down by the Neuse River. All our stuff is there, except what we have at the cleaner's. If we go now, we'll never see any of it again."

A twinkle came to his sleep-starved eyes. "Okay, Porter, I'll give the two of you a half-hour. Be back by then or we'll take off without you."

Bob and I hopped into my red convertible—what was I going to do with it?!—and darted off the base amidst a cold blast of December air. When we arrived at the boarding house, I backed the red Ford right up beneath the window of our second-story room while Bob dashed up the stairs. Moments later, Bob opened a window and started throwing clothes into the back seat (and the front seat, and onto the hood, and all over the ground around the car). Our landlady was out, so I wrote her a note while Bob scoured our room. Fortunately, our rent was up to date, so we would not be hearing from the law on this skip.

After we collected the last of our belongings, Bob jumped into the rear seat to keep our clothing from blowing away in my slipstream.

We arrived at the base as other pilots were turning up their F4F engines. I helped Bob stuff—literally, stuff—his belongings into the tiny storage compartment beneath the cockpit, then dashed over to my airplane and did the same. As I jumped up onto the wing on my way to the cockpit, I handed my car keys to my plane captain, the same trustworthy sergeant who had kept mum over my hitting the trees months earlier. "Please see if you can get the car to me in Quantico." I really hated to leave it, for it was like my oldest, best friend, the one constant in my life since flight school.

I joined up on Bob's wing as soon as we got airborne, and we pushed our throttles to the wall in order to catch up with the rest of the squadron, which was a few minutes ahead.

We made the 300-mile hop in a little over two hours and landed at Quantico's Turner Field. There, we faced a whirlwind of activity, packing and fine-tuning the Wildcats. We also had to absorb some new pilots and bid farewell to several comrades who were posted to brand-new squadrons. Among other things, all the airplanes were equipped with armor-plated seat backs and self-sealing tanks.

On the second day after we reached Turner Field, we were told at a squadron meeting that Germany had declared war on us. Major Jack also told us that VMF-121 would be reinforced to a total of 28 Wildcats and then leave the next day to fly cross-country to San Diego for possible future deployment to the Pacific.

★

The morning VMF-121 was slated to take off for San Diego, December 12, was bitterly cold, easily the coldest day I could recall experiencing in my whole life. I was glad to have been issued the bulky winter flight gear.

None of us had flown since the armor plate, new fuel tanks, and other heavy modifications had been installed. And no one told us about the extra weight, so I never thought about the potential differences in handling characteristics they would impose.

First a dive-bomber squadron took off, also bound for the West Coast, then VMF-121. I was next to last in the squadron formation, and behind me was Techical Sergeant Kenny Walsh, an extremely talented airman who had been denied a commission by one of the hardbitten oldtime air colonels who still believed that a Marine officer had to be a college-educated gentleman.

Each pilot who took off over the Potomac commented on the open tactical radio that the extra wingload gave him trouble, so, by the time my turn came, I was prepared to put on a little extra power. I revved the F4F's engine and came off the brakes but immediately ran into trouble as my F4F surged down the runway. We had been having problems with the electrical propeller-pitch controls for some time, and now my F4F's propeller blades would not go into full pitch, which was essential for getting that heavy fighter airborne. I was halfway down the runway when I knew I was not going to make it. The problem was that Kenny Walsh was right behind me, committed to his own takeoff. To make matters worse, the airplane got away from me when I momentarily put my head down to check the magnetos. I slewed to the right and actually felt Kenny Walsh's fighter pass right behind me, no doubt inches from a collision with my tail.

When I recovered my composure, which is not to say control of the airplane, I saw that I was heading right for the hangars, where many of the Marine Corps' limited aviation assets were parked. As I focused on this new danger, I saw that dozens of Marines and the families of the men who had just taken off were standing in front of the parked airplanes. I could plainly see their confused, onrushing faces.

I stomped on the right brake and tried to follow the circular taxiway farther to the right, to slew away from the transfixed crowd of well-wishers who had just seen their loved ones and comrades off to an uncertain future in the war.

Suddenly, I was speeding between two rows of parked SBC-4s, biwing dive-bombers. My F4F's wingtips were inches away from striking the precious warplanes as I fought to slow down and regain control without dodging to one side or the other. For all I knew, the SBC-4s were armed and fueled, so hitting them could easily roast me and numerous others.

I somehow made it into the clear and audibly sighed. But my travail was not quite over, for a silver-colored SNJ trainer taxied directly into my path. I squinched up my eyes in anticipation of killing myself and the unknown pilot before either of us met the enemy, but he saw me coming and really gunned his engine. My left wingtip missed his tail by a foot.

By this time, I had the F4F under control, but my landing gear dropped into a ditch moments before I would have rolled to a stop on my own. The propeller hit a post, and the nose pitched forward into the ground. Though I was securely strapped in, I managed to bash my head into the gunsight. Then I was thrown back against the headrest as the tail levered back to the ground. My head hurt, and I could feel a trickle of blood running down the side of my nose from my forehead.

I shook my head once or twice, then lapsed back into pure terror as I saw that a brown Marine Corps staff car had already pulled up in front of the ditch. The base commander, Lieutenant Colonel C. I. Campbell, was already walking toward my F4F. Hell, I thought, they've already sent the colonel to fire me! Wow, a million bucks for flight training down the drain!

Lieutenant Colonel Campbell, the same oldtime aviator who had blocked Kenny Walsh's commission, climbed up onto the wing as I pulled back my canopy in preparation of hearing a reading of my fate. I actually had my head appropriately hung in shame by the time the older man reached over and gently patted me on the shoulder, "Lieutenant, are you all right?"

"Uh, oh, ah, no, er, I mean, yes, Sir! I think I'm okay."

"Well, you seem to have a cut on your forehead. Here, use this." And he handed me a clean, white handkerchief to dab away the sticky blood. "I think we can have your airplane ready to fly within forty-eight hours. I'm pretty certain you can catch up with your squadron. Or they'll be there when you get there."

I fretted and fumed as a double groundcrew fixed the landing gear, installed a new propeller and pitch-control system, and pulled the engine for repairs and adjustments (and finally wound up replacing it with a new one). The mechanics went over the F4F from stem to stern to see what else I had broken.

Lieutenant Colonel Campbell was as good as his word. I took off exactly forty-eight hours after my first attempt, this time without excitement or mishap. I flawlessly rolled up my abused-thencodddled Wildcat's landing gear as I turned out over the Potomac and headed southwest toward Texas.

★

I was frightened out of my mind on that long, lonely flight. I could not help thanking God every hour on the hour for the hard work of the Red-and-Blue Maneuvers, which is where I had learned what I really needed to know about cross-country navigation to survive this journey.

I also kept thinking about an incident at New River, North Carolina, where VMF-121 spent a few days training with Marine infantry after the larger maneuvers. Two Army P-40 fighters had gone off course on a cross-country training flight. The two Air Corps lieutenants must have gotten it into their heads to try to find our little strip at New River, and they actually got to within ten miles of us when their fuel supply became critical. They tried to land abreast in a wide, fallow tobacco field, but both of them piled up on contact with the ground. Both pilots were dead in their crumpled factory-fresh fighters by the time we arrived with crash trucks and an ambulance. Aside from being the first dead bodies I had ever seen, the unlucky fate of those two young lieutenants painted a grim image for me, and that image grew ever grimmer as I headed deeper into the great unknown, completely in my own unsteady hands.

The whole world looked the same from 10,000 feet as I flew from navigational beam to navigational beam along the great transcontinental air highway the military had only recently established. After a while, I could no longer discern between the going-away and coming-toward $_opings_o$ in my headphones, and I became groggy from paying so much attention to my wind headings and so many other life-or-death details. Of course, I had been among the loudest moaners during navigation training at Pensacola. But I had also had to pay more attention to it because I was so bad at it. That sheer awfulness no doubt saved my life that bleak December week in 1941. My only ace in the hole was in knowing that the services had built or were building literally scores of bases in proximity to my flight path. Every time I figured out where I was, I plotted a contingency course to the nearest of them: I did not want to wind up like those two unlucky Air Corps lieutenants.

I do not know how many times I checked the wind direction by monitoring smokestacks and chimneys, looking for clothes drying on clotheslines, or observing which way cows were facing (they almost always face into the wind).

After hours of seesawing between boredom and terror, I began to notice how cramped the cockpit had become. For all practical purposes, this was my first long flight in the bulky winter flight suit, which was further bulked out by the parachute on my back and the rubber boat beneath my buttocks. I had not noticed until I was somewhere over Tennessee that I had barely enough room to move around and no room in which to rest any of my limbs or even reach the pisstube the F4F's designers had thoughtfully provided for our flying comfort.

I flew the prescribed 450 miles before landing to refuel and pick up weather information. I was thankful to stretch my kinked legs and slurp down some hot coffee and a quick meal. I had no idea where I was, but I kept on going. I am sure I slept at a military field that night, but I have no idea where.

I landed at Dallas late the next afternoon through a thick, unhealthy fog. Almost as soon as I climbed from the cramped cockpit, I spotted VMF-121's familiar F4Fs parked by the taxi apron. The plane captain told me that the squadron had been weathered in, but they hoped to leave in the morning if the fog lifted.

I was dog-tired and wanted to get some sleep, but I learned at the transient pilot's quarters that some of the local oilmen had chipped in and invited VMF-121 to a "little get-together" to show their appreciation for the fine job we had been doing thus far in keeping Japanese and German bombers from their oilfields. My leaden body perked right up at the news, and I caught a ride into town to find my comrades.

My fellow pilots patiently listened to my over excited, slightly drunken prattle about my narrow escape at Quantico and my self-esteemed tales of flying alone across the great unknown. They rejoined by telling me how 1st Lieutenant Ham Lawrence had collided with a buzzard over Baton Rouge; he was somewhere between there and Dallas seeing to his F4F's damaged wing.

We partied on right through to the next foggy dawn and slept it off back at the base.

We took off the next morning and flew in formation across the Southwest directly to El Paso. After stretching our legs and refueling at El Paso, we headed for Yuma, Arizona. As we were crossing

Guadalupe Pass at a mere 11,000 feet, 2nd Lieutenant Tolar Bryan, a Floridian on his first journey out of the Old South, blurted out over the squadron net, "I never seen snow before!"

We were just east of Yuma when 1st Lieutenant Paul Ashley, who had been a flight instructor while I was at Pensacola, calmly announced that his engine was dying and that he was going to attempt a deadstick landing on the highway we had been following across the state. Paul got his wheels onto the ground okay, but he found himself heading straight for an oncoming car. The pilot and the driver played chicken for a few moments, then Paul veered off the highway and upended his F4F when the right wheel stuck fast in the loose roadside sand. In fact, he did a pretty good imitation of my ignominious stop at Quantico. The rest of us landed at Yuma to refuel and heard the story when Paul phoned in to say he was unhurt.

We finally took off on the last leg of the transcontinental flight. After an uneventful hop across California's high Mojave Desert, we landed at North Island in San Diego on December 16, 1941. We hung around North Island for the day, which gave me an opportunity to phone my folks, and then we left the next day for our permanent training base at Kearney Mesa (now Miramar) in San Diego County.

The new field, which had been a blimp mooring mast until a few months earlier, sported a single, narrow 2,280-foot runway and minimum facililties. There were no taxiways, and the mud around the dispersal areas was so bad that any plane that rolled off the hardstand had to be dug out by hand.

We found ourselves on a total-war footing. Each morning, six pilots and airplanes, a full division of two three-plane elements, had to stand ready to take off at a moment's notice. That meant sitting in our cockpits for hours, keeping the engines warm so we could instantly get aloft to intercept Japanese bombers or chase off Japanese submarines.

The West Coast was populated by millions of people who expected a Japanese invasion, and the pilots of VMF-121 did, too.

The Navy gave us a special Christmas present that year. Fleet carrier *Saratoga* was in port at North Island to have some torpedo damage repaired. Since she was due to sail back to the war, her fighter-squadron commander arranged to trade all of his F2A Brewster Buffalo fighters for our well-tuned, thoroughly debugged modern F4Fs. The Brewster Buffalo was a thoroughly inadequate model that had been tested in quantity and rejected a year earlier by both services. (Six months later, at least three of my Pensacola classmates were killed at Midway flying F2As. In fact, every Marine Buffalo launched from Midway was shot down.)

★

We did a lot of running around during those first uncertain months of the war. Young men who expect to die soon have a tendency to raise hell, and VMF-121 did its share. I hooked up with Jeff Poindexter, Jack Amende, and other friends from my cadet days as soon as VMF-111 joined us at Kearney Mesa. Together, we cut a wide swath through the ladies of the region.

The only inhibiting factor was that my red convertible had not yet appeared. I received a letter in January from my old plane captain, who said that he was trying to find someone reliable to drive it to the West Coast, but that did not solve my immediate problem or my diminished social standing. What I really needed, I realized, was a girlfriend with a car. I got one. Boy, did I get one!

As time wore on, I became increasingly philosophical—which is to say, maudlin—over my chances of surviving the war. I came to question the wisdom of getting an early start in the service, for even I could see that my nation was woefully unprepared to meet the Japanese in combat. The first of my Pensacola classmates had already been posted as Missing in Action at Wake Island, where a single, totally unsupported F4F squadron had fought itself out against a Japanese fleet that included at least two full Japanese carrier air groups. We had nothing with which to match the awesome power of the Imperial Navy's carrier air arm, not to mention its hundreds of modern land-based Navy and Army warplanes.

I suppose I did what many thousands of young men have done since war was invented. I became involved in a whirlwind romance that resulted in a wedding I only dimly desired. The girl was wealthy, sophisticated, smart, and fun to be with. She dazzled me and I dazzled her; we swept one another off our feet. It was great fun to be together. And it was great fun when the time came to dress up in my white formal dress uniform and leave the church beneath the crossed swords of my fellow pilots, to honeymoon in a lavishly appointed hotel, and to play at being a married couple with long years of life and love stretched endlessly before us. I knew even then, as my training schedule picked up and as the inevitability of shipping out loomed closer, that I had rushed into a situation I would not have been able to handle under any other circumstances. But I had fallen in love with her, so I trusted more than hoped that time would work things out. But I had no time then, so I simply put the doubts aside for the rest of my stay at Kearney Mesa; I buried my fears and self-doubts, as did we all, in partying and love-making, in role-playing.

10

I was suddenly transferred into VMF-111, an F4F squadron, with several other VMF-121 pilots in early February, 1942.

The 1st Marine Air Wing, which the two squadrons had been a part of since before the war, was rapidly expanding in the face of burgeoning wartime needs, and new squadrons and air groups were being formed and reformed faster than anyone could keep track of them.

At the same time I was transferred, Sam Jack was promoted to lieutenant colonel and placed in command of a new group, MAG-12, which was to consist of four fighter squadrons: 121, 122, 123 and 124. In order to assure that each of the three new squadrons had an adequate cadre of trained professionals, VMF-121 was broken up, and about half of its pilots were transferred to the new squadrons, which would continue to train under Sam Jack's careful scrutiny at Kearney Mesa.

The rest of us were transferred into Major Dan Torrey's VMF-111, which was itself broken up to staff new squadrons in Lieutenant Colonel T. J. Walker's new MAG-13, which 111 was a part of. I and my fellow transferees were frankly put out by the change of venue, and we tried to wrangle our way back into MAG-12 so we could continue to serve under Sam Jack. But the new lieutenant colonel only smiled and told us to make the best of it.

Jack knew something we did not know: VMF-111 was to sail into the Pacific to guard one of the forwardmost Allied holdings in the face of the whirlwind Japanese amphibious drive across the Pacific. We were slated to plunge into the Pacific in early March to become part of America's forward shield in the Pacific.

★

The squadron flight and ground personnel joined a Marine coast artillery detachment aboard the former civilian liner *President Garfield* at San Diego's North Island on March 8, 1942, and immediately set sail—alone, without a warship escort—into the vast, hostile Pacific.

The ship was well away from the West Coast before our destination was revealed at an officers' call by Major Brown, the infantry commander, and Lieutenant Colonel Walker, the air group commander. We were headed for the lush, tropical, threatened Samoan Islands, specifically Pago Pago, in American Samoa, where we would support a Marine ground brigade that would be sailing in a month's time.

None of the pilots I talked with—including my old buddies, Stan Tutton, Jeff Poindexter, Jack Amende, and Louis Gordon— initially gave more than a hoot and a holler at the prospects we might face in Samoa. Our immediate concern was surviving the journey on a sea we knew was infested by bloodthirsty Japanese submarine skippers. Our first and only line of defense was keeping our ship completely blacked out. Major Brown, a really tough old bird, let it out that he would personally execute any Marine or sailor caught showing a light between an hour before sunset and an hour after sunrise. No one, absolutely no one, tested the major's resolve to carry out the sentence.

My fellow pilots and I were a wisecracking bunch who normally affected a cynical devil-may-care attitude toward all public displays of concern, but we all took lifeboat drills and similar activities *very* seriously.

The level of fear was running so high aboard *President Garfield* that some of the ground troops living below decks went off their rockers and had to be locked away in a section that had been converted to serve as the former luxury liner's brig.

As we gained our sea legs and confidence—we had not been torpedoed yet—we had more time and inclination to talk about what we were going to do to the enemy. The war was going badly, and the prospects of our nation holding the line forward of Samoa were bleak, absolutely grim. We bragged among ourselves that we wished no harm upon our fellow Marine, Navy and Air Corps pilots, but we did not exactly wish the squadrons based forward of Samoa all that much success in holding the line. How else would we get to fight? We did not know then that there *were* no squadrons based forward of Samoa and the Fijis. We were the proverbial *it!*

★

President Garfield arrived safely late on March 11, 1942. Our destination was the port of Pago Pago (pronounced *pongo-pongo*) on the island of Tutuila, which boasted one of the Earth's great natural harbors and one of its most beautiful natural wonders. High above us, the trade winds daily gathered the rain clouds as a mantle around the summit of Rain Mountain, and sunny beaches backed by waving palms spread in all directions. The splendor I saw that day took my breath away; I have never been so exhilarated by anything I saw before or since.

We slowly eased into the port and came to rest beside a quay for unloading. One of the first buildings I focused on was a nondescript commercial establishment whose weather beaten sign proclaimed it to be "Goat Island," a bar. I made a mental note and vowed to return to drink a toast to my safe landing.

Everyone just hung around on the main deck while the sailors and Samoan longshoremen unloaded jeeps, trucks, and tentage from the ship's holds. During that time, everyone bemoaned the fact that we saw not one bare-breasted South Seas damsel.

Finally, the squadron personnel were loaded aboard the vehicles and driven from the port area to our new home, Tafuna Field, which was located across the island on the south shore.

★

The United States, Great Britain, and Germany had squabbled over ownership of the Samoas through the latter half of the nineteenth century, but none could permanently gain the upper hand over the others. The island group was ideally located along the trade routes and was ideally suited to serve as a major naval base.

Finally, after years of arguing, all three nations signed the Tripartate Treaty of 1899. Germany was awarded the two largest islands in the group, Savaii and Upola, and the United States got

Tutuila, which, though smaller, boasted the best harbor, at Pago Pago. The U.S. government turned American Samoa, which also included numerous smaller islands, over to the Navy to administer, a natural progression in view of the reasons for acquiring the possession in the first place.

The Germans commercially dominated the region until the end of World War I, when all their colonies were turned over to the League of Nations for redistribution as nominal trusteeships. The German holdings in Western Samoa were ultimately mandated to the care of New Zealand.

When we arrived, Eastern, or American, Samoa was the only United States possession anywhere in the world where the national sport was cricket.

The United States Navy decided to build an airbase complex on Tutuila in the late 1930s, and engineers selected Tafuna. However, nothing would be done until the naval base at Pago Pago had been upgraded and modernized. A $10 million contract was awarded for the naval base upgrade in 1940, and work began in early 1941. The civilian contractors were in the process of installing oil storage tanks and station facilities when the Japanese struck Pearl Harbor.

The naval base was hurriedly finished, and the center of the construction activity was centered on Tafuna at last. However, a snag quickly arose. Following the tragic involvement of civilian construction workers in the battle for Wake Island, all civilians working on constructing military bases in the Pacific were withdrawn and replaced, wherever possible, by naval construction battalions, Seabees. Fortunately, a Seabee battalion was immediately made available to work on Tafuna, and it was shipped in even before any significant defense forces left the United States. The Seabees worked like mad to hew a 2,500-foot-by-250-foot runway out of the jungle toward the sea and then cover it with tons of crushed coral and volcanic rock, which were also used to lengthen the seaward end of the runway right out into the shallow lagoon.

The major work—but none of the finishing touches—was completed only days before VMF-111's arrival. Then the Seabees departed to undertake necessary construction work elsewhere in the group and throughout the dwindling Allied bastions in the South Pacific.

★

Our living conditions at Tafuna were rustic, and the heat was all but unbearable. We had to contend with swarms of coconut bugs and mosquitos, knee-deep mud, and daily rainstorms that dropped literally inches of rainwater within minutes.

The rain rendered typical service-type housing out of the question. Native workers were hired to build numerous fales (pronounced *follies*) for us. This native construction, adapted locally over hundreds of years, consisted of a light, airy prefabricated structure with 8'-by-8' wall sections built over a 16'-by-16' base. The squadron buildings, completely fitted out with furniture and mosquito nets, had been built in the week or two before our arrival, and we moved right in.

All we needed was our airplanes, but they were on another ship about a week behind us.

While we were waiting for the planes, our MAG-13 commander, Lieutenant Colonel T. J. Walker, mobilized all squadron personnel into an ad hoc infantry company to support the small Marine infantry contingent assigned to guard the base. This was the first contact any of us but the most senior pilots had had with Marine infantry tactics. Again, despite the wisecracking that was our trademark, all the young pilots listened as attentively to experienced infantrymen as we had to our flight instructors before our first solos.

Our dedication was considerably enhanced, if it needed to be, by news that a Japanese submarine had surfaced off the Pago Pago naval station on January 11 and shelled the place, wounding a Navy officer and several members of the local defense force.

Lieutenant Colonel Walker and others stressed again and again how vulnerable we were and would be, with or without our F4Fs. To call ourselves a "leading edge" was to raise our status by hundreds of degrees. Except for a large and growing air establishment in Hawaii, the line in the Pacific was being held by about a half-dozen fighter squadrons and even fewer dive-bomber squadrons. The Navy had five operational fleet carriers and their complete air groups based in the Pacific at the time, but we knew that they would not come to our aid unless the Japanese committed their own, more numerous carriers. Our job was simply to attack Japanese warships as far out at sea as we could find them and, failing that, to defend the beaches when the dreaded invasion force landed. As had already happened at Wake, those of us who survived air combat were expected to fight on as infantry once our Wildcats could no longer be flown.

We were expendable. Our only purpose out there was to buy time for our nation to train and equip the hundreds of Navy, Marine, and Air Corps squadrons yet to be formed.

Our squadron's nineteen F4F-3 Wildcat fighters arrived aboard U.S.S. *Procyon* about a week after us, along with our second echelon of groundcrewmen and clerks. The airplanes, which arrived with their wings removed so they could be carried in *Procyon's* cargo holds, were carefully unloaded and uncrated. The wings were winched aboard flatbed trucks, as was the tail section of each fighter. Then the precious warplanes were pulled backward through the streets of Pago Pago and fifteen miles across the island by way of twisting mountain roads. It rained unmercifully all day.

The occasion marked our first trip out of Tafuna, and Lieutenant Colonel Walker enforced the standing order that military personnel go everywhere wearing a steel helmet and carrying at least a .45-caliber pistol and a gasmask. That worried us.

As soon as our mechanics had rebuilt the F4Fs, VMF-111 was on constant alert. Every day, from at least an hour before dawn until after breakfast, at least six pilots at a time were geared up and sitting in their cockpits, ready to take off at a moment's notice. There were always armed aircraft in the air after breakfast, for our training schedule was absolutely unrelenting. In addition, from the first day we had airplanes, all of us flew sector searches at least 100 miles out to sea at least once a day on a rotating basis.

On April 6, we were reinforced, if that is the word, by Marine Observation Squadron (VMO) 151, which arrived with a large Marine infantry contingent in four ships directly from Norfolk, Virginia, by way of the Panama Canal. The new squadron was equipped with a dozen ancient, underpowered SBC-4 biplanes, ostensibly for the purpose of dive-bombing the Japanese fleet into submission. The only real boost in our morale brought on by the convoy's arrival was news that it had been escorted across most of the Pacific by a carrier task force commanded by Vice Admiral William Halsey; at least we knew that someone else was out there with us.

The best part of having VMO-151 sharing Tafuna with us was the easing of our sector-search schedule. This was the dive-bomber squadron's specialty, and they did most of the work, though VMF-111 retained responsibility for covering a half-dozen of the fixed pie-shaped sectors. That left us with more time to practice fighter tactics and aerial gunnery.

We suffered our first fatality during this period, while six of us, in two three-plane elements, were practicing formation dogfighting. The two elements had just completed a head-on mock firing pass and I was recovering to the left, when I saw that 2nd Lieutenant Jack Lyons's F4F had broken from the opposing formation and was spiralling nose-first toward the sea. I had no idea why Lyons was diving, but he looked to be in trouble, and I instinctively dived away after him. Jack never got out of the airplane; I saw no sign of life in the cockpit. The F4F plunged straight into the water and was never seen again. I learned within a minute that Jack had swept ahead of and too close to his element leader and that the element leader's propeller had cut through Jack's F4F right behind the cockpit. Jack doubtless had zero control over his fighter in the wake of the collision, and he could very well have been too dazed or injured to react. Or perhaps his cockpit canopy had become stuck on its rails while Jack was trying to bail out. Whatever the case, Jack Lyons died when his Wildcat dived into the water.

I was royally chewed out after we landed by the flight leader, Captain Don Yost, our squadron exec; he said, correctly, that I had no business breaking formation for any reason unless I was told to do so.

Right after VMO-151 arrived, the Navy merged its only flight increment in American Samoa with MAG-13. This was VS-1-D14 (Scouting Squadron 1, Detachment 14), which had arrived on January 23 to fly virtually unarmed OS2U fleet scout seaplanes. This administrative merging, the first of its kind, was highly unusual, in that the Marine Corps was considered the junior naval service. However, the departure from tradition was short-lived, for VS-1-D14 was transferred west to British Samoa in early May.

While we were racing to catch up with ourselves, news arrived that all the American garrisons in the Philippines had accepted Japanese surrender terms. As far as we were concerned, that could only mean that the huge Japanese resources that had been tied down in the Philippines since December would be available for work elsewhere in the Pacific.

The nearest Marine fighter squadron to Tafuna was VMF-211, which flew fourteen F2A Brewster Buffalo fighters from the carrier *Lexington* at Palmyra Island on April 18. We also heard that a new F4F squadron, VMF-212, was slated to occupy Efate, in the French New Hebrides, to guard the southern flank.

We had no offensive power in the South Pacific, and very few defensive options. On the other hand, the Japanese had maintained the initiative from the first day of the war. They had demonstrably superior weapons in the hands of trained, *experienced* soldiers, sailors, and airmen. Their tactics were proven successful. And there were far more of them in the arena than us. All we could do was train and wait. Our fate would be decided in Tokyo.

11

We heard in the second week of May that U.S. Navy carriers had blunted a major Japanese amphibious foray through the Coral Sea a week earlier. As details mounted, it became evident that the two fleets had fought the first carrier-versus-carrier battle in history—without the warships of either side ever seeing the warships of the other—and that our naval aviators had sunk at least one of their carriers and several surface ships. We were also saddened to learn, however, that our carrier *Lexington* was lost with several smaller vessels.

The Coral Sea Battle was our very first Pacific victory, but it remained to be seen if we could take the initiative. We remained spread thin in the air and on the ground throughout the South Pacific.

The biggest worry we had in Samoa and other bases along the thin, porous forward shield was that the Japanese would go all out to destroy us as a way of mitigating its setback in early May. Our vigilance and training were redoubled. We really expected to see the Japanese fleet sail over our horizon.

Intelligence briefs throughout the remainder of May gave credence to our self-generated fears. There was no doubt that Japan was going to mount a major fleet strike using many carriers somewhere in our vast region. Follow-up attacks were planned throughout the region if the first strike was successful and if our our main battle fleet, including the precious carriers, was drawn out and destroyed.

The showdown came during the first week in June, when six Japanese fleet carriers bypassed us in Samoa and lashed out against Midway, which was to be amphibiously invaded once the beach defenses and air squadrons had been destroyed. Marine, and Air Corps squadrons flying out of Midway, and Navy carrier air groups over the horizon, retaliated in an all-or-nothing gamble to defend Midway. When the smoke cleared, Midway was secure, four of the six Japanese fleet carriers had been sunk, and about a dozen of my former Pensacola and Opa-Locka classmates were dead.

We learned within a week that the Japanese master plan called for serious raids against Samoa after Midway had been finished off. We were marked for eventual invasion.

The pressure lifted not one iota, though our relief at not being invaded raised our morale. If anything, our vigilance was redoubled yet again in anticipation of retaliatory raids or, worse, an all-or-nothing bid by the Japanese to conclude the war by force of arms.

★

In addition to our normal complement of F4F Wildcat fighters, we also owned a Grumman J2F Duck, a tiny two-place amphibious spotter plane used for courier service, antisubmarine patrols, or rescuing downed pilots.

Interestingly, very few VMF-111 pilots had ever checked out in water landings before arriving in Samoa. Since all of us were liable for courier service, we all had to learn to land on the water, for our runs usually took us to British Samoa or the outer islands, which had no runways. We were also liable for undertaking antisubmarine patrols in the Duck, which could carry a depth charge slung under each wing. The usual manner of checking out in the Duck was to fly rear-seat on an antisubmarine patrol with an "expert" who knew how to land in the water. The second time I flew the Duck, I was responsible for "training" one of my comrades.

We carried literally everything in the Duck: mail, passengers, the paymaster, beer, even coconuts. We always took off (and, as it happened, returned) with our two depth charges. Our usual destination was Satapaula in Western Samoa, where VS-1-D14 had taken up residence in April to serve as our "distant" early warning system. Satapaula is 100 miles west of Tutuila, which was 100 miles closer to the Japanese.

There was, at the time, a new airstrip under construction at Faleola, about twenty miles north of Apia, the capital of British Samoa. Until the strip could be finished, VS-1-D14 and our Duck landed and took off from the lagoon beside the construction site.

One of the most important things we learned in our check-flights in the Duck was to roll up the landing gear after taking off from Tafuna. The Duck was so slow in the air that it lost nothing to wind drag, so having the gear up had nothing to do with its airworthiness—it was just impossible to bring her in for a safe water landing with the gear down.

Lieutenant Spud Miller forgot the lesson one day when he and Lieutenant Pete Peterson were charged with flying the paymaster to Faleola. As I recall, Spud was the command pilot and Pete was checking out for the first time in the Duck. The paymaster was riding in the spacious, hollow pontoon, which we often fitted out with mattresses to provide a modicum of comfort for our passengers. I am sure that the little amphibian was also carrying supplies and perhaps a few cases of beer to brighten the day for the Navy search pilots. As usual, the Duck had two 500-lb bombs strapped under its wings. These bombs would double as depth charges if they were dropped on enemy submarines; if they were dropped armed, they would detonate on contact, but if they were dropped unarmed, they were set to detonate 50 feet beneath the waves.

As was our custom, Spud made a low pass over the lagoon to draw the Navy pilots and groundcrewmen out to give the brave fighter pilot a rousing welcome. Or maybe it was the paymaster who drew the crowd. Whatever the case, Spud drew a respectable audience, and every man there seemed to be yelling and waving. In sheer joy, Spud thought.

There was a radio aboard the Duck but no control tower on the ground, so no one could tell Spud that his gear was down. All the yelling and waving was a game effort by fellow airmen to warn the Gyrene pilot that he was about to screw up. But Spud could not hear them over the engine noise, and he preferred to believe that they were all admiring his technique. He made another pass over the lagoon and the adjacent base. Then he rolled out with a flourish and eased into his landing.

The landing gear hit the water before the pontoon did, and the lithe little airplane flipped right over on its back.

Spud, Pete, and the paymaster dived away from the submerged cockpits and pontoon and surfaced a moment later. There was cash all around the crash site, for the paymaster's satchel had been jarred open on impact. A crash boat was immediately dispatched, most likely more for the sake of rescuing the cash than the men. The two pilots and the paymaster thought they were in for a quick rescue, but the launch suddenly slowed and then circled away. Spud called out to ask what the trouble was, and one of the men in the launch said the crew was afraid to come closer because of the bombs attached to the bilged airplane. It took some sincere expletives from Spud, Pete, and the paymaster—who would control the money if it could be recovered—to entice the launch to within arm's length.

Until Pete was picked up and could explain his bizarre behavior, none of the onlookers could understand why the crazy Marine pilot was swimming with only one arm while holding the other arm high out of the water. Pete showed his rescuers the nifty new gold wrist-watch his family had sent him. It had arrived only a week before and was Pete's pride and joy. Of course, the brief dunking had destroyed the beautiful thing.

The story of Spud's landing made news throughout the naval aviation establishment. A few months later, Spud's photo appeared on the cover of our trade magazine, the *Gosport*. Beneath Spud's smiling likeness was the caption, "Dilbert of the Month." And a hand-drawn likeness of Pete graced one of the inside pages over the caption, "Keep your head out of your ass."

★

Captain Jake Meyers, commander of the Marine tank company based at nearby Trona, had wanted to become a pilot but had been turned down because of a physical problem that was discovered at his flight exam. Jake spent all his off-duty hours hanging out at Tafuna, shooting the breeze with the pilots and mechanics, providing liquor when we were dry, generally begging us to take him aloft for "some stick time." All Jake lived for was to fly an airplane just one time.

In addition to the fighters and the resurrected Duck, the squadron owned an SNJ instrument trainer, which we used to bone up on instrument flying. One day, after having heard Jake beg for months, one of the fighter pilots gave the tanker the nod and took him up for a spin. If all went according to plan, Jake would have an opportunity to run a few simple maneuvers.

They had been aloft for only a few minutes and were running through a series of aerobatics over the sea when, for no reason the pilot could fathom, the usually responsive SNJ fell into an inverted spin from 10,000 feet—the same sort of spin that had killed three of my classmates at Opa-Locka in a single week.

The SNJ was falling quite fast and the pilot needed all his concentration and strength to recover, but he took time out for his passenger: "Jake, bail out!" he called over the intercom.

Jake had never had a parachute on before that day, but he was a good Marine, which means he did exactly what he was told by the man in authority. Out he went.

Immediately after Jake left the SNJ, the pilot came up with the right combination of corrective actions and brought the airplane to straight, level flight. He looked around for his former passenger and saw that Jake was okay, floating beneath a huge white silk canopy over the stunning blue Pacific. The Duck was in use elsewhere, so the pilot arranged for the crash boat to leave Tafuna while the SNJ slowly circled overhead.

Jake landed in the water without difficulty, but no one had told him how to spill air out of the chute to keep from being dragged along the surface by the wind. This day, there was a 15-to-20-knot offshore surface breeze, which pushed Jake farther out to sea. The crash boat was a speedy little thing, but it had to overcome Jake's surface speed as well as the initial distance.

The wind also whipped a great deal of water into Jake's face, and the gyrating chute kept dragging him under for unpredictable periods. Jake was certain he was going to drown, but he was eventually rescued and returned to the beach.

The SNJ pilot was brought up on charges for taking an unauthorized passenger aloft, but it came to nothing because, frankly, we had too few pilots in forward areas, or anywhere, to ground a competent man for a relatively minor infraction that turned out well in the end. The rest of us filed that information for future use.

★

The F4F was a formidable weapon against friend or foe.

The prevailing wind at Tafuna obliged us to take off over the lagoon, which was the safer way in any case because the flight path was clear in that direction but was dominated by hills and trees at the inland end.

The group dentist, Dr. Jones, had a little shack set up as a dental dispensary about two-thirds the way down the runway, on the left side as we took off. One day, one of the F4Fs ground-looped to the left (in the direction of the engine torque) right in front of Dr. Jones's dispensary. The force of the unexpected turn was so great that the 100-lb bomb slung beneath one of the fighter's wings came loose from its shackles and skipped across the runway right up to Dr. Jones's door. The bomb did not detonate, but Dr. Jones did; he never set foot in that shack again.

The group maintenance shop was on the opposite side of the runway from Dr. Jones's dispensary and farthest from the lagoon end of the coral-topped strip. One day, an F4F was landing from over the lagoon, toward the hills, when the pilot lost control and ground-looped to the left, as usual. The airplane headed for the group maintenance hangar and rolled right through the open door before it could be stopped. The group maintenance chief, a leathery old warrant officer named Gadje, jumped out of his skin and came thoroughly unglued when he looked up just in time to see the silvery, transluscent propeller disc heading right at him. Gunner Gadje jumped up and ran. But, instead of going out the side door, he headed straight back into the hangar and knocked himself out on the rear wall.

A bizarre series of accidents nearly claimed the lives of several Marine SBC-4 dive-bomber crews when collapsed landing gear sent three of the ancient airplanes sliding across the runway on takeoffs and landings in only a week's time. There was no ready explanation. The SBC-4 had been in service for years, and the problem was a new one. Finally, it was discovered that someone had been tapping alcohol from the landing-gear struts to fire a boring stay. We never found out who the culprit was, but he apparently stopped when he realized that lives were at stake. Meantime, three of our precious warplanes were out of service for a while.

★

Several of us made first lieutenant during the early summer, and not by the usual means.

Lieutenant Colonel T. J. Walker, the group commander, called a number of young Reserve lieutenants into his office one day and

pitched us on the advantages of signing up as Regular Marine officers, which would allow us to stay in after the war and *might* give
us an advantage when promotions came due. Since the colonel had
gone to the trouble of having the contracts drawn up, we all signed.

A few weeks later, Jeff Poindexter, Louis Gordon, Jack Amende,
and several others, including me, received our promotions. I have no
idea whether they would have come through anyway; but there
wasn't a second lieutenant of my flight school generation in MAG-
13 who had not succumbed to Walker's pitch.

It did not dawn on us then, but our move to the Regulars invali-
dated the flight bonus we had all earned when we signed up for the
Naval Aviation Cadet program and accepted Reserve commissions.
The $500 per year I was to receive for four years — my college nest-
egg—was completely wiped out; I never received a dime of it.

12

The new runway the Seabees had been building at Faleola, on Upolu in Western Samoa, was completed late the first week of August, 1942, and I was ordered out of Tafuna with the first mixed detachment of F4Fs and SBC-4s.

Momentous news arrived as we were preparing to leave Tafuna. A U.S. Navy amphibious force had penetrated to the Japanese-held Eastern Solomon Islands, and a reinforced division of Marines had landed on August 7 at Tulagi and Guadalcanal, seizing a nearly completed Japanese-built runway on the latter island. Early indications were that things were going well for our side.

We realized that a successful outcome of events in the Solomons would place us just over 1,000 miles behind the active war zone.

Six VMF-111 F4Fs, mine included, left Tafuna on the morning of August 10 for the short hop to Faleola's virgin 4,000-foot runway, which we found teeming with Samoans, none of whom had ever seen a modern land-based warplane before. It was all we could do to roll to a short stop and quickly cut our engines to avoid slicing some innocent islanders to pieces. When I climbed out of my cockpit, hundreds of islanders surrounded me and pulled at my clothing or slapped me on the back and shoulders as exuberant signs of welcome.

When I finally struggled free of the crowd, I walked alone the short distance to the bay shore and stared across the blue Pacific waters to Savaii, the largest of the Samoan islands. I could smell night-blooming jasmine, ginger, and other tropical aromas carried by the gentle offshore breeze. I wondered how long it would be before this gorgeous, uncluttered spot became overrun with Western technology and the rush to get somewhere else. I shook my head and worried that I was "going native."

When the welcome settled down, I returned to my airplane and pulled my belongings from the storage compartment, then walked to the tent in which I and another pilot would be quartered until Samoan workers could build fales for us.

Late that afternoon, the elderly chief of a nearby village came to greet us. Three of the Wildcat pilots had already left for parts unknown, so only Jack Amende, Norm Mitchell, and I were on hand to accept his invitation to join him at his home and meet his family.

When we arrived, the chief's wife offered us each a lavalava, a bright-colored wrap-around dress, worn by men and women, which reminded me of a festive tablecloth. The three of us readily acceeded to the wish, for we wanted to show proper respect and, while we were at it, have fun.

Then, following the lead of our hosts, we sat cross-legged on coconut mats in the chief's fale before a huge bowl filled with kava, a mildly intoxicating nonalcoholic drink made from the roots of a pepper plant mixed with coconut milk. The chief gave me the first bowl of kava and beckoned that I drink. I found the taste pleasing. Soon, I was matching the chief and all the other Samoan men who were there toast for toast while a number of beautiful girls sat behind us preparing mounds of food.

For all the months I had lived in Samoa, it turned out that this was my first meal of palusami, a thick coconut cream cooked in taro leaves and served on thick slices of taro topped with green bananas.

After everyone ate and drank to bursting, the girls began singing Polynesian songs and, following the chief's lead, Jack, Norm, and I joined in. I was utterly transported, keenly aware of all the pleasant breezes riffling through the open sides of the fale, of the chirping of night creatures, of the murmuring surf on the nearby beach, of the peace and community that transcended my warlike presence.

★

Lieutenant Bill Deuterman was killed off Savaii on September 9, 1942. Bill, who had always said that he would never bail out of a crippled airplane, ran into trouble over the bay and could not make it back to Faleola. He tried to set his F4F down on the water. Jeff Poindexter, who was flying on Bill's wing all the way down, saw Bill stand up in the cockpit at about the last minute before the airplane impacted. Bill was clearly trying to bail out, but he was too low in any case for his chute to have deployed. Jeff watched in sheer horror as the F4F's propeller bit into the waves. This flipped the airplane over at great speed and threw Bill against the windscreen and instrument panel. Jeff was certain that Bill died on impact. If not, he was certainly unconscious when he sank forever beneath the waves.

★

When the squadron finally got itself sorted out at Faleola, we discovered that we had somehow acquired a station wagon. Though we were told this civilian-type vehicle was to be used only for official business and transport to the flight line, we all had different ideas. Four of us simply stole the station wagon one late August afternoon and drove it the twenty miles to Apia on our first real leave since our arrival in Samoa in March.

The boys from VS-1-D14 had told us to spend our two free nights (barring the intervention of military policemen) at a hotel run by Aggie Grey, a gracious lady who later served in small part as the model for Bloody Mary in James Michener's book, *Tales of the South Pacific*.

The drive itself was a bit shocking, for we constantly had to slow down or stop along the newly paved road through unforgettable scenery to avoid hitting pigs and the islanders who were driving them along or across the roadway.

We followed the Navy pilots' directions and found the hotel without difficulty. It was located right on the beach overlooking Apia Bay. Beside the main structure was a tropical river in which naked children were splashing while their mothers sat on the banks gossiping and laughing as I have only heard Polynesians laugh. I also heard strains of what I took to be German in their conversation, a holdover from the decades of German colonial stewardship.

The hotel itself was a monument of pleasure to us fighter pilots; we had seen nothing like it in six war-weary months. It was a white three-story structure with living and working quarters on the top two stories and the more-or-less open ground floor reserved for the storage of nonessential items that could be sacrificed in the event of a flood or a tidal wave, which apparently were common enough to warrant the arrangement.

The four of us climbed the stairs to the front verandah and entered. Aggie Grey was on hand to greet us and make us welcome. She also warned us to be quiet because the Marine general in command of the troops in Western Samoa was at that moment ensconced in a third-story bedroom.

In time, Aggie Grey's hotel became the headquarters of all the American pilots who worked in or passed through Apia during the war. In time, Aggie learned how to cook hamburgers to suit our American tastes, and she earned more money providing them than she ever did running a hotel.

The only problem that arose at Aggie Grey's was the wholesale theft of gasoline, tires, and other movable bounty from the hordes of jeeps that eventually could be found parked there every evening. Sometimes, if a jeep was foolishly parked beneath an overhanging tree branch, brave thieves would winch out the engine. In time, military policemen were permanently stationed around the hotel, just to keep an eye on government property and not to monitor the officers within.

Aggie also provided an important service to enlisted soldiers, sailors, and Marines, who were barred from within the hotel when it was eventually turned into an officers' club. Officers had access to a reasonable supply of beer and stronger spirits, but enlisted personnel could only purchase beer in limited, strictly rationed quantities. However, there was nothing but the laws of supply and demand stopping them from buying locally supplied liquor on the open market.

In return for providing raisins, rice, corn, and other such ingredients (at a fair price), Aggie was able to provide the teeming masses of enlisted personnel, and not a few officers, with her own varying recipe of booze, sold under the sobriquet Bush Gin, for $2.00 a bottle.

Another local resident turned out a passable if illegal home-made beer, and it seemed as though everyone in Samoa was making money selling Palm Toddy to American servicemen. This age-old brew had been prohibited on the open market since the earliest days of the British mandate, but the toddy-tappers, the islanders who turned out the unsophisticated brew, had a thousand ways to dodge the law.

The sale of Palm Toddy was usually consummated only after the toddy-tapper had shinnied up a thirty-foot palm to retrieve the needed supply. This requirement came about as a result of the method of making Palm Toddy. Coconut buds had earlier been selected by the toddy-tapper and scored with a knife and bound tightly in palm fronds. Glass jam jars hanging beneath the selected buds collected the slow trickle of juice from the cuts. The result, which resembled barley juice, was nonalcoholic, but it produced a mild, laughing intoxication and ended with a very mild, not-altogether-unpleasant hangover.

★

The emphasis on having a good time and attendant heavy drinking came in the wake of the Guadalcanal invasion. The battle was not going well for our Marines and sailors through September, but the focus of the war had moved a thousand miles from Samoa and, though we still felt vulnerable, the sheer terror of the early days was slowly dissipating. By then, new airbases were being built well forward. (An Air Corps P-39 squadron had been sent to the Fijis in January, 1942, and another was working out of Noumea in the New Hebrides. A growing number of Marine and Navy squadrons and a group of Air Corps B-17s were based in the New Hebrides, at Efate and on New Caledonia.) Increasingly, we felt that we had arrived at a great impasse, that our presence was less and less important, that we were missing out on the real war. Fighter pilots with whom we had trained or who had graduated from flight school long after us were knocking down Japanese planes every day of the week in the hotly contested skies over Guadalcanal, and our months of intense, dangerous training were coming to nothing except fates like Bill Deuterman's and Jack Lyons's. None of us minded risking our lives at the outer limits of personal combat, but no one wanted to die in this backwater.

Still, since nothing much threatened us, we relaxed, unwound, and sought solace from the intense pressures we had allowed to build up when little besides ourselves stood between the Japanese and our last Pacific battle line.

The rush to fun nearly cost four of us twenty years apiece in Leavenworth.

One September evening, Louis Gordon, Jeff Poindexter, a Marine infantry officer, and I dug up a like number of island girls and about a gallon of medicinal alcohol mixed with grape juice and ice, with which we repaired to sleepy Pago Pago. We met our dates in town and headed for the home of one of them, a gorgeous two-story fale overlooking the moonlit lagoon.

We were gassed pretty early, singing Polynesian love chants to the accompaniment of a ukelele and rubbing cheeks with the Samoan lovelies. Suddenly, I looked up to see that Louis was duking it out with an enlisted Marine on the verandah.

Louis had been a fine intercollegiate boxer before going to flight school, and he was easily holding his own against the inexpert, brawling style of his adversary until a second Marine jumped him from behind. Louis looked stunned for a second, then he recovered and commenced to hit both Marines with lightning left and right jabs. I could clearly hear the *thud* and *smack* of Louis's fists on their bodies.

A third Marine got into the fray and round-housed Louis in the back of the head. At that point, I stopped enjoying the spectacle and decided to get actively involved. I dropped the Samoan girl who was in my lap to the coconut-mat floor and charged across the room at the third assailant. A fourth Marine appeared out of nowhere and caught me with a flying right hook that threw me back into the chair. I was so dazed I could actually see stars and hear strange sounds going off in my head.

By the time I finished shaking my head to refocus my vision, the fight had moved out to the verandah, four enlisted Marines against 1st Lieutenant Louis Gordon.

I saw what was coming but could do nothing to stop it.

Jeff Poindexter looked up from his conversation on the verandah with the infantry officer just as Louis stepped backward through the fale's doorway. I saw Jeff's eyes take in the scene, and I saw his hand come up with his heavy .45-caliber automatic pistol, which we were all obliged to have with us at all times. Jeff hesitated for only a second, I am sure to decide how to use the weapon, then swung it around, butt-first, and cracked the nearest Marine right across the head. I heard the sound of breaking bone and saw the Marine lifted from his feet by the force of the blow, for Jeff was a huge, powerful man in top physical condition. The Marine's body hung in midair for an instant as Jeff's arm followed through. I saw a look of horror on the big pilot's face and felt a grimace on my own. Then I heard a *crack* that sounded like a gunshot. I could only think: Did Jeff shoot the guy, too?!?

Then it was deadly silent.

Everyone else was gathered around the injured man by the time I got outside. He had been flipped into the air and had come down on his back right across the verandah railing. The "gunshot" I had heard was the victim's back breaking.

Someone, perhaps it was me, ended the tremendous burden of silence by say, "Oh boy!"

Next morning, Lieutenant Colonel T. J. Walker and Major Dan Torrey, our group and squadron commanders, ordered us into Walker's office and really dressed us down. Walker, whose huge handlebar moustache looked like it was going to fall off his face from the sheer exertion of yelling, told us that we each faced a prison sentence. It scared the hell out of me, and I'm sure that Louis and Jeff were equally impressed.

When Walker ran out of words, Dan Torrey chimed in with his opinion of us as human beings, but he softened after a while and said, "The only thing that's keeping you three out of prison is the misfortune of others. We're losing too many fighter pilots at Guadalcanal to waste three of you in Leavenworth. You all deserve to be there, but maybe you'll have a chance to set things right in combat before this matter ever comes up again."

Then Lieutenant Colonel Walker dismissed us in a cold, even voice.

The incident never resurfaced.

★

In mid September, Faleola was overrun for a few days by several Marine fighter and dive-bomber squadrons from MAG-12, whose ships put in at Apia on the way to the New Hebrides, from which they would fly to Guadalcanal in a few weeks. All the VMF-111 pilots were incensed at the notion of being left behind, and many of us let it be known that we were senior to and had more hours in the air than most of the lieutenants who were passing through. Some of the dive-bomber pilots, who were now flying relatively modern Douglas SBD Dauntlesses, had less than thirty hours in the air with an active squadron.

The thing that really irked me was that one of the squadrons that stopped over was VMF-121, my old unit. Very few of the original pilots I had trained with before the war were still aboard, but it was *my* squadron, and it was on its way to combat while I was literally stranded on the beach. Captain Joe Foss, who went out with VMF-121, became the first American World War II pilot to match the 26-kill World War I record of Captain Eddie Ricken-backer; Joe also earned a Medal of Honor.

In the end, all we could do was offer our condolences and see our fellow pilots off to the war.

★

We buried our frustrations in training aimed at making us irre-futably the best fighter pilots in the world.

One of our most talented pilots was a Texan in his mid twenties, Captain Hunter, Reinburg. It soon fell to Hunter to put us all through our paces, developing our skills to the utmost in the sort of all-out hair-raising aerobatics our combat pilots were finding themselves employing to stay alive in the Solomons.

Hunter was a nerveless flier who insisted on risk-taking for the sake of honing our predatory and survival skills. As close as we had learned to fly to one another at flight school and Opa-Locka, Hunter insisted that we keep on closing in and, to prevent accidents, that we think in terms of maneuvering two or four—or eight or sixteen—high-speed, throttle-to-the-wall fighters as if they comprised a sin-gle mass.

Hunter's training syllabus scared the hell out of most of us, but our reputations as men and as fighter pilots forced us to follow him on some of the most harrowing noncombat flight paths ever devised.

One day we were up at about 16,000 feet chasing tails, a mere warm-up. Suddenly, Hunter peeled out of the gaggle and dived, nearly vertical, right at the sea. By then, we had been conditioned to instantly respond to our flight leader's every move, so we all lined up on Hunter's tail in a great long line doing well over 400 knots.

Hunter pulled out of the dive and flat-hatted right over the waves. Every one of us followed his lead; we maintained a straight, nose-to-tail formation and began chewing up the miles at wavetop height. We were really moving!

I was about halfway back in the formation and things were going a mite too fast for me, but I had no time to panic or even think about what might happen. Every iota of my attention was riveted on the tail of the F4F right in front of my prop disc.

When I did finally focus on the airspace ahead, I saw that we were headed straight at a pair of huge rocks I knew to be about a quarter-mile offshore. I nearly closed my eyes I was so taken aback by fear and anticipation of death. I knew there was not enough room for the wings to go through.

I did not actually think the consequences through until later, for I was flying on pure instinct; there was no time to think. But in my soul I knew that pulling up—even if there had been time—would lead to a fate worse than death: I would be branded as a chicken-shit.

Hunter flew right between the rocks at 400 knots, and so did we all. I swear I heard my wingtips scrape the rocks on either side. When I realized that I was alive, I felt that I could have flown without the Wildcat, so great was my relief and pride.

★

All the training and alerts finally paid off in the form of a scramble in early October in response to a radar fix on a large mass of "bogies" approaching from the hostile west and quite close to Faleola.

We had switched over to four-plane divisions of two two-plane elements after the three-plane element had fallen from grace at Midway. Two four-plane fighter divisions were sent southwest to pick up the unidentified targets.

Though officers senior to me were also launched, a scramble is a scramble, and I somehow wound up leading the eight F4Fs to fighting altitude.

Before we could rearrange the two divisions to reflect seniority, my wingman and I spotted the targets at 8,000 feet. There were about twenty of them flying in a large box formation, which marked them as bombers. They were . . . Air Corps B-17s!

I yelled into my throat mike to tell everyone to hold fire, then switched frequencies to tell our ground controllers that we had found friendly bombers. As I hurtled across the top of the bomber formation, I waggled my wings in salute and they waggled theirs in acknowledgment. I had been so keyed up and ended up so relieved that I could feel the sweat dripping off the point of my chin, though I rarely perspired at altitude.

We escorted the B-17s to Tafuna and stayed the night.

Late that evening, I was having a beer at the Goat Island, which I had seen on my first day in Pago Pago, with the bomber squadron commander, Colonel Richard Carmichael. In March, Carmichael had flown General Douglas MacArthur out of the Philippines in a B-17. I learned that the squadron was on its way to Hawaii (the first warplanes I knew of to take that road) for a well-deserved rest after seeing intense combat out of the Philippines, Australia, and New Guinea. We talked of little things for a while, and then Carmichael predicted, "You and the other Marine fighter pilots here will not leave Samoa for Guadalcanal simply because it's doubtful our Marines can hold on there."

We had been kept abreast of the situation at Guadalcanal through top-secret briefings, but the reports had always been at least slightly optimistic. We knew that our aircraft and pilot losses had been steady from the beginning, but we also believed that our pilots were bleeding the Japanese dry; we had seen enough credits for confirmed kills posted to believe that. The implications of my talk over a beer with Colonel Carmichael were simply too chilling to consider.

Within a week, word arrived from the front that the Japanese had mounted a massive aerial and naval assault against Guadalcanal's main runway, Henderson Field, and the situation there was in serious doubt. Some reports said it was grave.

New bases were being built or becoming operational between us and Guadalcanal, but we wondered what the loss of so many of our ships, troops, pilots, and airplanes might do to our ability to defend those intermediate bases. Since May, the U.S. Fleet had lost three carriers sunk (*Lexington* in the Coral Sea in May, *Yorktown* at Midway in June, and *Wasp* to a Japanese submarine north of Guadalcanal in September) and two severely damaged (*Enterperise* to Japanese bombs in the Stewart Islands in August and *Saratoga* to a torpedo north of Guadalcanal in September.)

Another cause for anxiety was that Carmichael's B-17s had approached so close to our base without our knowing in advance. That alone was chilling confirmation of our leaders' long-abused admonitions about our need to remain vigilant.

So, some days we felt we were being left behind, and other days we felt we were again at the forefront of the war effort. But, every day, we felt we were being unfairly deprived of a chance to test our mettle in combat.

13

MAG-13 was bolstered on October 1, 1942, when a brand new fighter squadron, VMF-441, was formed and commissioned in Samoa by a levy of replacement pilots manning fresh F4Fs. Within a week of the formation of the new F4F squadron, Major Dan Torrey was transferred to command it, and several of the senior VMF-111 pilots—including me—were reassigned to it to oversee and train its fresh lieutenants.

My first real command as a Marine officer came within a week of my transfer, when I was elevated to the rank of captain and went to work as a full-time division leader.

In early December, Captain Waldo Meyer, who had just taken command of VMF-441 from Dan Torrey, selected my division and one other to accompany him for temporary duty guarding the brand new airstrip at Funafuti, wherever that was.

Funafuti is a seven-mile-long, 100-yard-wide sandspit that had been occupied by elements of the 5th Marine Defense Battalion and 120 Seabees on October 2, 1942. As soon as the defense battalion set up coastal and antiaircraft gun positions, the Seabees began work on a new airstrip, which would place our reconnaissance aircraft and warplanes within 700 miles of the Japanese-held Gilbert Islands, a former British possession in the eastern reaches of the Central Pacific. Within 30 days of the felling of the first palm, Major General Charles Price, the commanding general of the Samoan sector, was flown into the new runway aboard a PBY5A

Catalina patrol bomber to mark another astounding accomplishment of the tireless Seabees, who did so much to bolster our aerial offensive against Japan.

Within days of General Price's landing at Funafuti Airfield, four OS2U scouts from VS-1-D14 were sent up to join groundcrewmen who had been at work readying maintenance facilities. Since the OS2Us were within range of Japanese float warplanes in the Gilberts—at Tarawa—the decision was made to provide an advance fighter-and-dive-bomber detachment to protect them. Naturally, MAG-13 drew the job.

Even as we were preparing to mount out a detachment for Funafuti, an urgent message from Pearl Harbor revealed that the Japanese were sending two fleet carriers with complete air groups into the waters near the base. Our travel plans were pushed up — but our detachment was not strengthened.

This was definitely not the way I wanted to experience first combat.

Our nine F4Fs and six SBD dive-bombers were led out of Faleola by General Price's PBY5A, which would handle navigation on the long over-water flight. Our first stop was for refueling at Wallis Island, a French possession about midway between our base and our destination. We were told that Wallis had been the regional leper colony and were warned that we might see some grotesque sights. It had been proven that leprosy was not contagious, as had been thought in earlier years, so the quarantine at Wallis was lifted and their colony was closed down. Still, many of the surviving lepers had stayed on.

We no sooner landed at Wallis and taxied to the dispersal area than my wingman, 1st Lieutenant Sam Logan, who had joined VMF-111 in Samoa in April, was accosted by dozens of laughing islanders who pointed at him and shouted, "Half-a-caste."

Then one of the islanders climbed a tall, stately coconut palm in back of the dispersal area and returned with a ripe coconut, which he cracked with his huge, formidable-looking knife and presented to Sam.

Sam took the attention good-naturedly, but he was a little confused until one of the groundcrewmen told him the islanders were referring to his features and dark skin. Sam, who was from Kansas, was part Indian, but the islanders took him to be the scion of a marriage between a Frenchman and an islander; he looked like a Samoan, one of them.

We flew on to Funafuti and arrived after a long but thoroughly uneventful flight.

In the end, the Japanese carriers never materialized.

★

My being assigned to Funafuti—my still being in the hands of the Samoan defense establishment—was a source of considerable bitterness. Just before my half-squadron flew to Funafuti, thirty of my former VMF-111 comrades—including Jack Amende—were replaced by a number of combat veterans and many fresh lieutenants and were reassigned to VMF-121, which had been withdrawn from Guadalcanal to Espiritu Santo following a meteoric combat tour in which many dozens of Japanese warplanes fell before its guns. As soon as our pilots and some people fresh from the States could be absorbed into VMF-121, that squadron was going back to Guadalcanal for more combat. For all practical purposes, the new VMF-121 was the old VMF-111, and vice versa. Even the two squadron commanders swapped jobs: Major Duke Davis came to VMF-111, and Major Don Yost, our former VMF-111 exec, went up to command VMF-121.

I was naturally let down about my ill-starred luck. I had joined the Marine Corps early in the hope of getting into the war early. I had been an early member of VMF-121 but had been detached to make the move to Samoa, so I had missed out on VMF-121's combat debut at Guadalcanal. Now, because I was a "valuable" and highly skilled senior pilot, I was relegated to the role of trainer of new kids, who would probably benefit from my guidance to the point where they would be committed to battle before me. At the rate things were going, I was destined to be just about the oldest virgin fighter pilot in the service, and I was only 22.

There was absolutely nothing to do on Funafuti except fly sector searches, train the new kids, and brood. One little ray of sunshine glimmered through my personal gloom as a result of my running into Navy Lieutenant Art Redding of VS-1-D14. Art and I had been friends at USC. He was a track star and I was on the water polo team, so we spent a lot of time working out together. I had seen Art earlier, when we first arrived at Faleola, but he had gone on to Funafuti, and I expected that that would be the last I would see of him. We alleviated scores of potentially boring off-duty hours by literally reliving our college bull sessions.

Long after I had left Funafuti, Art had been out on a routine sector search and had had to ditch at dusk when his engine failed. He landed his float scout in the water, but the OS2U was quickly swamped, and Art and his radioman had to get into the water. Art had on a Mae West life vest, but his radioman did not, so Art held the other man up and just swam around. After only a few minutes, in which Art had time to tell the radioman that hope of their being found was slim, a tiger shark attacked and ripped off part of one of Art's legs. Art realized that he was bleeding to death, so he slipped out of his Mae West and helped the radioman into it. Then he slipped beneath the waves, where he died. The radioman was not molested by the shark, but he was on the brink of giving up, when, in the darkest hour of the night, an American PT boat passed so close to him that he was able to make his presence known. He was rescued from waters the PT-boatmen said were teeming with sharks. The radioman later told his story to a doctor at Funafuti, then went totally out of his mind.

We stayed at Funafuti for only three weeks, then nine fresh VMF-441 pilots and F4Fs replaced us. We returned to Faleola by way of Wallis to resume our new squadron's intense training schedule for all the green second lieutenants who had replaced my thoroughly trained comrades in December.

As January passed, we stay-behinds began hearing good things about our former VMF-111 comrades. Several of them downed Japanese planes, including Hunter Reinburg, who bagged a total of three Zeros fighters, including a double kill on January 27. I was happy for Hunter and the others, but I was furious with my superiors and the Marine Corps.

But my chance was coming.

PART III

Combat

14

Several of VMF-441's senior pilots—including Captains Bruce Porter, Jeff Poindexter, and Louis Gordon—were ordered to leave Samoa and proceed to the airbase at Turtle Bay, on Espiritu Santo, in late February, 1943—nearly a year after we had sailed from San Diego into the vast, unknown war zone.

Turtle Bay, which was about 450 air miles from Guadalcanal's Henderson Field, was not exactly the front line, but it was no backwater, either. To us, anything was better than remaining marooned in Samoa or, worse, Funafuti, which is where VMF-441 was permanently transferred just after our departure.

All we could bring with us was our flight gear and a minimum of toilet articles and personal possessions—whatever we could cram into the single seabag and one flight bag we were allowed to carry aboard the R4D transport (a military version of the DC-3 airliner) that flew us from Tutuila to Nandi, in the Fijis, and then on to our destination in the the New Hebrides.

An early rumor we had picked up while still at Tutuila was that we were being transferred into VMF-121, the squadron that had absorbed many of our fellow VMF-111 pilots at the beginning of the year. Since our friends had been gone, they had entered combat along with a solid remnant of the original VMF-121 pilots who had passed through Samoa in September, 1942, and who had gone on to achieve astonishing successes over the Japanese during the really grim middle period of the Guadalcanal Campaign.

By the time we reached Turtle Bay, the rumors and the reality of our situation had changed. We were immediately assigned to a "casual" squadron, which is to say we were not assigned at all. For the time being, we would be ferrying new warplanes to active units operating out of Henderson Field and its two satellite fighter strips on Guadalcanal. For purposes of administration, we were assigned to MAG-11 at Turtle Bay, but we also lived at Tontouta with MAG-25, a transport group that mainly flew R4Ds between the front and the rear. One good thing to come of this was my reunion with Captain Lee "Chirp" Sparrow, an R4D driver who had been on my Los Angeles High School water-polo team in the late 1930s. Chirp offered me a place in his tent, and I readily accepted his hospitality.

Our hopefully temporary status was the result of the strategic situation in the South Pacific area at that time.

Guadalcanal had been declared "secure" in early February, and the air war (though not our ground forces) was advancing up the 600-mile-long Solomons chain. Our fighter and bomber sorties were still well short of the ultimate goal, the main Japanese bases around Rabaul, in the Bismarck Archipelago, but they were hitting targets around New Georgia, Bougainville and other islands in the Central and Northern Solomons.

The replacement aircraft we casuals were to ferry to Guadalcanal all arrived in the region aboard escort ("jeep") carriers, which put in at Noumea, in New Caledonia. Generally, the airplanes were winched down to the quay from the tiny flight decks and taxied to a nearby runway, where mechanics tinkered with them. The new airplanes were next fueled for the brief flight to Tontouta. Usually on the morning following the arrival of the new warplanes, we would fly them to Turtle Bay. From there, generally in the company of a pathfinding multiengine airplane that had a navigator aboard, we flew the last leg to Guadalcanal. If we were flying F4Fs, we would set down at either Fighter-1 or Fighter-2. If we were flying Douglas SBD Dauntless dive-bombers or Grumman TBF Avenger torpedo bombers, we landed on the main runway at Henderson Field. Depending on the time of day we arrived, we would stay overnight at Guadalcanal or we were flown right back to Turtle Bay or Tontouta aboard any sort of multiengine airplane that happened to be going our way.

The overnight stays were often exciting, for the Japanese frequently sent over single Betty bombers with maddeningly unsynchronized engines. These usually flew lazily over the airdrome complex and dropped 250-kg bombs at odd intervals to keep us awake and pit the runways or destroy depot facilities. The threat could not be taken lightly—casualties resulted on many nights—so we often spent sleepless hours in bomb shelters.

Every time we went to Guadalcanal, we saw our warplanes take off for or return from missions up the Solomons. It killed us to know that most of us were captains with many hundreds of hours in F4Fs and that most of the pilots in the active squadrons were youngsters (they *seemed* young to me, though I was all of 22) with under 300 hours of flying time noted in their logbooks. We begged friends in the active squadrons for a chance to sneak out on just one mission, but we never got the chance.

One March morning, after tedious weeks of ferrying warplanes from the rear to the front, we were finally given a reason for all the ill will that had built up between ourselves and our unreasonable superiors. There came the day in late March when I went aboard one of the jeep carriers with Jeff Poindexter, Louis Gordon, and several other casuals to pick up what we thought would be replacement airplanes for VMF-124, the first Marine F4U Corsair fighter squadron to be deployed in the Pacific.

When we landed at Tontouta following the minutes-long hop from Noumea Harbor, we were told to taxi to the dispersal area and stand by for orders. Something was in the wind, but we had no idea what. We shut down the airplanes and stood around shooting the breeze until a senior officer drove up and told us that we were being reassigned to VMF-121, which had just gotten in to Turtle Bay to prepare for its third tour on Guadalcanal. The Corsairs we had just flown ashore were the first of the type to be assigned to the squadron, which would spend up to several months absorbing new pilots from the States and transitioning from F4Fs. We were to report to the new squadron commander, Major Ray Vroome, as soon as we could.

★

The Vought Corsair was designed in 1938 by an engineering team headed by Rex Beisel. Unlike many of the naval-type warplanes designed in the United States at that time, including the F4F Wildcat, the Corsair started out as a single-wing fighter. Even more unusual was its distinctive bent-wing platform, an inverted gullwing.

The gull wing did little or nothing for the new fighter's performance in the air, but neither was it merely a mark of distinction. It provided ground clearance for the Corsair's huge thirteen-foot-four-inch three-bladed propeller, which did everything for the new fighter's performance in the air. It also allowed the landing gear to be shortened, and it simplified the storage of the retractable landing gear.

The Corsair's 2,000-horsepower Pratt & Whitney R-2800-8(B) air-cooled radial engine was the most powerful engine available at the time the fighter was designed.

Unlike the Army Air Corps, which had largely switched over to liquid-cooled aircraft power plants because of their inherent streamlining qualities, the Navy still favored the more traditional air-cooled radial engines because they were less likely to fail under the impact of enemy bullets. This says something about the perceived differences in missions of the two services: the Air Corps was content to have its pilots bail out over land, on which they could make their own way to friendly lines, while the Navy did not want to lose pilots or have to rescue so many of them if they had to bail out over water. Thus, the Air Corps appeared to be more concerned with flying characteristics, and the Navy, with pilot survival. Besides that, the air-cooled engines were easier to maintain and less expensive to build.

The Corsair was the first all-metal fighter to which the skin was attached to the airframe by the spot-welding method. (Previous models were riveted.) The result was a lighter, smoother, drag-free finish.

The XF4U1's first flight took place on May 28, 1940, and the prototypes were delivered a short time later to the Anacostia Naval Air Station for extensive flight testing. On July 27, 1940, an XF4U1 exceeded 400 miles per hour in level flight.

The Navy test pilots recommended several modifications to facilitate carrier operations. The fuselage was extended 40 inches, and extra fuel tanks were installed, which raised the flight range to 2,000 miles. Machine guns placed on the engine cowling were eliminated, and six .50-caliber machine guns were placed in the wings. The original fabric-covered wingtips were extended twelve inches and covered with spot-welded metal.

The redesigned prototypes were turned over to Navy test pilots in early 1942, and the airplane was soon accepted and placed under a full-production contract.

The first production-model F4U-1s were delivered to the Navy for full operational flight testing in July, 1942. VMF-124 took delivery of its first F4U-1 production fighter shortly after it was commissioned at Kearney Mesa on September 7, 1942. However, the airplanes arrived in tiny batches over so long a period of time that the squadron, which was scheduled to deploy overseas in January, 1943, nearly switched over to older F4F Wildcats. On February 1, 1943, 2nd Lieutenant Kenny Walsh—my former prewar wingman, the NAP who had almost followed me into the Potomac during my memorable takeoff from Quantico in December, 1941—had the dubious honor of becoming the first Corsair pilot to make a water landing; Kenny went in because of an engine failure and nearly drowned before swimming 150 feet to the surface and eventual rescue.

The first U.S. Navy Corsair squadron was Fighting Squadron 12 (VF-12), which was commanded by my former fighter-tactics instructor, Lieutenant Commander Jumpin' Joe Clifton. VF-12 was based at North Island, San Diego, from which it had access to the type of aircraft carriers on which the F4U was slated to serve in the Pacific. It took VF-12 until mid January, 1943, to amass ten operational Corsairs with which to hammer out revised fighter tactics.

VMF-124 and VF-12 were the *real* test beds for the Corsair. Until it got into the hands of each squadron's least experienced, least talented pilots, the new fighter had been flown only by the very best test pilots wearing Wings of Gold, an unfair test despite the rigors to which it had been subjected. Until the *worst* operational pilot successfully recovered from an emergency, no operational pilot would fully trust the new design.

There was reason for worry. While VF-12 was testing the F4U on carriers and on multiplane formation sweeps out over the Pacific, tyros at Opa-Locka and newer advanced fighter schools were checking out in F4Us. And they were having fatal accidents.

As had occurred at Opa-Locka during my first weeks in F3Fs there in mid 1941, the flurry of accidents was initially difficult to explain. There is no one to say precisely what is going wrong with single-seat airplanes that crash and kill their pilots. But a pattern eventually emerged. Most of the F4Us went in while in steep vertical dives, so flight instructors tested new recovery methods and instructed new F4U pilots on new ways to pull out. (Identification of the problem and its solution both arose from the accidental survival of a lucky pilot like the solver of our 1941 F3F riddle, Wortham Ashcroft—who, incidentally, was killed at Guadalcanal.)

Training accidents aside, VF-12 had problems landing its new fighters on carrier flight decks, and that resulted in the cancellation of the Navy's F4U program in favor of the soon-to-be-delivered Grumman F6F Hellcat. All the VF-12 F4Us were turned over to the Marine Corps. At the same time, the F4Us used for advanced fighter training were also turned over for the exclusive use of Marine pilots fresh from flight school, an indication of the Marine Corps' total commitment to the F4U program.

The Marine Corps made the firm decision to transition all existing F4F squadrons to F4Us and to equip all new fighter squadrons with its new windfall fighter.

Before VMF-124 deployed to the Pacific, and just before VF-12 began receiving its first Corsairs, Lieutenant Commander Jumpin' Joe Clifton spent many hours with the Marine pilots to help prepare them for the rigors of combat against the Japanese Zero fighter. Fortunately, Joe was one of the very few Americans who had flown an intact A6M2 Zero fighter captured in the Aleutians in June, 1942 and refurbished at North Island. Talented fighter pilot that he was, Joe was able to extrapolate his knowledge of the Zero and the F4U into workable schemes and tactics aimed at readily defeating the Zero or, at worst, saving the F4U pilot. His findings and suggestions went a very long way toward assuring VMF-124's successful combat debut and, indeed, the success of the F4U in combat during the balance of the Pacific War.

Clifton's pivotal observation was that the F4U enjoyed a decided advantage in speed over the Zero. Until the F4U arrived, Marine (and Navy) pilots flying F4Fs could gain on a Zero—or get away from one—only in a dive. This was because of the Wildcat's heavier airframe. Joe had already developed the basic evasion tactic—a hard, diving turn to starboard at speeds in excess of 240 knots was guaranteed to lose a Zero. This was essentially the same as the F4F's basic evasion tactic. But the F4U could recover more quickly and could thus chase a Zero with some hope of catching up. Early operational models were hard pressed to get to the 400-knot test speed achieved at Anacostia, but the F4U's huge engine gave it an awesome advantage over the relatively underpowered F4F.

Also, an F4U could overtake a Zero in a climb. The Japanese fighter was lighter and thus more nimble until 10,000 feet, but the F4U would nearly always prevail in a race for altitude over 10,000 feet.

★

My first impressions of the Corsair were mixed. I had already ferried several to VMF-124 at Guadalcanal by the time I was reassigned to VMF-121, and I was still undecided whether I preferred it over my beloved F4F.

The first thing I noticed on my first takeoff from Tontouta was the very limited visibility from the cockpit. This was due in part to the birdcage canopy (done away with in later models in favor of a bubble-type canopy) and also to the Corsair's nose-high three-point attitude, the result of its rather long front-wheel struts and rather short tail-wheel struts, which were required because of the inordinately large propeller. The new fighter was three feet taller than the F4F and 3,000 pounds heavier.

My first landing at Tontouta confirmed the Navy's decision to reject the Corsair for carrier operations. I found that the rigid landing gear oleo strut caused a potentially disastrous bounce in anything but a smooth touchdown. I had zero carrier experience at the time, but even I could see that it would be difficult for an average pilot to control the airplane if the carrier deck was moving up and down in rough seas.

As experienced and polished as I was at that time, I had a great deal of difficulty breaking in with the F4Us I was shuttling to Guadalcanal. Another difficulty that must have been behind the Navy's decision to terminate its F4U program was that the low tail wheel placed the very large flaps too close to the ground. This affected the pilot's ability to control a moving Corsair on the ground, during takeoff, landing, and on taxiways. It was, I realized, one thing to have directional problems on an airfield, and another to lose absolute control on a narrow, crowded carrier deck in heavy seas.

On the other hand, I found the F4U cockpit to be complete and comfortable and particularly well suited for combat. Many former F4F pilots climbing into an F4U cockpit for the first time literally got lost in the vast stretches of comfortable space. The new fighter even had two foot rails running toward the rudder pedals, and these only served to heighten the sense of vastness.

In the air on my first long hop to Turtle Bay, I glanced down between my knees, and all I could see was a deep darkness. It was a positively eerie sensation. I had no idea what might be lurking down there, but I did know a way to find out. I nudged the virgin airplane over into a roll and allowed everything on the deck to fall "up" to the canopy. I got lots of dust in my nose and was nearly brained by a screwdriver.

15

Jeff Poindexter, Louis Gordon, and I started our tour with VMF-121 at a distinct disadvantage. We were all captains, so we all immediately qualified as division leaders. All of us had in our four-plane divisions lieutenants who had served with VMF-121 during its second tour at Guadalcanal in January, 1943. Some of those kids had flown under us in VMF-111 before they left us in Samoa, and a few even had kills to their credit.

Despite my many hundreds of hours as a seasoned fighter pilot and trainer, I found it difficult to exert any real influence over blooded combat veterans. I had to impose discipline on them, I knew, but I also had to remain flexible enough to be able to learn from them.

Fortunately, I was only at the middle level of the problem. Our squadron's new skipper, Major Ray Vroome, was a former ground officer who had only recently qualified as a fighter pilot. He not only faced commanding battle-experienced lieutenants, but all his squadron's captains had hundreds more hours in fighters than he did. Ray was a very patient man and a good leader. He recognized his shortcomings and helped his unblooded flight leaders work within the constraints of theirs. That alleviated a lot of potential friction and, more important, established an environment in which knowledge passed up as well as down the command chain with equal efficiency.

Including pilots who had flown during VMF-121's second Guadalcanal tour, former VMF-111 and VMF-441 pilots, and new arrivals from the States, the squadron comprised 23 F4F pilots who had to transition to the hot, new F4Us.

I considered the Samoan group (including the former VMF-111 pilots who had seen combat in January with VMF-121) to be the best-trained contingent in the squadron. Many of us had never fired a shot in anger, but we all had a solid year of combat-ready training experience. Since there had always been the possibility of attack on Samoa, we had all flown combat air patrols and sector searches from dawn to dusk, or, if we were not on combat-alert missions, we had been training for them. Every moment aloft at Samoa had been flown as if the next moment would find us face to face with enemy aircraft or surface targets. We had flown in literally every type of weather, and all of us had many hundreds of successful hours of over-water navigation under our belts—just the experience we would need as flight leaders in the Solomons.

As soon as we had all read the Corsair manuals and tested ourselves and the individual airplanes in the air, we began the usual transition up the formation ladder to full-squadron practice missions: first in two-plane elements, then in four-plane divisions, then in mixed division groupings, then as a full fighter squadron. Every pilot had an opportunity to fly lead and wing positions on every other pilot, and we constantly juggled the composition of elements and divisions to build on the strengths of each man and reduce the effects of the weaknesses in many. I was fortunate to draw Lieutenant Phil Leeds as my wingman very early in the training schedule, and I was so impressed with his skills that I made sure he stayed with me throughout.

Our problem of seeking everyone's true level as pilots was compounded by the usual comings and goings that plague any operational squadron. We had a few accidents in the air and on the ground, and we had a few pilots opt out of flying altogether or request transfers to transport or other noncombatant squadrons. No request of the sort was ever denied; no one wanted a wingman who was not flying his fighter with all his heart and soul on the line.

Once the composition of the four-plane divisions were more or less fixed, competition between the divisions became super-heated. Aerial gunnery, fighter tactics, and navigation were all practiced daily, and every pilot stood regular combat alerts at the end of the runway. At odd intervals, and without warning, the alert pilots were scrambled and vectored out against targets that, as far as they knew, were real. Often as not, the alert pilots were sent out to find and "destroy" scouts returning from their own routine sector searches far out to sea. Or we went after formations of dive-bombers or torpedo bombers or transports—whatever our friendly radar operators turned up for us. At times, by prior arrangement or on the spur of the moment, we even staged mock fights with the other fighter squadrons also training at Turtle Bay.

The pressure was turned on all the way to see who would crack and to prepare us for our inevitable transfer to Guadalcanal and the real war.

The Samoan pilots liked to think that our solid year of similar training exercises and mock dogfights rendered us better overall pilots than many of the younger combat-experienced men, and they liked to think the opposite. The friendly rivalry served us well and, above all, provided a framework for bringing the newly arrived lieutenants or inexperienced senior pilots like Ray Vroome up to a level at which they stood a good chance of surviving aerial combat. Since none of us could rely on luck (nor discount it), we were unanimous in our decision to rely on skill to get us home alive.

*

Turtle Bay was overrun by overly aggressive fighter pilots unable to requite their thirsts for revenge and adventure. The result was a madcap atmosphere and the emergence of legendary, flamboyant personalities.

One of the most flamboyant was Major Greg Boyington, a former aeronautical engineering student who had entered the Marine Corps as a pilot candidate in 1935 and who, in 1941, had resigned his commission to fly and fight in China with General Clair Chennault's American Volunteer Group—the Flying Tigers.

Greg had scored six kills in China while flying P-40s, but he had gotten into a hassle over money and had returned to the United States by way of India after the start of the Pacific War. He had then fought his way back into the Marine Corps and had eventually been assigned as executive officer of VMF-122 under my former nemesis, Captain Elmer Brackett. Greg succeeded to the command of VMF-122 in April, 1943, just in time to take it up to Guadalcanal for a four-week break-in tour (a normal tour was six weeks by then) escorting bombers up to hit Munda Field, on New Georgia. VMF-

122 was withdrawn before it ever saw a Japanese warplane and was shipped to Turtle Bay to transition to F4Us.

However, before getting back to work, VMF-122 was shipped to Sydney, Australia, for a week of rest and rehabilitation—which is to say wallowing in drink and sex. Greg overdid things a bit and thus earned the ire of our MAG-11 operations officer, a tough, old-line disciplinarian who had come to resent Greg's ability to have a good time under even the most-trying circumstances.

I met Greg Boyington on his return from Sydney. I went out to the airstrip to pick up Jeff Poindexter, who had managed to steal a leave in Australia. Jeff introduced me to Major Boyington as we walked back to my jeep, but we talked for only a few minutes.

I next laid eyes on Boyington late in the afternoon of June 7, 1943, as I was leaving the base skeet range with two lieutenants who had served with me in Samoa but who had gone off to Guadalcanal when so many of the VMF-111 pilots were transferred to VMF-121. It happened that Hunter Reinburg and others had subsequently been transferred to VMF-122—Boyington's squadron—for its upcoming second tour. The two lieutenants—Harold "Fateye" Gardner and Bartel "Ras" Rasmussen—were among Hunter's group of transferees. Since both VMF-121 and VMF-122 were scheduled to fly their newly acquired Corsairs to Guadalcanal within a few days, I had arranged to get in some last-minute shooting practice with Ras and Fateye.

As we were leaving the skeet range, I saw Greg Boyington wander by in an aimless daze, muttering to himself. I am sure he was looking for someone to kill. Suddenly, I found him walking in step with us, and we fell into conversation. Almost immediately, Greg revealed that he had just received word from the stiff-necked group operations officer that he was to turn VMF-122 over to another major and report to group headquarters in the morning to assume command of a desk as MAG-11's new *assistant* operations officer.

Greg simply would not stand—or sit—for the new assignment. I somehow became his jeep driver, and together with Fateye and Ras we drove around the bay through a teeming downpour to the quarters of Brigadier General James "Nuts" Moore, chief of staff of the 1st Marine Aircraft Wing.

Major Boyington assured Ras, Fateye, and me that he and General Moore were old friends and that the general could be counted upon to get Greg put back on flying status.

We roared along the jungle tracks through the downpour and

safely arrived at the general's door. Greg told us he would meet us at the nearby officers' club as soon as he could, then he hopped out of the jeep and approached the general's door.

Ras, Fateye and I repaired to the nearby bar and ordered stiff drinks to chase off the chill of the rainy night. I liked being with Ras and Fateye. The two were utterly inseparable, fun-loving All-American sports who were liked by everyone. In a way, they were the squadron's mascots. Fateye was one of the finest chess players I ever ran across and was usually the champion of whatever unit he happened to be serving with. He was a good teacher, too; he even managed to force a few pointers through my otherwise uncomprehending brain as we sat at the generals' bar waiting for Greg Boyington.

After a few drinks, I began wondering aloud at the huge mirror that was hanging behind the bar, and I finally asked the bartender where on Earth it had been dug up.

"Hell, Captain," the sergeant-bartender told me, "they brought that over here from the Fijis in a B-24." I gathered that at least one of the several generals then headquartered in Espiritu Santo was behind the acquisition, but before I could ask, Major Boyington blew in out of the rain. "Guess what? The general has given me a chance at combat again!"

Greg had already amply celebrated his return to flight status with General Moore, but he insisted on celebrating with his good buddies, Ras, Fateye, and Bruce. The bartender poured us each a stiff drink, and we all downed them in a swallow. Greg was so excited that he gave out a great yell of joy and hurled his shot glass right through the big imported mirror.

The four of us were gone from there before the last of the glass slivers had cascaded to the deck. As Ras slewed the jeep around the first corner on the the way out of the headquarters compound, someone thrust a bottle he had grabbed off the bar into my hand, and I chugged a swallow, fighting to stay in the jeep as it slid all over the rain-soaked track. By the time the bottle came back to me, I was not paying any attention to the road. Suddenly, Greg leaned over beside me and delivered a sharp blow across the back of Ras's neck. The jeep swerved off the road and lurched to a stop in the viscous mud.

We all jumped out of the jeep, hooting and hollering, and singing in the rain. We played in the mud until all the liquor was gone, then we all pushed the mired jeep back to the roadway and pointed it in the direction of the fighter strip.

As soon as we arrived at the tent camp, we heard a lot of noise emanating from one of the tents. A party!

We joined the festivities, downing liquor no doubt provided by an R4D transport returning from Sydney with a load of pilots fresh from a week of boisterous drinking and sex down under.

After a while, Greg Boyington challenged someone to one of his famous wrestling matches (Greg had been a noted college wrestler) and, before many minutes had passed, the newly reinstated squadron commander was blind-sided and went down with a broken ankle. It was painfully obvious that Greg would not be going to Guadalcanal with his squadron.

★

VMF-121 left for Guadalcanal two days after Greg Boyington broke his ankle.

16

VMF-121 was ordered to leave Turtle Bay for Guadalcanal on June 9, 1943. Ahead of us was a six-week combat tour.

I had been a naval aviator for about two years and had been posted to the Pacific for fifteen months, but I had never fired in anger or been fired upon. I had no sense of fear or trepidation. I knew how well trained I was, how utterly prepared I was to face the enemy and to overcome him. My only desire was to put myself to the test. I had no other ambitions. I had no other plans.

The entire squadron, divided into a perfect formation of elements and divisions, followed an R4D navigation plane from Turtle Bay to Henderson Field early in the morning.

As we approached the airport complex following our 450-mile flight, ground controllers warned us that Condition Red was in effect; an enemy airstrike had been picked up by our coastwatchers far up the Solomons chain and was then being followed in by our radar. The strike was still quite far away, so we would have time to land and disperse our Corsairs. Other squadrons operating out of Fighter-1 and Fighter-2, the main runway's smaller satellites, would intercept the attackers while we refueled. We never saw or heard a Japanese airplane that afternoon, so effective was the multisquadron intercept.

Guadalcanal is *not* a tropical paradise; it is quite unlike Samoa. Located less than ten degrees south of the Equator, its climate is wet and hot, with an average temperature well into the eighties.

The combination of heat, humidity, and a dense interior rain forest provide for daily showers, which only increases from November through March, the season of the northwest monsoon. Rainfall over land in the Solomons is far greater than rainfall over the water. The island, like all the major islands in the Solomons, is volcanic in nature, though coral reefs and islets abound. Guadalcanal, which has a land area close to that of Long Island, is quite mountainous, and some of those mountains rise to well over 8,000 feet.

Our landing instructions were to approach Henderson Field from around Cape Esperance, the northwest tip of the island. We were to remain just offshore, over Lengo Channel, which was known at the time as Ironbottom Sound in commemoration of the many major American, Australian, and Japanese warships sunk there during the vicious Guadalcanal Campaign of August, 1942, to February, 1943.

As I passed over Cape Esperance and turned in over Lengo Channel, I saw the ominous conical bulk of Savo Island, off which most of the major naval engagements had been fought. Only seven months earlier, in November, 1942, Guadalcanal-based dive-bombers and torpedo bombers had spent a full day sinking the Japanese battlecruiser *Hiei* off Savo after she had been robbed of her steering control in a vicious night battle in which many ships of both sides had been mortally damaged or sunk outright. Beneath my right wing, at Doma Cove, were the rusting hulks of several Japanese troop transports that had been run aground during the November battle. Intentional grounding was the only way the Imperial Navy had been able to ensure delivery of the ships' precious cargoes of reinforcements and material to the desperate soldiers ashore.

I knew from my earlier ferry flights that hundreds if not thousands of Japanese soldiers and sailors remained trapped on the big island, having been left behind in February, when crack infantry units had been evacuated from Cape Esperance. Even as I approached Henderson Field, I knew that newly arrived U.S. Army divisions were undertaking live-fire training exercises against those hundreds of miserable, dangerous castaways in the dense woods along Guadalcanal's northern coast. On all my previous flights to Henderson Field or the fighter strips, I had been warned to stay out of the rain forest, for Japanese raiders desperate for food or revenge often struck small combat patrols, and individuals and small groups had gone missing in areas quite close to the immensely built-up airfield complex.

We set down on the main runway in perfect formation and taxied out behind guide jeeps to our squadron's new dispersal area, which had revetments literally carved out of high stands of palm trees to protect the Corsairs from the effects of bombing.

After turning the airplanes over to waiting groundcrewmen, we pulled our meager belongings from where we had crammed them into our cockpits and our fighters' tiny storage compartments as well as from free space aboard the navigational guide plane. Then we followed our ground officers, who had gone up a few days earlier, to our new home.

The squadron's entire flight echelon was housed in a single quonset hut. We slept on canvas cots protected by mosquito nets, which were absolutely obligatory in this mosquito-infested place. We were shown our large bomb shelters as well as the locations of numerous foxhole-type one-man shelters that dotted the squadron area. I already knew how to use these amenities as I had been awakened virtually every time I had overnighted at Henderson Field during my ferrying duties.

★

By June, 1943, the night drill was fairly standard. The Japanese sent over one bomber—usually a twin-engined Betty with intentionally unsynchronized engines—every two hours beginning at midnight. Each of them would slowly buzz around overhead, dropping single 250-kg bombs at odd intervals to either pit one of the runways or damage warplanes, pilots, aircrewmen, or facilities. Each new arrival would be greeted by a wailing air raid siren, which was guaranteed to awaken the most exhausted pilot.

That very first night of my first operational tour, I sat out in the open beside a one-man foxhole and watched long cones of light from our searchlight batteries stab through the night sky while the automatic antiaircraft batteries hurled streams of gorgeous red and yellow tracer after the night's first circling Betty, which we had dubbed Washing Machine Charlie after her unsynchronized engines. (Single-engine night harassers were called Louie the Louse.) Now and again, when the heavy 90mm antiaircraft batteries operating under radar control locked on and fired at Charlie, the entire encampment was dazzlingly lighted by bright muzzle flashes.

On this night, I had been told, several Army Air Corps P-38 pilots had volunteered to go aloft early and try to intercept the raiders. I was wondering where the Air Corps pilots could be—and what would happen to them if they were found by the searchlights or the gunnery radar. Suddenly, a stream of red tracer burst out of the darkness overhead, and I could hear the distinctive steady *thrum* of a P-38's powerful twin high-performance engines. Before I could open my mouth to cheer my brother pilot on, the sky right over my head erupted in a great ball of red-gold flame, which slowly dropped behind the tops of intervening trees and, I suppose, into Lengo Channel.

The P-38 had made a night kill!

Cheers and yells of excitement and acclamation rose from hundreds of throats as the invisible P-38 swooped down the length of the main runway before turning in to land. I could imagine the satisfied Air Corps pilot executing an ecstatic victory roll in the dark despite the danger of hitting a tree or becoming temporarily disoriented and crashing into the channel or the jungle on either side of our relatively small human enclave.

I was utterly transfixed by the sheer complexity of what that P-38 pilot had done, and I made up my mind right then and there to sign up for night-fighter training if the Marine Corps ever announced the formation a night-fighter program.

★

Meals were served in a central quonset hut accomodating several fighter squadrons that were operating off the main runway. There was no refrigeration available for our food. (We heard that the senior brass not only had refrigeration for their food but an ice plant as well, one that had been captured intact from the Japanese when our Marines first landed in August, 1942.) The lack of refrigeration obviated our ever seeing fresh vegetables or real, unprocessed meat—unless our friends from the transport squadrons remembered us when they smuggled in their own fresh victuals from the civilized rear areas.

Everything we ate was canned or dehydrated. For example, our first squadron breakfast at Henderson Field consisted of powdered eggs, pancakes, and chipped beef on toast. Coffee was always plentiful, and I have to believe that most of us got our essential vitamins and protein from it. Once in a very great while, we were served severely rationed treats of powdered milk.

Our lunch and dinner menus varied among canned spam, canned corned beef, canned beef stew, canned chicken, and canned hash. At odd and infrequent intervals, we were treated to fresh Australian mutton, which many of us had thrived on while we were based in Samoa.

Many of the pilots, including Captain Bruce Porter, suffered from dysentery brought on by the improper diet as well as improper cleaning of our metal feeding trays or even improperly washed cooking vats. The trays were the real problem, however. After we ate, we dumped leftovers into a garbage can and then dipped the trays in a vat of boiling water and stacked them for the next meal. Well, the water bath was not always boiling, but it was always greasy from all the trays that had been dipped earlier. (It was often thick enough to mistake for a meat soup.) It was not uncommon for forward-based pilots to return from combat or escort missions befouled in the results of a wide assortment of stomach and lower-tract ailments. The problem was so universal, in fact, that we stopped kidding one another about it.

Between the unremitting heat and humidity, the lousy food (which we ate as little of as we could), and the recurrent dysentery, nearly all of us lost weight and suffered from obvious loss of energy and the general sense of well-being that fighter pilots find absolutely essential for making the clear-headed, split-second decisions required to keep us alive and knocking down enemy planes. I have no doubt that lack of essential vitamins caused physical problems that literally killed pilots called upon, for example, to navigate their airplanes down a darkened runway before sunrise.

We never looked forward to mealtimes. We simply ate to try to stay alive, and we were slowly losing the struggle.

★

By the time we reached Henderson Field, I had been advanced to the position of squadron flight officer, behind the CO, Major Ray Vroome, and the exec, Captain Perry Shuman.

In addition to my flight duties, which were minimal during our first few days ashore, I was required to attend group operations meetings, where I was fed a steady diet of operational and contingency plans and orders. More important, I had an opportunity to meet my fellow senior pilots and discuss with them the real nature of the Solomons air war of the period.

During one such conversation on my second or third day at Henderson Field, I was given some details of a huge air battle that had occurred near Bougainville on June 7, the day Greg Boyington broke his ankle.

One of the top-scoring squadrons that day had been VMF-112, which would not have been of particularly compelling interest to me but for the fact that it had been commanded by my first operational flight leader, Bob Fraser, now a major, and had involved my old "half-a-caste" wingman, 1st Lieutenant Sam Logan, in a heart-stopping role.

It took me some time to piece together the news because VMF-112 had been relieved and sent south the day after the battle, which was the day before our own trip from Turtle Bay to Henderson Field.

Sam had scored his first kill over Bougainville on June 5, right after joining VMF-112 as a replacement for a downed lieutenant. The June 7 battle was only his second combat mission.

Sam's second combat intercept was made at 20,000 feet, when he went after a Zero that was plainly getting the better of a Royal New Zealand Air Force P-40 fighter. Unfortunately, Sam failed to notice that a second Zero had picked him up and was boring in from behind. Within a minute, Sam's Corsair was vibrating badly from a number of rounds through the engine. When Sam looked back to see where his attacker was, he saw instead that his airplane's tail surfaces that been hit by numerous bullets and were beginning to peel away from the framework.

There was no way Sam was going to get that fighter home, so he pushed back the canopy, unbuckled his seat harness, and jumped away into thin air. His chute deployed without any problems, and he began drifting toward the spectacularly beautiful sea thousands of feet below. All around Sam, Corsairs, Zeros, and P-40s were tangling in mortal combat. Here and there, Zeros fell away from the battle, trailing long plumes of smoke and flame. Large, expanding brownish splotches marked the spots where warplanes had blown up in mid air.

But Sam Logan was out of it, reduced to the role of a mere observer.

From out of nowhere, the Zero that had shot up Sam's Corsair dived on the helpless Marine, its machine guns blazing. The stream of tracer fell away beneath Sam's feet, and the Zero flashed by before the pilot could correct his aim.

The Japanese pilot pulled up and around and prepared to make another firing pass at Sam. As he came on, Sam pulled up on the chute shrouds and tucked his knees against his chest to make a smaller target of himself.

Suddenly, Sam realized that there were no bullets coming his way. With crystal clarity, Sam realized that the pilot was going to try to hack him to death with the Zero's propeller.

Sam lowered himself in the chute as the Zero came out of its shallow dive at dazzling speed. At the last possible instant, Sam pulled up on the shrouds with all his strength and again yanked his knees to his chest. The metal propeller blades missed his feet by inches. The Zero passed so close that it was all Sam could do to keep from trying to kick in the windscreen with his only weapons, his two combat boots.

As the Zero climbed around for another pass, Sam spilled his chute in the hope of dropping toward the sea with far greater speed, at least to make the Japanese pilot's next pass harder to line up.

Then the Zero was coming at him again. He tried to pull up on the shrouds and shorten his body. But he was either too slow or the Zero pilot had learned something from his previous pass. Sam felt a wrenching bump and a piercing stab of pain. Dumbfounded, he looked down and saw that his entire right foot was gone and that a gory stream of blood was pouring from the stump. Blood was also pouring from his left foot, which, though the heel had been sliced off, was still attached to his leg.

As if this was not enough, the Zero was banking around for its fourth pass on the helpless Marine. Sam's mind focused upon just one simple thought, "This is the *end!*"

Sam's good judgment and nerves never deserted him. As he prepared to pull up on the shrouds and shorten his body once again, the New Zealander he had saved minutes earlier dived out of the blue, all guns blazing, and chased the Zero away.

The New Zealander followed Sam all the way to the sea, where Sam made a soft landing. Sam's instincts were terrific; they completely overcame the pain and loss of blood. He efficiently slipped out of the parachute harness and twisted the knob that activated the rubber raft he carried in his ass pack. There was a comforting hiss and crackle, and the raft quickly expanded beside Sam, who used the last of his composure and strength to heave his mutilated body aboard, out of the shark-infested water.

Sam rolled over onto his back and fumbled with his emergency pack. He unwrapped a gauze bandage and pulled out his K-bar knife, from which he fashioned a passable tourniquet. By then, the blood loss and shock were fuddling Sam's mind, but he held on to that tourniquet and even released it at regular intervals, despite a creeping sense that he was locked in a bad dream. In that dream state, he popped several sulfa tablets into his mouth to combat infection and then stabbed a full syrette of morphine into the mutilated leg to combat an awesome pain.

After an hour, Sam was jarred from his reveries by the puny rumble of an approaching Grumman J2F Duck. He removed his highly polished metal mirror from his emergency pack and flashed it at the approaching amphibian.

High above, Lieutenant Colonel Nathaniel Clifford, temporary commander of MAG-21, immediately spotted the mirror flashes from the surface and made a water landing right beside the tiny yellow liferaft bearing Half-a-Caste Logan. Clifford flew Sam straight to our new base in the Russell Islands, and Sam's right leg and bleeding left foot were promptly treated. Then Lieutenant Colonel Clifford flew Sam back to Henderson Field. Sam was safely in the base hospital at Turtle Bay by nightfall, receiving the finest medical care available in the South Pacific. Within days, he was safely in an Australian military hospital.

The story, related to me in far less detail only a few days after the event, shocked me to the core of my being. I swore that I would get a Zero for Sam.

17

Following several days of getting VMF-121 familiarized with the Henderson Field complex and the islands and waters around Guadalcanal, we were assigned duties as one of several combat-alert squadrons. Upon hearing of the approach of enemy warplanes ours would be among the first to scramble aloft. Other fighter squadrons based at Cactus, as Guadalcanal was known, escorted bombers on raids up The Slot, the double chain of islands stretching from southeast of Guadalcanal to Bougainville, which was about as far as our fighters could reach.

This was all familiar stuff for both the squadron's combat veterans of previous Guadalcanal tours and for the squadron's Samoa-trained contingent.

★

My first air-alert scramble at Guadalcanal was on June 12, 1943. It was to be my first intercept and my first combat.

I was then the squadron flight officer and, on June 12, was flight leader of VMF-121's two four-plane alert divisions.

Pilots not already waiting in their cockpits were in the squadron ready room, a large tent near the edge of the main runway, within sprinting distance of our Corsairs.

At the alert, I ran toward the airplanes, which were waiting like cow ponies in the dispersal revetments beside the taxiway.

I climbed up on the left wing of the first plane I could find and vaulted into the cockpit. With the aid of the plane captain, I shrugged into my seat and parachute harnesses and plugged in my throat mike and earphones. As the plane captain climbed down off the wing and got out of the way, I checked the lever that was set to lock me into the cockpit.

Then, one by one, I heard the thrumming high-performance engines, which had already been turned up by the plane captains, roar to full power. At this point, all pilots checked the two magnetos to be sure they were each bearing a full power load. If the magnetos gave a low reading, or if some other problem was noted, the pilot would quickly shut off the engine, reverse the entry procedure, and head for the nearest spare plane, of which there were always one or two. Sometimes, if too many airplanes were down, some pilots would miss getting into the air.

The eerie thing about scrambles was the complete absence of radio chatter. The entire evolution was so automatic that, except in an extreme emergency, there was zero conversation. We just boosted power and rolled out to take off into the wind.

As my airplane vaulted into the air, I pulled up its landing gear lever with my left hand. Then, as I climbed beyond danger of hitting the earth, I switched the joystick to my left hand and pulled my birdcage canopy shut with my right. Then I strapped on my oxygen mask, which was mandatory above 10,000 feet.

Within a very few minutes, my half-squadron was clawing for an altitude advantage over the onrushing enemy, seeking to meet that enemy as far from friendly bases as we could manage. As we climbed, each of us charged and test-fired all of his Corsair's six .50-caliber wing guns. There was no point in flying on if the guns were inoperable.

The formation pretty much took care of itself. We nearly always had a few stragglers or gaps in our formation right after reaching altitude. That meant we had to reconstitute two-plane elements and divisions on the way to combat.

★

We were at 18,000 feet and heading northwest, toward the Russell Islands, which were about 80 miles from Henderson Field. The remainder of the squadron, and three other alert squadrons, were dispersed nearby or right behind us, covering different altitudes and sectors. Thus, we had 32 Corsairs and Wildcats flying as a leading wedge and nearly an identical number coming on as a follow-up force. The New Zealanders managed to launch another 30 P-40 fighters.

For all the long months of practice and performance in Samoa and at Turtle Bay, I did not have a calm cell in my body. It is unusual to sweat at altitude, even in the tropics, but bodily fluids were running off me in rivulets. I was even concerned that my canopy would fog up from so much moisture. I had no fear, but my bloodstream had an overabundance of adrenalin and, I'm sure, other life-preserving substances that gave off a rank odor and copious amounts of perspiration. In a way, my discomfort shielded me from dwelling too much on the possible consequences of the onrushing confrontation.

I do not think I was ever as exhilarated as I was during that flight.

The Russells had been recently seized by Marine Raiders, and a new forward fighter strip was under construction. It was unclear if the approaching Japanese wanted to strike at the new base or if they were bound for Guadalcanal. Whatever the case, we had barely enough time to intercept them just to the northwest of the Russells.

There was no end of chatter among the Corsair pilots, especially "bogies"—unconfirmed, presumably hostile radar contacts from our ground controllers at Guadalcanal.

We were over the Russell Islands within 30 minutes of the alert. Below, I could see the wakes of boats as they plied the blue waters. I was scanning the entire sky, looking for telltale movement among the distant thunderheads and the lacy white cumulus clouds set against a splendid blue canopy.

I was just commenting to myself what a beautiful day it was when my earphones suddenly crackled with an incoming all-squadrons message: "Tally ho! Zeros at eleven o'clock. Angels 25." This meant that enemy fighters had been spotted as they flew at an altitude of 25,000 feet and on a bearing just to the left of dead center. (Imagine a clock. Dead ahead is 12 o'clock, dead astern is six o'clock, right is three o'clock, and left is nine o'clock.)

I charged my guns and turned on my reflector sight, which cast an image of a gunsight, complete with distance calibrations, on the windscreen in front of my face.

Within seconds, I saw silvery glints against the bright blue background of the sky. The enemy fighter formations were coming in from all directions.

No enemy bombers had been reported by coastwatchers occupying various covert observation posts farther up the Solomons, and none was sighted as the opposing forces rushed at one another in excess of 500 miles per hour. We were encountering a fighter sweep, pure and simple. Over 70 Zeros had come only to challenge our fighters.

Well.

★

As I approached the swift silver streaks and tried to lock onto one of my own, I could see in the middle distance that other Corsairs—from my two divisions, as it turned out—had already engaged, for there was a large brown smudge set against a lacy cumulus cloud to mark the spot where a Zero had blown up. I saw no parachute.

Then we were into it.

To my left, my own division's second element suddenly broke away to take on an oncoming Zero. But I had only enough time to watch the first spurt of tracer erupt from one of the Corsair's six .50-caliber wing guns.

All the best training in the world could not abate the instant of sheer surprise when my eyes locked onto a target of their own.

The Zero was going to pass me from the right front to left rear as he dived on one of the Corsairs of my engaged second element, which by then was behind and below me. I was sure the Japanese pilot never saw me as he opened with his two .30-caliber machine guns. I saw his pink tracer reach out past my line of vision, which was obscured by my Corsair's long nose. Then, for good measure, he fired four 20mm cannon rounds, which passed in front of me like fiery popcorn balls; I was shocked to see how slowly they seemed to travel.

I never consciously pressed my gun-button knob. I had practiced this encounter a thousand times, and I seemed to know enough to allow my instincts to prevail over my mind. My guns were bore-sighted to converge in a cone about 300 yards ahead of my Corsair's propeller spinner. Anything within that cone would be hit by a stream of half-inch steel-jacketed bullets.

My Corsair shuddered slightly as all the guns fired, and I saw my tracer passing just over the Zero's long birdcage canopy.

Then he was past me. I pulled around after him, to my left. So, I hoped, did my wingman, 1st Lieutenant Phil Leeds, who was echeloned to the right and rear, just off my right wing.

My turn was easy. I did not pull many Gs, so my head was absolutely clear. I came up with a far deflection shot and decided to go for it. I gave the Zero a good lead and fired all my guns again. As planned, my tracers went ahead of him, but at just the right level. I kicked my left rudder to pull my rounds in toward his nose.

If that Japanese pilot had flown straight ahead, he would have been a dead man.

Instead, that superb pilot presented me with a demonstration of the Zero's best flight characteristic, the one thing a Zero could do that could carry its pilot from the jaws of death just about every time. I had heard of the maneuver I was about to experience from scores of awed F4F and F4U pilots, but I had no conception of how aerodynamically fantastic the Zero fighter really was until that split second.

As soon as my quarry saw my tracer pass in front of his airplane's nose, he simply pulled straight up and literally disappeared from within my reflector sight and, indeed, my entire line of sight. My tracer reached out into empty space. I was so in awe of the maneuver that I was literally shaking with envy.

I had time to inscribe a fleeting image of my surroundings upon my mind's eye—the sky was filled with weaving airplanes, streamers of smoke and flame, winking guns, and lines of tracer set against that superb blue background, with its distant thunderheads and lacy cumulus clouds. Then I pulled my joystick into my belly and banked as hard to the left as I dared.

There he was! My reflector sight ring lay just to the right of him. He was just beyond my reach. If I was to get a clear shot, I would have to pull up in an even steeper climb. Even then, he had the better climbing speed, and he was steadily opening the range.

But I wanted the son of a bitch to avenge Sam Logan.

I held my breath and sucked in my gut to counteract the pressure, but I felt the forces of gravity steadily mount up and press me into my seat; I felt the thought-carrying blood being sucked from my brain. I could not quite get him into my sights; he was just a little too high and a little too far to the right.

He had me in a tight loop by then. I knew I would not be able to maintain the mind-expanding maneuver indefinitely. It struck me that I might be running low on ammunition.

All the alarm bells went off in my head at the same time, but I hung on despite the gray pall that was simultaneously passing over my eyes and my mind.

I finally reached the top of the loop, a point where all the forces were in equilibrium. Suddenly, the G forces relaxed. I was not quite weightless, but neither was I quite my full body weight. There was a moment of grogginess, then the gray pall totally cleared. I noticed that the horizon was upside down and that the Zero was . . . in my sights!

He was about 300 yards ahead of me, at extreme range, and slowly pulling away.

It was now or never.

I blocked out everything else in the world except that silver Zero and the tools I had at my disposal, now mere extensions of my mind and my senses. Nothing else in the world mattered more than staying on that Zero's tail. I would have flown into the ocean at full throttle if that enemy pilot led me there.

I squeezed the gun-button knob beneath my right index finger. The eerie silence in my cockpit was broken by the steady roar of my machine guns.

The Zero never had a chance. It flew directly into the cone of deadly half-inch bullets. I was easily able to stay on it as the stream of tracer first sawed into the leading edge of the left wing. I saw little pieces of metal fly away from the impact area and clearly thought I should nudge my gunsight—which is to say, my entire Corsair—a hair to the right. The stream of tracer worked its way to the cockpit. I clearly saw the glass canopy shatter, but there was so much glinting, roiling glass and debris that I could not see the pilot. The Zero wobbled, and my tracer fell into first one wing root, then the other, striking the enemy's unprotected fuel tanks.

The Zero suddenly blew up, evaporated.

★

I instinctively ducked, certain that I would be struck by the debris, which was hurtling by at many hundreds of miles per hour. I could feel things hitting the Corsair, but I was quickly through the expanding greasy cloud of detritus and soaring through clear sky.

As I fell back into the ironclad routine of rotating my head left, right and up in search of enemy planes, I felt rather than saw Phil Leeds closing in on my tail. Only then did I realize that trusty Phil had followed me all the way through the grueling chase and on through the debris cloud of the evaporated Zero.

Now it was his turn.

Only seconds after passing through the debris of my kill, another Zero flashed by directly in front of us, from right to left and a hair above us. Phil was in the best position to get him; we both knew that. While Phil went after him like a hawk after a mouse, I dropped back and locked on to Phil's wing.

Phil peeled off to the left and struggled mightily to grab hold of the Zero's tail. As he turned, however, I saw a stream of pink tracer flash past his windscreen from the right rear.

My eyes quickly shifted to my rear-view mirror on the right and caught the glint of the sun on our assailant's silvery fuselage. Phil saw the second Zero too and led me sharply around to the left.

There, we both saw that a third Zero was coming toward us from below!

Phil followed through right into a diving head-on attack against the third Zero. Even as pink tracer from the second Zero's guns flashed by from the right rear, I saw that Phil was scoring solid hits on the third Zero. I also noted that there was no return fire from the third Zero.

Then it was time to get out of the way. We reversed course by flying up into a tight loop. The instant we completed the high-G maneuver, the second Zero overtook us and hurtled out from under my wing. Phil simply fired all his guns at the second Zero as it passed beneath his wing.

I lost track of Phil's bullets and all the Zeros for just an instant as I checked to see if any more Zeros were converging on us. When I next looked around, all I could see was a huge white parachute opening beneath a great puff of black smoke. Nearby, the remains of the lifeless second Zero spiralled down toward the sea. Neither the first nor third Zeros were anywhere in our part of the sky.

I don't think Phil's kill took more than ten seconds.

★

The sky around us was empty; the air battle had passed us by. Far off, I could see airplanes maneuvering against the backdrop of clouds. I briefly considered joining the action, but I was worried about our supply of .50-caliber ammunition. I well knew that only very foolish pilots knowingly use all their bullets when enemy fighters are still around.

I motioned Phil to fall back on my tail, which he did as I checked our position on my strip map. As soon as I had a fix on a distinctive island below, I climbed back to 18,000 feet and shaped a course for home, well to the southeast.

Only then did I realize that my flight suit was dripping wet from perspiration. And I could feel a heavy pounding in my temples, indicating that a vast quantity of adrenalin was coursing through my bloodstream. My breathing became shallow, and I felt ever so faint. I took a few deep pulls of pure oxygen, and that cleared me right up.

★

After a return flight of under 30 minutes, we made landfall over Cape Esperance, Guadalcanal's northwestern tip. It was about 1130. Then and there, Phil and I both spotted a solitary Zero circling right over the beach at about 5,000 feet, well below us. I had the vague impression that the pilot might have been speaking by radio with someone on the ground.

I knew I was very low on ammunition and would have left that Zero alone, but Phil radioed that he wanted to take a crack at him, though he had no idea how many bullets he had left.

I turned the lead over to Phil and followed him in a steep dive right out of the sun. The whole thing was over in seconds. Phil simply nailed the Zero, which turned its nose down and dived straight into the sea. It never even flamed.

We circled the Zero's grave once, then turned for home, where we made a routine landing and taxied out to the dispersal area to see how our comrades had fared. As it happened, Phil and I were the first ones back. We accepted handshakes from our plane captains after telling them the good news, and then we bided our time by checking our Corsairs for damage. Neither of the airplanes had sustained any bullet holes, but my airplane's nose and leading wing edges were pitted from debris, and there was a large black smudge, probably flaming oil or aviation gasoline, on my prop spinner and the nose of my fighter.

Everyone was back within 30 minutes or so. It turned out that VMF-121 was the only squadron that scored that day. Captain Bob Baker was credited with a probable Zero; Captain Ken Ford got two solid kills and a probable; Captain Bill Harlan got one kill and two probables; Captain Bruce Porter got a kill; and 1st Lieutenant Phil

Leeds got two kills. That is six kills and four probables against no losses of our own. A *very* good day!

★

I had not only weathered first combat, I had scored my first kill. I had been baptised. I had won my spurs.

It did not dawn on me until late that night that I had also killed a man.

18

Shortly after I broke the ice *over* the Russell Islands, VMF-121 was ordered to pack up and move forward *to* the Russells to become the first fighter squadron to operate out of Advance Base Knucklehead, the brand new runway on Banika Island.

Advance Base Knucklehead, which was 80 miles closer to the main Japanese bases on Bougainville and around Rabaul, was a beautiful, new, all-weather, coral-topped strip, built by our friends the Seabees. It was rather primitive by Guadalcanal standards, but far better than Tutuila had been when I had arrived in Samoa in March, 1942. It was extremely well defended by antiaircraft batteries established by a Marine defense battalion, and there were thousands of Army infantrymen on hand to protect us.

We were attached to MAG-21, which had established an advanced headquarters and supply and repair facilities several weeks before our arrival.

All of the confrontations associated with the major Japanese air offensive in early June were fought over the Russells. The Japanese offensive culminated in a mixed fighter-and-dive-bomber sweep on June 16, four days after my kill, but we did not know it then. The result of our anticipation was that VMF-121 was placed on full-time air-alert status, ready to launch as soon as news of renewed Japanese aerial sweeps was passed along from the north. Our job was simply to be the first squadron to confront oncoming raiders. We were 80 miles closer to the Japanese fields, so we could either blunt the Japanese sweeps farther away from our own bases, or, closer to home, we would be able to hang around in a fight longer than Henderson-based fighters.

In any event, there were no raids. Except for tracking lone snoopers and responding to false alarms, we sat tight on Banika while the air war intensified to the north.

That intensification was our doing. Before the Japanese evacuated Guadalcanal in February, 1943, they had nearly completed a new all-weather bomber strip at Munda, on New Georgia Island. Once Henderson Field was considered secure, the thrust of the Allied air effort in the Solomons had been aimed at neutralizing all the Japanese air bases in the Central and Northern Solomons as far north as Bougainville. Munda was the closest Japanese base to our sphere, so it received the brunt of the attention.

It was clearly just a matter of time before our ground forces invaded New Georgia. In fact, it was a fairly open secret that at least one of three Army infantry divisions occupying Guadalcanal and the Russells would launch the invasion. No one at my level knew precisely when or where the new offensive would be launched, but it was quite clear that heavy bomber and fighter-bomber strikes from Henderson Field were aimed at clearing the way and softening up the main objective. It was also clear, after we moved to the Russells, that MAG-21, including VMF-121, would be at the leading edge on invasion day.

In the meantime, as more squadrons followed us to Knucklehead, we drew escort missions to Munda and beyond. Our increased range was ideally suited for seeing flights of Navy and Marine SBD dive-bombers and TBF torpedo bombers all the way through to the Bougainville bases. We even escorted Army B-17 and B-24 heavy bombers. Whenever possible, we strafed enemy runways, defenses, and base and port facilities.

On rare occasions, we took part in "Dumbo" rescue missions, either to help find a downed aircrew or to fly top cover for Grumman Ducks or PBY patrol bombers.

★

Banika was a beautiful place. It was composed of volcanic matter, as were all the larger Solomon Islands, but it had the same lush, tropical environment as the better coastal areas around Henderson Field. It had been formerly used as a cattle-feeding range by Lever Brothers.

One of the first "fixtures" of the new base we met was an old Navy chief who called himself South Pacific Joe. I do not know how that old man did it, but he sort of left the Navy and set up a hamburger stand right next to the main runway. He called his place South Pacific Joe's Hamburger Spot.

To a man, VMF-121 began patronizing the Hamburger Spot as soon as the dust settled from our first landing at Knucklehead.

As at Guadalcanal, the Russells base was harassed every night by Washing Machine Charlie or Louie the Louse, the twin-engine or single-engine night bombers that scattered their payloads on and around the airbase facilities to keep us awake and damage our equipment. Among other wildlife that fell victim to Japanese bombs were the fat remnants of the Lever Brothers herd that had fed wild for decades before the war.

Nearly every night raid produced at least one freshly butchered Lever's cow or bull, and these were dutifully ground to hamburger meat by South Pacific Joe and his motley crew of "sanitation engineers." Joe also managed to corner the market on canned milk and canned ice-cream powder. These he concocted into a very passable imitation of a milkshake to go with the superb burgers and occasional french fries.

The most amazing aspect of Joe's enterprise was the price of the hamburgers, fries and shakes. They were free to pilots.

As The Word about South Pacific Joe's Hamburger Spot spread to other squadrons and groups, South Pacific aircraft plying their trade between Henderson Field and Japanese bases far up The Slot suffered a sudden rise in the number of intermittent engine failures requiring emergency landings at Advance Base Knucklehead.

Joe could have retired from the Navy as a millionaire, but he chose to give his product away.

★

Our squadron quonset huts—ready room, offices, and mess hall— were on a hill overlooking the strip, scattered through the sparse trees that provided overhead protection from the sun and falling objects. In addition to the larger quonsets there were smaller Dallas huts, each of which housed two or three pilots.

One night early in our stay, by which time we had been joined by at least one other F4U squadron, a Betty bomber slipped through our early warning system and arrived overhead with stunning swiftness.

By the time the air-raid siren sounded, I was already wide awake and alert, listening with intent interest to the regular *carumph* of bombs as they walked up the hill right toward our bivouac.

I headed for the door of my Dallas hut, intent upon reaching one of the large open-topped "bombproof" pits that were scattered throughout the area. I made the run without difficulty and leaped into the hole in one piece. Immediately, I heard and felt a bomb go off close by.

As my ears were clearing, I heard the sound of laughter coming from the far corner of the bombproof, nearest the VMF-121 bivouac.

Within a minute, I joined the crowd that quickly formed around the source of the laughter.

One of our Samoa vets, Captain Bob Schneider, was a very sound sleeper who had not been awakened by the distant sound of the exploding bombs. However, his roommate had been pulled from his sleep by the sound of the first detonation. Before the roommate quite woke up, he pulled on his boondockers and headed through the door, which he thoughtfully closed as he passed through—an ingrained gesture aimed at keeping mosquitos out.

Bob Schneider finally stirred when the air-raid siren went off. He was not quite awake yet, but he knew enough to run out of the Dallas hut. He was just getting into high gear when he ran smack into the closed door at full speed. The impact jarred him from his feet and knocked him silly.

The roommate, whom I had heard laughing, was the first to see Schneider crawl to the lip of the bombproof pit on his knees and one arm. The other arm was raised to protect the dazed pilot's nose, which, though not broken, was bloody and tender as a result of its leading impact with the door. Legend has it that the wounded man's eyes intently stared at one another for the balance of the night.

Bob showed up at breakfast the next morning with the most garish shiner I have ever seen.

★

This was sort of a slack period for us. We owned the sky during the latter half of June. The Japanese had been amply bloodied in early June and, except for launching intercepts against our raids to the north, they left us alone. We flew a lot during our first ten days at Knucklehead, but none of us even saw a Japanese warplane.

It was during the so-called slack period that Captain Bob Baker and I managed to swipe a box of two-ounce bottles of medicinal brandy from the group sickbay. We were feeling absolutely no pain by the time we decided to shower before going to evening chow.

We were lathered up and just rinsing off when two old geezers with towels wrapped around their middles clomped in. They hung their towels up and isolated themselves at the far end of the line of showers, all the way down the row from Bake and me.

The two freely used their soap and rinsed off for an incredibly long period of time, despite the fact that they were standing beside a prominent sign reading, "CONSERVE WATER! USE ONLY TO RINSE THE SOAP OFF."

The constant noise of running water and the low muttering of old voices that accompanied it finally got under Bake's skin. He suddenly turned and yelled at the two geezers, "Hey, Sawtooth and Pinhead! Can't you read?" He pointed ominously to the sign.

The two old men wordlessly turned and pondered the message, then they meekly turned off the water, collected their towels and hobbled from our sight.

Bob felt like a million bucks.

Next morning, Bake and I were in the squadron mess hall, easing coffee into our systems to counteract the alcohol poisoning we had acquired all through the previous afternoon and evening. The hubbub of the cavernous quonset hut was suddenly broken by a call to attention. Everyone mindlessly rose to obey. The screen door flew open and in strode Sawtooth and Pinhead. Each was turned out in a freshly starched khaki uniform. Each sported a wide smile on his face. On their shirt collars were lots of shiny stars. Sawtooth had three stars and Pinhead had two. They both looked freshly showered.

Bake groaned out loud while I just turned improbable colors and strangled on my heart as Pinhead and Sawtooth strode straight forward to join our skipper, Major Ray Vroome, at the commanding officer's table. The two never so much as looked in our direction as we gulped the dregs of our coffee and hurriedly left the premises.

Lieutenant General Alexander Archer Vandegrift had commanded 1st Marine Division at the invasion of Guadalcanal and had run the ground war there for four months, until his Marines were relieved and sent to Australia for rest and rehabilitation. Vandegrift had subsequently been elevated to command I Marine Amphibious Corps, with headquarters in Noumea. He was the senior Marine officer in the Pacific. It was common knowledge that he was slated to become the next Commandant of the Marine Corps.

Major General Roy Geiger was the senior aviator on active duty in the Marine Corps. He had commanded 1st Marine Aircraft Wing during the dark days at Guadalcanal. At the time of our meeting, Geiger was deputy commander of I Marine Amphibious Corps. He was slated to become Vandegrift's successor as corps commander later in the year, an unprecedented assignment for an aviator.

The two generals had arrived late the previous afternoon to inspect the Marine Corps' newest and most advanced operational base and to overnight with VMF-121. They arrived with so little fanfare that most of us never got The Word.

A year later, Bake was stationed at the Marine Corps Air Station at Goleta, near Santa Barbara, California. One day, he spotted a notice that General Vandegrift, by then a four-star general and Commandant of the Marine Corps, was due to arrive to conduct an official inspection. During the general's tour of the base, Bake was standing at attention with a large group of other pilots in front of the squadron offices. Vandegrift stopped right in front of Bake, looked him square in the eye, and asked, "Captain, do you have enough water here?" Bake did not bat an eye when he barked, "Yes, Sir!" at the Commandant, who moved on up the line without saying another word.

★

One of the great difficulties in breaking in a new operational base (Knucklehead was my third, after Tafuna and Faleola) was overcoming primitive repair facilities.

While the airplanes we flew in World War II do not compare in complexity and number of parts with the operational jet fighters flying today, they were highly complex machines that required constant maintenance.

Also, the F4U was still a new fighter. We had not ironed out all the bugs or absorbed all the minor adjustments and other officially sanctioned changes that came on line almost every day.

Not enough can be said about the devotion and pivotal importance of our groundcrewmen. They labored mightily out of the limelight while young kids like me sucked up all the glory. Factors of heredity—great eyesight and reflexes—placed us in the cockpits of airplanes that could never have gotten airborne without the loving attention provided by our plane captains and mechanics.

Often, groundcrewmen worked 24-hour days, with little time off for meals or catnaps. They suffered debilitating illnesses and life-threatening diseases because they took better care of our Corsairs than their own bodies.

Unlike bases to the rear, Knucklehead had not built up the needed boneyard of scrapped airplanes that could be cannibalized for spare parts. Parts literally had to be machined from other parts or raw metal stock. That meant long hours for the machinists who had to do the fabrications. Our machinists, electricians, armorers, and radio technicians also lost sleep over ongoing problems that resulted in field innovations—new designs handled in the field before the factories in the States ever found out there was a need to make changes.

It quickly got to the point where all our Corsairs were flying with little things wrong with them—things that would have seen them grounded for days or weeks in the States. We drew the line at hazarding our lives in clearly unsafe airplanes, but we gave up the fine edge of speed or performance in the interest of getting marginal fighters airborne to protect friendly bombers and shipping.

The Corsair had been designed to fly from carriers, so our early models retained wing-fold mechanisms, a useless affair that endangered us because of hydraulic leaks. I never heard of a Corsair's wing folding in mid air, but the danger was present in high-stress combat flying, so the problem could well have led to deaths in cases where pilots did not push their airplanes to the limit because they were favoring those wings.

I do know that hydraulic leaks in landing gear mechanisms caused operational accidents and, I am sure, direct and indirect deaths. Who can say how many people died during the war because a fighter was in for repair and *not* covering someone's "six" in a fight?

I knowingly took off in fighters with only four of six wing guns operational or with a faulty radio.

The aft part of the Corsair's wings and control surfaces were made of fabric, which was easily patched when bullets passed through. But most of the Corsair had a metal skin, which had to be replaced by new metal when it was damaged. The metalsmiths used so-called "cherry rivets" to tack on the new skin. These were small explosive rivets that were detonated within a wing panel or other tight area by means of a bucking bar. The detonation flattened the inner end of the rivet against the inner side of the new skin, thus providing a permanent seal. There were never enough cherry rivets at the front.

Early model Corsairs suffered from chronic leaky wing tanks. This was a real enough hazard in ordinary flight, but it was particularly so in combat, where all sorts of fire and flame leap through the air.

In the end, over its nearly ten operational years and five separate major iterations, the F4U Corsair underwent 2,800 minor standard changes and over 500 major upgrades. Many of those changes were specified and initially handled by our groundcrewmen at the leading edge, where they counted the most.

19

One morning very late in June, 1943, all the pilots and staff officers of all the squadrons based on Banika were called to a special briefing conducted by Lieutenant Colonel Luther "Sad Sam" Moore.

It was at this unprecedented meeting that we learned the exact time and place of the New Georgia invasion. In fact, it was a matter of learning times and places, for there were to be a half-dozen landings and assaults throughout the morning of June 30, 1943. The big show, the one to which we were assigned, was at Rendova, an island near Munda Field, the main objective of the operation.

The bulk of the ground work would be undertaken by the 43rd Infantry Division, a relatively unblooded collection of New England National Guard units that had seen some action mopping up at Guadalcanal and had supplied a regiment earlier in the year to seize Banika. A number of Marine Raider battalions would launch several side operations to sweep up outlying Japanese detachments and base units.

The aerial part of the assault was to be massive, the largest continuous blow to be administered thus far on one day by Allied air units in the Pacific. Our leaders anticipated huge Japanese counterthrusts in the form of air and naval attacks on our shipping. Guadalcanal-and Banika-based Corsair and Wildcat units were to strafe ground targets, provide top cover for bombing missions, protect the landing beaches, and execute on-call air support missions.

We were told to expect days or weeks of steady combat, culminating in the capture and rehabilitation of Munda Field as well as the construction of several outlying airfields by our Seabees.

★

On the night of June 29, I was told that my division and another commanded by Captain Louis Gordon would be the first Banika-based fighters to launch on invasion day. The eight of us were to get airborne before dawn and fly up to Rendova to help guard the invasion fleet against incoming Japanese warplanes.

I hated predawn takeoffs. We all did. They were extremely dangerous from those small, primitive airstrips. We had airfield lights to delimit the edges and ends of the narrow, tree-hemmed runway. To avoid hitting those trees, we had to carefully line up on the flickering lights, make certain we were going down the center of the strip, and sharply pull up just as soon as we became airborne. Any sort of engine trouble or a ground loop could easily be fatal. As it was, we always had a little trouble getting off of Knucklehead because our tail wheels, which were built for steel-braced hardwood carrier decks, always stuck a little and slowed us down. I even hated daytime takeoffs at Knucklehead.

We awakened at 0400 and trudged down to the mess hall for breakfast. As usual, all I could get into me that early was a cup of coffee, which I drank scalding hot to mask the flavor. I spent the rest of the pretakeoff time with our group meteorologist, who had nothing but bad news. The weather up north had turned foul, which was great for the Army infantrymen because it was bad for Japanese aviators—and us.

The weather front had moved in by the time we were turning up the engines of our eight Corsairs. As I was getting set to taxi out, my earphones told me that two of my eight F4Us were unable to launch because of engine trouble. The decision was made to send me north with just six fighters.

I had the lead. Phil Leeds was on my wing, as usual. I have no idea who the next two pilots were. Then there was the other division leader, my old and dear friend, Louis Gordon. The last man was 1st Lieutenant Bill Snee.

After I carefully lined up on the two smudge pots at the far end of the runway, I took a deep breath and turned my engine all the way up. Then I came off the brakes and rode my Corsair into the air.

I had my wheels up and canopy closed by the time I scraped across the first line of tall palm trees and flew over the lagoon.

As Leeds and I pulled away from Banika, my earphones crackled with a tortured "Mayday! Mayday!" Then silence. We were supposed to be maintaining radio silence, so I mouthed a heartfelt "Hang in there" and turned my attention back to topping the low-lying cloud cover.

I finally broke out of the weather at 10,000 feet and circled to allow my extended division to join up. Leeds easily found my wing lights, as did the two pilots following him. And so did Gordon. Snee was missing. I had to assume that he had failed to get up enough air speed and had aborted, spun in, or collided with the trees.

Leeds smoothly joined on my wing, and I managed to convey that the other two pilots were to join on Gordon in an old-fashioned three-plane element.

It was pitch black up there, without any sign of the sun. As soon as everyone who was going to join had sorted themselves out, I circled one more time to orient myself. Then I headed on up the compass bearing I had been given before takeoff. We would slowly climb all the way to Rendova and report to an air coordination center located aboard one of the warships covering the landing. They would do with us as they chose.

The sun was just peeking up over the horizon when we arrived over Rendova fifteen minutes after starting out. The clouds were stacked up as far as I could see. After I reported in, we flew lazy circles over the fleet and watched tiny landing craft dart between the larger ships and head for the beaches. After a short time, I was ordered down to 10,000 feet. The view was much better for a brief interval, then the clouds moved in.

I was particularly worried about the clouds. They might have hampered Japanese flight operations, but it was certain that they would not prevent our enemies from making a game try at the fleet.

★

We had a total of 29 fighters from VMF-121, 122, 213, and 221 flying fleet cover when the first cobbled-together bomber strike came down from the large Japanese base at Kahili. Nearby, there were at least 32 additional, later-arriving Corsairs and Wildcats from the same squadrons flying other sector patrols. Several Marine and Navy Wildcat squadrons out of Guadalcanal were also in the vicinity.

The first inkling I had that we were under attack came when forty or fifty Zeros suddenly emerged from around the cloud cover right in front of my face. It happened that fast.

Their nine-plane fighter V's simultaneously struck from several directions. They all had the advantage of altitude and they all arrived out of what little sun there was. Our shipborne radar had completely dropped the ball.

I also saw bomber formations slip through far below, but there was no way I or any other Corsair or Wildcat pilot could attack the bombers when there were so many Zeros to fend off.

The chatter in my earphones overwhelmed my efforts to exert any influence on my flight's actions.

Initially, there were at most 29 of us, so we were badly outnumbered for the minutes it would take the second echelon to get the news and pitch itself into the battle.

★

The first individual Japanese warplane I focused on was a Zero, which was passing a dozen feet below my nose at high speed from left to right. He was smack on the tail of a smoking Corsair. I instinctively yanked around sharply to my right to try to get on the assailant's tail, at least to scare him off my damaged fellow Marine.

The Zero was less than 300 yards ahead and I was closing when my reflector gunsight fell right on his nose. I coldly squeezed my gun button knob for three seconds. Every third round out of my six wing guns was a tracer. I saw a whole line of them fall right into the Zero's engine cowling.

First I saw pieces fly off the engine. Then the Zero disintegrated right in front of me, and I flew through the maelstrom of metal and burning fuel.

The kill had taken less than seven seconds from the moment I first saw the Zero flash by.

I had not yet recovered from my right turn when a blue Corsair passed from right to left in front of my propeller disc. It was Phil Leeds. I must have shaken him loose when I turned into my Zero seconds earlier. He was at just my altitude and 500 yards to my left by the time I boosted power to follow him. I only then noticed the twin streams of pink tracer chasing his tail. A Zero flashed into view from over my left shoulder. I was stunned by the size of the red "meatball" set against the Japanese fighter's shiny aluminum fuse-lage.

"No way you're getting my wingman," I thought.

I immediately reversed course by turning hard to the left, and I quickly brought my reflector sight onto the Zero chasing Leeds. I had him in a split second and fired a full four-second burst, which struck him in the starboard side, in the engine and around the cockpit. He kept flying after Leeds, so I gave him another burst. And another. And a fourth. By then, I could see smoke trailing from the Zero's engine. I had an instant to see him pull up, but I lost him when my attention was wrenched to thoughts of my own survival.

My first knowledge that my exposed rear had acquired a stalker came in the form of a brief, bright flash to my right. I caught the 20mm round in the corner of my eye just as it blooped into my wing and created a two-inch hole between the aileron and the wing-gun magazine. He had me! My Corsair shook and jerked as dual streams of .30-caliber rounds hit the same wing.

I saw the Zero flicker past my rearview mirror, but before I could do anything, a .30-caliber bullet passed through my Corsair's plexiglas canopy. It did no noticeable damage, but it did scare the hell out of me.

I could not shake the Zero. He followed me move for move for agonizing seconds. I was growing desperate as I realized that only a lucky break could save me from death.

Without warning, the stream of bullets let up. I followed through with my next two or three maneuvers before I realized that the Zero was gone. I flicked a peek into my rearview mirror and saw that Phil Leeds was closing into his usual off-wing position. Clearly, he had returned my earlier favor by chasing my tormentor off my tail.

★

I saw that Phil and I were in open sky, cut off from the battle by a high mountain of clouds.

"Was that Gordon's Corsair we saw smoking back there?" I was referring to the Corsair from whose tail I had blown the first Zero only a minute earlier. I was very worried. Of all the friends I had made at flight school, only Jeff Poindexter and Louis Gordon were still with me.

Phil told me he was not sure who it had been, but he reluctantly reported that he thought he had seen the pilot bail out over the beach off Munda Point just as I broke away after the first Zero.

"Well, let's take a run over Munda to see if the pilot is down and got out of his chute okay."

We turned over Munda Field and followed the beach around from northwest to southeast.

I saw the spilled chute right up against the beach beside the main runway. A khaki coverall-clad body was gently rocking in the surf. I saw no sign of blood or any movement as I rocketed past. Another pass would have been foolhardy; we had beaten Japanese antiaircraft gunners once, and that was as much as we could expect.

My feeling of remorse was total.

All I could do was report in to the shipborne flight operations center, which had been dubbed "Pluto."

"Pluto from Black One. Reporting a downed Corsair pilot on the beach near Munda airstrip."

I realized that the tactical channel was clogged with hoots and hollers and warnings and curses from temporarily unhinged young pilots in combat. I received no acknowledgment, tried again with no success, and gave up.

I led Phil back up to 8,000 feet and circled over the fleet to find the rest of the VMF-121 fighters in action that morning.

By then my engine was smoking and it faltered a few times. I guessed that my oil system had been damaged, which was a good reason to head for home. If the cooling system failed, the high performance engine was bound to burn itself out. Every second counted.

I signalled for Phil to follow, then shaped a course for Knucklehead, which was only 60 air miles away. As we flew, I tried to assess the damage to my Corsair. My first point of interest, after seeing to the knocking engine, was the round that had passed through the cockpit. I easily found the starred plexiglas where it had come in. It was evident that the round had barely missed my head. There seemed to be no damage to my instrument panel or to any of the levers I needed to keep the airplane aloft. The bullet had exited low on the the windscreen, and a tiny stream of cold air was playing right on my face. I counted ten other small holes from the Zero's .30-caliber rounds, and the one big 20mm hole on the starboard wing. It was also obvious, since the Japanese pilot was above me when he fired, that he had put at least one round through the top of my engine cowling.

As Phil and I reviewed the fight in excited tones, he told me that

I had one definite kill and had also badly damaged the one I had pried off his tail. However, neither of us saw the smoker go down, so I would not be able to claim a victory—unless someone else saw it fall to earth.

We spotted our sanctuary at Banika in only fifteen minutes and flared out to approach upwind. That took us over the lagoon, where I saw the wreckage of a Corsair. I knew then what fate had befallen Lieutenant Bill Snee. It was clear from the position of the wreckage that he had lost power after becoming airborne and had tried to land on his belly in the water following a tight turn to starboard. Clearly, the turn had gone badly—it was a longshot to begin with—and Snee had crashed. It remained to be seen if he had survived, but I made a silent bet against him on the basis of the mangled wreckage.

My Corsair's engine held up through the rigors of landing and I taxied into the dispersal revetment. There, my plane captain jumped up on the wing to help me out of my harness. "Did you get any of the bastards, Sir?" I nodded and accepted his handshake. Then he saw the bullet holes and muttered a low, "For Christ's sake." I quickly deduced that he was blaming *me* for the damage!

I joined Phil for the short, dusty walk to the operations shack, and there we heard the early news from Rendova. The day thus far was considered a disaster. The Zeros had completely suckered the Corsairs and Wildcats into a fight, while, as I suspected, low-flying Betty medium bombers had dodged in to strike at the fleet. The weather had played havoc with our fighter tactics, and our radar was deemed worse than useless.

We had taken losses. Bill Snee had indeed died on takeoff, and one of Louis Gordon's wingmen had already reported that Louis had definitely bailed out over Munda. My report pretty much confirmed my friend's demise.

The group operations people also told me that Ras Rasmussen, of VMF-122, had been critically injured in his Corsair in a preflight mishap. It was an unusual accident in that the refueling crew had apparently allowed some gasoline to dribble into Ras's cockpit while the refueler truck was alongside before dawn. No one had noticed; the smell of aviation gasoline was so commonplace on the flight line as to be beyond anyone's notice. The fuel had evaporated to fumes by the time Ras climbed into the cockpit. He had his goggles up and his sleeves rolled up when the shotgun-shell engine starter was fired. The fumes were immediately ignited, and Ras, who was already strapped in, was trapped by the flash fire. The plane captain had immediately headed for the nearby trees, causing everyone to think that he was running away. Far from it. He was back in seconds with a carbon dioxide fire extinguisher and bravely climbed through the flames to the wing. He put the fire out and pulled Ras from the cockpit. However, Ras was burned over most of his body. My friend died during the night.

By bizarre coincidence, Ras's bosom buddy, Fateye Gardner, was shot down and killed on the same late-morning mission Ras was to have flown. He was last seen running at full speed with a Zero on his tail. No one ever heard a peep from him. His grave was never found.

So, the Knucklehead Corsair squadrons lost four men on June 30. Against our side of Death's ledger, Marine pilots claimed 101 kills for the day. This number was reduced after a thorough investigation to 66 kills and fifteen probables, plus two Japanese airplanes definitely damaged.

I was credited with one kill and one probable. Captains Bob Baker, Perry Shuman, and Ken Ford each got three kills. Altogether, the squadron was officially credited with nineteen confirmed kills and two probables on June 30, 1943.

I'm not sure all those kills were worth two of our pilots killed in combat and two killed in operational accidents.

20

Although the Japanese failed to repulse the Rendova landings on the first day, the battles over the beaches continued for the next two weeks. The Japanese suffered crippling losses in airplanes and aircrews, but they only scored hits on four of our ships—a fine testimonial to the skill of both our fighter pilots and our radar controllers.

I took no direct part in the New Georgia operation after the June 30 kickoff. While Guadalcanal-based fighters continued to fly over Rendova and New Georgia, the extra range afforded us by our being based at Knucklehead was used to provide our bombers with escorts as they ranged farther up the Solomons chain to interdict Japanese airstrikes and naval forces at or nearer their sources.

We flew three types of missions—dumbo escort, strafing, and bomber escort.

The strafing missions were always hair-raising. Typically, a single F4U division was sent to a set of map coordinates, usually the beach of one of the larger islands beyond New Georgia. While two of the Corsairs circled high above to ward off enemy fighters (which almost never appeared), the other two dived on the coordinates and fired about half their .50-caliber ammunition. We visually acquired targets only about half the time. The other half, we just sprayed an area of jungle or beach, allowing our half-inch bullets to search for something a coastwatcher or passing aviator thought he might have seen at that particular spot. Once the first element had fired, it climbed to take up the guard station, and the other element ran its strafing mission. It usually took each plane two passes to fire half its ammunition. We never knew what might be lurking in the rain forest. Usually, it was nothing. However, other squadrons, and other divisions in our squadron, lost pilots and planes during these blind-shooting episodes.

The dumbo rescue missions were universally boring because we had to fly our fighters dead slow to remain on station with twin-engine PBY flying boats or single-engine Grumman Ducks, neither of which could fly straight and level at over 125 miles per hour. On the other hand, the payoff for these missions was usually the rescue of a downed aviator. It was nerve-wracking work none of us would have passed up; we all knew how easy it was to become a downed fighter pilot stranded in enemy territory.

The bombing escort missions filled most of my days for the first three weeks in July.

I and my pilots—up to two or three divisions—were usually briefed in the group operations tent by Lieutenant Colonel Sad Sam Moore the night before the mission. Moore would tell us how many SBD Dauntless dive-bombers or TBF Avenger torpedo bombers would be going out, where they would be going, why they would be going, how they would be returning, and what sort of opposition could be expected. The targets were usually air or supply bases about halfway up The Slot, usually on Choiseul or Bougainville or any of the numerous smaller islands in the vicinity. The bombers also struck at Japanese shipping during this period, but I never drew a strike aimed exclusively at Japanese anchorages.

Our main purpose was to protect friendly bombers from preda-tory Zero fighters.

Our Marine and Navy single-engine bomber pilots had by then evolved tight antifighter formations, similar in principle to the familiar heavy-bomber boxes flown in the European Theater. The main difference was that the single-engine naval service bombers of the period had fewer machine guns. The Dauntless had a pair of .30-caliber guns mounted on the engine cowling that fired through the propeller disc, and a pair of free .30-caliber guns that could be fired to the rear. The pilot handled the forward guns, and the radioman handled the rear guns. The Avenger pilots could fire one .50-caliber gun through the propeller disc, while the radioman fired a single turret-mounted .50-caliber to the rear and the bombardier covered the lower tail quadrant with a single .30-caliber free gun. The extremely tight staggered-bomber formations of the mid 1943 period allowed almost any number of bombers to cover one another in the event enemy fighters penetrated their formation.

Our fighters typically flew a weaving pattern (partly to cover more sky and partly to match speed with the slower bombers) about 1,000 feet above the bomber formation.

During the first two weeks of July, no bomber formation I was escorting was even approached by enemy fighters. This in itself was a testament to the defeat we had administered the Japanese beginning in early June, when Allied fighters had obliterated one Japanese airstrike after another.

As far as we could determine, our TBF and SBD strikes caused severe damage to enemy installations. And they could not have helped enemy morale. However, we really had too few bombers dropping too few bombs to do any permanent damage. By and large, we were picking away at them and buying time in which to build up our ground and air forces to administer a series of killing blows.

At that time, our side really expected to slog up the Solomons chain and on into the Bismarck Archipelago, one island base at a time. The bypass strategy that saved so many of our lives and left so many Japanese rotting on the vine had not yet evolved.

★

On the evening of July 16, Sad Sam Moore told us, "We're planning a big strike for tomorrow. It will be the biggest strike we have ever mounted in the Solomons. We're going after Kahili."

Moore had assigned four Marine fighter squadrons to fly top cover on the strike against the big Japanese airbase in southern Bougainville. Also, a Royal New Zealand Air Force P-40 squadron would fly low cover, and an Army Air Forces P-38 squadron would fly far above the rest of the formation. The strike element would be composed of 36 Dauntless dive-bombers carrying one 500-lb or 1,000-lb bomb apiece, 35 Avenger torpedo bombers carrying four 500-lb bombs apiece (which would be dropped in a glide or from level flight), and seven Army four-engine B-24 Liberator heavy bombers carrying numerous 500-lb or 1,000-lb bombs each. The Liberators and many of the Navy and Marine bombers would strike the airbase while a number of Navy bombers went after shipping in the nearby Shortlands anchorage.

VMF-121—the entire squadron—was to cover the Liberators. VMF-122, 213, and 221 would cover the Marine and Navy bombers.

We rendezvoused over Munda at 25,000 feet at about 0815, July 17, 1943. By the time everyone who was going along had joined the formation, we had 78 bombers (7 B-24s, 36 SBDs, and 35 TBFs) and 114 fighters (44 F4Us, 35 F4Fs, 12 P-38s, and 23 P-40s). It was the most impressive friendly formation I had seen up to that time.

It was a gorgeous morning, with a high blue canopy overhead. Visibility was unlimited.

The approach was largely uneventful. The volcano that looms over Kahili was drawing closer, and I was looking down at the Japanese shipping in the Shortlands anchorage. Suddenly, my earphones crackled with the news that many Japanese fighters were scrambling from Kahili and the nearby airstrip at Ballale.

Within a minute of the warning, the first wave of Japanese fighters were on us. My division was at 27,000 feet when we were ordered to break off to meet the challenge.

I barely saw the Japanese fighters as they passed from high and right and slightly from front to back to go after the bombers. As I pulled the release to drop my belly fuel tank, I guessed that there were three or four dozen of them.

★

I was bent around in a tight G-turn to the left, looking after two silver streaks I had caught in the corner of my eye just as my order to break formation had come through.

The first airplane I saw in front of me was a Corsair, which I supposed was going after a target blocked from my view by my engine or left wing.

I continued on through my diving turn to look for those two silver glints. I did not see anyone approach me, but one enemy fighter suddenly filled my field of vision as it climbed past me from right to left.

I simply reacted. Although I was pulling very heavy G's, I squeezed off an instant two-second burst as we hurtled past one another 800 feet apart. I saw the Zero's canopy shatter and the broken pieces of glass trail off in a sparkling shower. I recovered from the tight turn in time to watch the Zero roll off in a steep spiral. A thickening plume of white smoke was billowing from just behind the engine. As I turned in to follow him down, his spiral flattened out. Suddenly, he was spinning nose-down and in flames from nose to tail. There was no doubt that we was bound to fall all the way into the deep blue water far below.

My third confirmed kill!

To gain better visibility, I pulled up sharply to the right— and nearly blacked out from the stress of the high G forces to which I was being subjected. As it was, my vision went blurry with tinges of red.

I levelled off at 19,000 feet and scanned the sky around me in search of enemy planes. My heart skipped a beat when I saw that Phil Leeds had been unable to cling to my tail through the tortuous turns and spirals of the last minute or two.

At just that moment, Phil passed me. A Zero was on his tail, pumping .30-caliber bullets into his Corsair.

I pulled a very tight turn to the right to join the parade. At the same time, I two-blocked the throttle—pushed it to the firewall and then eased back to keep my engine from burning out— and immediately squeezed off a trailing burst. I had little hope of hitting the Zero, but I wanted to shake the enemy pilot's concentration.

The Japanese pilot saw my tracer just as I was able to pull my bullets in to strike his tail. Chunks of metal were streaming off the Zero's tail when the Japanese pilot used his best stock evasion tactic. In the twinkling of my eye, he pulled straight up, away from the deadly bullets. I was unable to follow; I did not even try. I knew I had done the Zero harm, but there was no way I could tell if I had done enough to cause him to crash. I would have to settle for a probable, or even a "damaged."

★

When I first had time to breathe, I realized that my earphones were filled with the bleats, yells, warnings, and trailing verbal thoughts of scores of Marine fighter pilots. As always, radio discipline had instantly declined to the point where we would have been better off without radios.

My eyes told me that the entire fighter force had disintegrated to a visual jumble of individual, disconnected fights across the entire sky.

The B-24s our squadron was supposed to be protecting were by then coming up on their bomb-release point. The bright blue sky around those rock-steady Liberators was a kaleidoscope of burning airplanes, colorful tracer streams, billowing parachute canopies, and falling debris.

I saw then that most of the Zeros had drawn away from the bomber formation. We clearly had given them a fight they could not match. Now they were looping and rolling just outside our range. I was certain they would stay there until after our fighters had gone. Then they would dog our tails to get at crippled or straggling bombers and fighters out to the extremity of their operational range.

★

The Corsairs and Wildcats had been instructed to strafe "targets of opportunity" if we could. As I watched the B-24s release bombs and turn to the left for home with the P-38s and P-40s, I saw tiny-looking Wildcats and Corsairs far below whip across the smoke-shrouded airdrome and anchorage.

Phil Leeds and several other Corsair pilots had formed on my tail by then. We were diving past 3,000 feet over the Shortlands. I was getting set to lead the group against the shipping when Phil yelled, "Hey, Bruce! Look down there!"

Right above the water, at an altitude of no more than 500 feet, was a Navy Wildcat with a Zero right smack on its tail. The Japanese airplane was pumping long streams of 20mm and .30-caliber rounds into the American, who simply could not shake his assailant. The bullets were slowly grinding the F4F to dust.

I told Phil, "Cover me. I'm going after him."

As I approached, I clearly saw that the American was hunched down in his seat to gain the full protection of the armor-plated seat back. I figured that his fighter's controls had been damaged and that he could not risk taking violent evasive maneuvers. Either way, he was in a bad place.

I executed a fast overhead pass and fired at the Zero with no visible result. Then I pulled in tight and went after the enemy fighter as hot and fast as I dared.

My gunnery had to be especially precise. The Zero was flying so close to the Wildcat's tail that any overshooting would certainly strike the Wildcat.

I decided at the last moment to make a high pass, which would minimize overstrikes on the friendly fighter.

I instantly maneuvered to bring the straight-flying Zero into my sights. My .50-calibers roared as I came down on the gun button knob. I immediately saw my tracer strike home. Pieces of the Zero's engine cowling were pulled free, and these hurtled away past me. Then I saw smoke billowing from the engine and stream back over the Zero's glass birdcage canopy.

The Zero was moments from blowing up when it simply vanished from my reflector sight. My eyes involuntarily rolled up, and I saw that silver beauty climbing straight out of view. I was stunned by that escape. I had never seen anything like it, and I never would again. I knew that Zero was dead, but I could not claim it. I hated to trade a sure kill for a probable, but I found myself secretly applauding that Japanese naval aviator.

★

The damaged Navy Wildcat went his own way, and Phil and I headed for home because I had used up nearly all of my ammunition.

We were getting close to New Georgia when I saw a Japanese armored landing barge chugging away between several green islands. I dropped down and buzzed the barge, but I dared not make a firing pass because I was so low on fuel. If he was bait for Zeros I could not see, there was no way I would ever be able to come out of a fight in one piece.

Phil and I eased back on our throttles and nursed our fuel supply all the way back to Knucklehead, where we made a routine landing and walked over to the group intelligence hut to debrief and trade war stories with our fellow pilots.

Marine pilots claimed 41 of the 52 kills recorded for the day; the New Zealanders and American Army pilots claimed the rest. VMF-121 was credited with seven of the kills.

I wound up the day with three official kills and four probables to my credit, but I know in my heart that the Zero I had shot off the Wildcat's tail never made it home.

★

A day or two after the big Kahili raid, Lieutenant Colonel Moore called four senior captains into his office and began his brief by saying, "I want to talk to you fellows. I've got a mission for you at Kahili."

Each captain in the tent was a combat veteran. Each of us had 500 to 800 operational hours aloft. Each of us smelled a fat rat.

"I want you fellows to think this over," Sad Sam went on, "because it will be a strafing raid. I want four of the top senior pilots."

It was getting worse!

The details slowly mounted until even the dullest of us realized that we were being asked to *volunteer* to mount an unsupported predawn strafing attack against Kahili, the most powerful Japanese base in our sector.

Jeff Poindexter spoke up after a long pause to ask Sad Sam if we could have a little time to talk it over among ourselves. The colonel nodded, but it was plain that he was not happy to let us get out of earshot.

The four of us walked to Jeff's nearby Dallas hut and sprawled on the bunks while Jeff wound up for his pitch.

"Well," he said in the most cautious tone I had ever heard him invoke, "let's look at it this way. We were all promised that, if nothing else, we would all get top decorations. Some of us have some already, and the rest of us are in line. A few of us are on our second combat tour. All of us have been out here for a long time. In the next few days, this combat tour is over. We're out of here in a week, at the outside.

Then Jeff got to the point. "I don't know about the rest of you, but I want to get to Sydney alive. They've been promising me a decent leave for a year. God knows, I've been saving it up for a long time, and I want to spend what I have with an Aussie girl, starting next week in Sydney."

(Good old Jeff! Only I knew that he had been to Sydney on a totally fabricated mission the last week of May, just before VMF-121 went back to Henderson Field.)

He went on. "Do any of you want to take the risk? Does anyone here want to go on this mission? Does anyone here want to miss the girls in Sydney because he got killed on this horse's-ass raid on Kahili? How should we handle it?"

We handled it by taking a vote. The decision was unanimous: As long as we were being *asked* to go, we would decline. The offer had all the earmarks of a suicide flight. We saw no pressing need to go; Sad Sam had given us none. The secretive nature of the offer seemed to be Sad Sam's way of saying that he was acting on a request from above but that he was not in favor of it himself.

Jeff acted as our spokesman a few minutes later when we turned the offer down.

Sad Sam just flashed as huge smile—was it relief?—and said, "That's okay, fellahs. I know how you feel." Then his eyes lit up and he added, "I'd do the same thing if I had been out here for nearly twenty months and was only a few days away from getting my hands on those man-starved Aussie girls."

As far as I know, that mission never did happen.

The squadron was relieved of flying duties on July 22.

21

After giving up our Corsairs and quarters to a newly arrived fighter squadron, VMF-121's entire flight echelon left Knucklehead aboard several R4D and PBY transports. We arrived at Henderson Field late in the afternoon and were put up at the Hotel De Gink, a strange jury-built series of little crackerbox cubicles that had been a sort of transient officers' quarters since the early days of the Guadalcanal fighting. Immediately upon arriving, many of us dropped our gear, shed our clothes, and waded into the swift, cool Lunga River, which was practically at our doorstep. This was but the first real step toward washing away the cares and tensions of our existence as combat pilots.

Next day, we all dressed in freshly laundered khakis and boarded jeeps for a quick drive out to the transport group's flight line. In the rush and confusion of getting out of there, I somehow became separated from the footlocker I had been dragging all through my Pacific escapades. I never saw it or anything I had stowed in it again, including a fine Japanese officer's sword and Luger-like 9mm automatic pistol. All I had when I took off was a small duffle stuffed with some of my clothing. Everything else was gone.

At Turtle Bay, we joined up with several other Sydney-bound squadrons and overnighted in the same transient officers' quarters I had occupied during my many ferry flights between New Caledonia and Guadalcanal in the early Spring. This stopover gave us the opportunity to catch up on war stories with many old friends we had not seen face to face in months. It turned out, however, that many of us had participated in many of the same big operations. Too many times, questions beginning with "What ever happened to old . . ." brought forth a chilling update.

The next stop was Tontouta, where I immediately looked up my old high school water polo teammate, Chirp Sparrow. It turned out that Chirp was scheduled to fly some of us down to Sydney, so I signed up with him and accepted his offer to spend the night in his big, sprawling tent overlooking a jungle river. Those R4D drivers really knew how to live!

At the first opportunity, I asked Chirp what I should take with me to Sydney. I expected to be told about clothing and the like, or even "plenty of condoms." But Chirp's immediate answer was "Cigarettes!"

"My God, Chirp! I never smoked in my life."

"Neither have I, Bruce. But take all the cigarettes you can get."

I shrugged and made my way straight to the Post Exchange, where I purchased a case of 50 cartons—500 packs of cigarettes! I realized that I still had some room in my duffle, so I bought another five cartons to stuff in there. The clerk who took my order looked me up and down and said, "Have a good leave in Sydney, Sir."

Next morning, I had no sooner boarded the R4D "Gooneybird" than one of my longtime buddies asked in a mocking tone, "Hey, whatcha got in that big box, Bruce?"

"Cigarettes!"

"Cigarettes?" The reply was incredulous. "Have you finally gone native this late in the game, Bruce? I have it on good authority that the Aussie girls'll take cash. This isn't the islands we're headed to, you know!"

The chatter continued in that vein as the Gooneybird droned on mile after endless mile all the way across the vast expanse of ocean between Tontouta and Sydney. The only relief was Chirp Sparrow's knowing smile every time he turned the controls over to his co-pilot and came by as he stretched his legs.

The landing at Sydney was accompanied by a long pass over the city's magnificent harbor. I became a little claustrophobic right away because I had not seen anything that resembled an American city for all of nineteen months.

★

Our first stop and last official way station was the Red Cross, which was located in the basement of an old department store I suppose was in the center of town. I was still a little put off by the general hubbub of the city; I suppose it was the city noises I found so unsettling.

The Red Cross ladies were stunning; every one of them was young and lush. These were the first desirable Caucasian ladies I had seen in nineteen months. My whole system just shuddered. If the look on Jeff Poindexter's face was any indication of the look I had on mine, I should have been embarrassed. Jeff was actually leering at them, and his tongue was hanging out.

The ladies calmly handed over a week's supply of food-ration stamps to each of us. Then they genially answered our questions about food rationing, for the older pilots who had gone out in February, 1942, had never seen such coupons as rationing had not then been instituted in the United States.

The lady at the last table was the most stunning of the bunch, a real knockout with a sweet, naive expression of open friendliness. She oversaw a supply of brown paper lunch bags, which she word-lessly handed to each pilot in turn. I was about midway back in the line, so I had an opportunity to view the red faces and embarrassed grins as the men ahead of me peeked into the bags. I joined the gabbling red-faced group and opened my bag of goodies, which con-tained disease-prevention pamphlets and a large supply of condoms that, on second thought, hardly seemed adequate for my built-up needs.

Next we crowded into a uniform shop to be fitted for new green wool uniforms. It had been quite a shock to find that July in Sydney was winter. The tailor was quite used to the arrival of many pilots and had enough semi-sewn greens on hand to be able to promise delivery in time for our planned evening outing.

It was very strange to experience the Australian winter weather in what I considered to be a summer month. However, that seasonal dislocation was considerably heightened by my hearing for the first time the strains of a popular new song from America that seemed to be playing on every radio in Sydney—Bing Crosby's "White Christ-mas."

Though it was only nine o'clock in the morning, many of us next crowded into the bar at the hotel Australia. I bought Chirp Sparrow a drink to thank him for his hospitality and smooth flying as soon as we landed. He gave me a few last-minute pointers on the action in Sydney and went off to do whatever he had gotten used to doing when he drew liberty flights. I knew that his return to Tontouta the next morning would be taken up with nursing boisterous, hungover pilots on their way back to combat.

Poindexter and I were sitting apart from the crowd when I felt a sharp pain in my shin. Jeff had kicked me under the table to draw my attention to the doorway, where two absolutely beautiful young women some years older were inspecting the day's catch of handsome American aviators. The two, who were dressed to the teeth, were even decked out with gloves and floppy wide-brimmed hats.

One of the girls was looking right at me, but I was so nonplussed that I instinctively turned to see who she was looking at over my shoulder. No one was there. She was looking at me!

For once, Jeff did not beat me across the room. I have no idea what anyone said after that. I don't think the ladies were interested in our scintillating conversation, anyway. Within a half-hour, Jeff and I were upstairs in the separate bedrooms of the apartment the ladies shared, and that's where we stayed until it was time to get to our own rooming house early in the afternoon. The really strange part was that, despite my early conviction to the contrary, the sack-time was free.

★

I was to room with Jeff Poindexter and Captain Herb Long, whose nom de guerre was Trigger. Herb had briefly flown with VMF-111 in Samoa and had joined VMF-121 for its second combat tour at Guadalcanal. Then he had gone with Hunter Reinburg and several other old friends to VMF-122 at about the time Jeff, Louis Gordon, and I joined VMF-121 from VMF-441. So far, Trigger had six kills. His last kill, like mine, had been on the big Kahili raid of July 17, 1943.

We wound up at a nice little place on Rose Bay, then a semi-fashionable middle-class neighborhood. The rooming house, which had catered to many returning combat pilots already, was operated by an elderly gray-haired lady. I have no idea what she was like before the war, but for a woman of my mother's generation, she was remarkably broad-minded.

No sooner had I finished stuffing my clothing into the dresser drawers than Trigger, who had already weathered one Sydney holiday, suggested, "Now's the time to move those cigarettes, Bruce."

I pulled out the slip of paper on which Chirp Sparrow had noted the phone number of his Sydney contact, and I rang it up. An expansive Aussie voice shouted "Allow" into my ear and waited to hear my request.

I told the man that I was Captain Sparrow's friend and that I had some cigarettes. The voice became high pitched and excited and told me he would be right over.

About twenty minutes later, as we sat around losing our patience, Trigger glanced out the window and shot to his feet in obvious alarm. "Jeez! Look out there! A taxicab is pulling up in front, and the sonovabitch is on fire!"

"Fire?" I asked. "What the hell do you mean 'on fire?'" But I got up and looked out the window, anyway. "My God! You're right! The sonovabitch *is* on fire."

We all piled downstairs, ready to bravely fight the fire.

An older man calmly climbed out of the vehicle and pasted a huge, benevolent smile on his face when he saw us thundering down the front garden path toward him. His unruffled demeanor brought us up short just as his smile collapsed in alarm over our obvious agitation.

We stared at one another for a moment, then all our eyes went to the smoldering taxicab.

The cabby finally got the point. "Oh, the smoke's put yer awf, 'as it?" He laughed a big belly laugh and explained in his slangy Aussie singsong that a brilliant engineer had designed a charcoal-burning engine for taxis to get around the very strict Australian fuel rationing. The taxi had no power to speak of, and a gasmask might be required if the breeze was off, but it ran. We learned soon enough that it and its kind could not quite top many of Sydney's numerous bayside hills. Whenever a taxi stalled partway up a hill, it would back down, turn around, and climb the hill in reverse. Such antics were very strange to my eyes.

The cabby was a huge man with a huge black beard and an open, expansive style. He followed us up to our room, accepted a tumblerful of American whiskey, and sat down in one of the plush armchairs, ready to haggle the afternoon away in quest of those 55 cartons of American cigarettes.

In the end, I swapped all my cigarettes for three cases of what was then the finest Scotch whiskey in the world, King George II.

As soon as the deal had been struck, the cabby told us, "I'll toss in me and that fire-burner out there for the whole time you're in

Sydney. I'll take you anywhere you want to go."

What a deal! We told this old pirate that we and numerous other Marine pilots had a big evening planned at Princess's, Sydney's most fashionable nightclub. I added, "Where do we get dates here?"

The cabby's face cracked into the biggest catbird grin I ever saw as he told us that the antiaircraft batteries at the Royal Australian Golf Course were "manned" exclusively by women. Though the gunners were usually restricted to quarters during their off-duty nights, the cabby had found a way to get word through to them whenever he could find dates for them. Ah, the deprivations of global war! All the Australian men worth having were at the front, so the man-starved women had to settle for Yank pilots to tide them over. For a small fee, the cabby would get a friend to help drive enough women for everyone and meet us at Princess's with "the goods." All we had to do was promise—on our honor as officers and gentlemen!—that we would have them back in their quarters by morning muster. At this last, I heard Jeff mutter under his breath, "Sure, and I guess rocks grow and cows fly in Australia."

★

While we were killing time that late afternoon waiting for our green winter uniforms to be delivered, I asked Trigger how he had gotten his nickname. I expected to hear a routine tale of deadly prowess in the skies, but I was treated instead to an absolutely classic "dumb second lieutenant" story.

Trigger had been an original and very junior member of VMSB-241, a dive-bomber squadron ultimately destined for Midway. (Its commanding officer was Major Lofton Henderson, who was killed at Midway and in whose memory Henderson Field was named.)

During a stopover in San Francisco, the squadron had been billeted at the luxurious Mark Hopkins Hotel. Typically, everyone drank too much, and, in one of the many episodes of comradely highjinks, young Herb Long had managed to fire his .45-caliber automatic pistol into one of the walls of the party suite.

Before the hotel security guards or shore patrol could arrive, Major Henderson decreed that Herb be tossed out of the room. And he was. His fellow pilots lifted him up and heaved him bodily into the corridor. The door was closed and bolted behind him.

As 2nd Lieutenant Long groggily oriented himself to his new surroundings, he heard the sound of voices approaching from the nether reaches of the long corridor. Since his fellow pilots would not have anything to do with him, he rose to his feet and reached down to smooth out his uniform. He wanted to make a good impression.

Unfortunately, all the young pilot had on was his skivvy shorts; he had become disassociated with the rest of his clothing sometime before the shooting incident (which never did draw the attention of the authorities).

At the precise moment of revelation, from out of the gloom there arrived several elderly, tuxedoed men and and gowned, bejeweled women.

The suddenly sobered and utterly embarrassed pilot pressed himself against the locked door and pleaded with his fellow pilots to let him back in. This was done after yet more well-dressed civilians passed the blubbering young man who was wearing only his shorts.

Herb Long, who was known evermore as Trigger, survived Midway by not being there. The squadron was split up to make way for more experienced fliers than Trigger Long, and he was sent to Palmyra at about the time VMF-111 was arriving in Samoa. He converted to F4Fs and was later sent to Samoa, where he briefly served with VMF-111. He joined VMF-121 for its second tour at Guadalcanal along with Don Yost, Hunter Reinburg, Jack Amende, Fateye Gardner, Ras Rasmussen, and so many other of my old flying buddies.

★

We were all decked out in our new greens when our cabby arrived to take us to Princess's. He told us that his rendezvous with the lady gunners was all arranged and that he would pick them up at the golf course battery site as soon as he dropped us off in town. A second cabby was collecting the other members of our group, and he would also pick up girls at the golf course.

At seven o'clock, right on time, not two but three charcoal-burning cabs pulled up in front of Princess's and deposited the loveliest herd of women I had ever seen at one time and in one place. I could not quite believe that these fashionably dressed young beauties had actually scaled a fence in order to get to the cabs, but they all said it was so.

We had all seen the paymaster at the airport and we all had converted at least $1,000 dollars apiece into Australian dollars. We were very rich men by Australian (and American) standards, and we spent like there was no end to the money. The champagne flowed by in buckets. Toast after toast was proposed to the living, to the dead, to the about-to-be-dead. Some of the girls drank out of their slippers. All that wine was just absorbed.

My memories of the later evening at Princess's remain dim; they were dim the next morning. I do know that we were thrown out of the place when we made too much of our freedom, but I have no idea what precipitated the final act.

I do know that I ended up back in my Rose Bay quarters and that I got in only after asking the landlady for another key. I have the sense that one of my roommates was in the room, too, but I could not have been less interested.

It was said that there were about fifteen ladies to every man in Australia at that time of the war. As appreciative as we pilots were of the attentions lavished on us by the man-starved ladies of the country, I have reason to believe that the appreciation was reciprocated in kind. The lady with whom I spent the rest of the night made an appreciable dent in my libido, and I did my best to do the same for her.

★

After seeing our dates off in the hands of the good cabby, Jeff Poindexter and I were joined early the next morning by Trigger Long, who had gone his own way after we were shown the door at Princess's. As soon as Trigger collapsed onto his bed, I was struck by a funny memory lapse and said out loud, "I don't remember kicking in for the bill last night."

Trigger wearily moaned, "That's because you didn't."

"Well, who paid, then?"

"I did. All you guys shoved off and I got stuck with the whole thing."

★

I wound up being the scoutmaster on the last of our ten libidinous days in Sydney. I was the senior captain, so I had to be the one to make sure that all hands reported in at the airfield in time to catch our Gooneybird back to Tontouta. It was the worst assignment of my young life.

We had completely avoided naming a common contact point when we had scattered to the winds on our first morning in town. I had steadily lost contact with more and more of the boys as my relationships with a long succession of female companions led me farther and farther astray from the pack. The result of my lack of foresight was that I had to give up most of my last day in town tracking down my fellow pilots. Fortunately, some of the boys had had enough running around by then or, worse, had run out of money. These I put to work searching for our companions.

I had accounted for all the pilots but one by midnight, so I released everyone who had helped me for their last night in town and went off to track down the lone ranger on my own. Fortunately, I had a days-old lead that led me down an hours-long path through the city and several suburbs. It was four o'clock in the morning and only two hours to muster when I rolled the dreadfully drunk pilot out of the bed he had been sharing with any equally saturated lady. I actually had to wrestle the sodden pilot to the ground in order to clothe his booze-ridden body in the semblance of a uniform. Then I carried him to the waiting taxi and made for the airport. We arrived in plenty of time to have him filled with strong black coffee and have his clothing straightened by pilots more willing than I to see the task through to a peaceable conclusion.

The barfing that went on in that R4D between Sydney and Tontouta would have set unbreakable world records if we had had any measuring devices aboard.

Elimination Cadet Bruce Porter at Long Beach, California, October, 1940.

SNJ Trainer

Grumman

Grumman F3F Fighter

2nd Lieutenant Bruce Porter
at home in Los Angeles,
September, 1941.

New Bern, North Carolina, September, 1941.
(L. to r.) Lieutenants Bob Fraser, Bruce Porter, and Tolar Bryan.

Kenneth A. Walsh

A VMF-121 F4F-3 Wildcat fighter at New Bern in October, 1941.

Technical Sergeant Kenneth Walsh, October, 1941.

2nd Lieutenant Jeff Poindexter

Kenneth A. Walsh

The VMF-121 flight line at New Bern in October, 1941.

Kenneth A. Walsh

Tafuna Airfield, Samoa, in mid-1942. Airplanes are SBC-4 dive-bombers flown by VMO-151. The large building is Gunner Gadje's maintenance hangar.

A Marine fighter pilot climbs aboard his F4U-1 Corsair at Guadalcanal's Henderson Field.

Captain Bruce Porter during
the Knucklehead deployment.

VMF-121 on May 11, 1943:
1st Row (seated, l. to r.): Leeds, Klas, Pierce, McPherson,
Rodes, Harlan
2nd Row: Snee, Schmitt, McCardy, Gordon, Porter, Morace
3rd Row: McEvoy, Trenchard, Barron, Baker,
Wilcox, Schneider, Bryson
4th Row (standing): Andre, Linde, Vroome, Hay,
Whittiker, Shuman, Ford.

Vought F4U-1 Corsair

Captain Bruce Porter with his father, Elmer Porter, in October, 1943.

Night-fighter class at Vero Beach, Florida, April, 1944.
The first four pilots kneeling (from l.) are Norm Mitchell, Jim Maguire, Bruce Porter, and Wally Sigler.

Major Bruce Porter and Patricia Leimert, December, 1944.

Robert Thayer

VMF(N)-533 Hellcat night fighters seen from an R5C guide plane on the way from Engebi to Saipan.

Robert Thayer

Japanese "giretsu" commando killed on runway of Yontan Airfield.

"Black Death," Major Bruce Porter's personal Grumman F6F-5N Hellcat Night Fighter.

PART IV

The Home Front

22

We got back to Turtle Bay by way of Tontouta without undue mishap and went got right to work preparing for another combat tour. We had many new pilots, mainly fresh-caught second lieutenants, to absorb and inculcate in the ways of our world. The training schedule was tortuous, as usual.

In late August, with a return to combat only days away, I got the word that I would not have to undertake my second tour at the front. By this time, Strike Command was filled to brimming with droves of replacements, some of them quite senior captains. So, all the senior pilots who had been in the Pacific for fifteen or more months were informed that we were going to be sent home by first available transport.

Within a matter of days, Jeff Poindexter's orders were cut, and he headed home. That made me the last of the original VMF-111 pilots still working with an operational fighter squadron in the war zone. But the distinction was a brief one.

I hung around Turtle Bay for only a few days, trying to get used to the idea that combat was behind me. Then, quite suddenly, I was flown back to Tontouta and immediately ordered aboard a Liberty ship for the trip back to California.

By great good luck, my cabinmate turned out to be 1st Lieutenant Kenny Walsh, the former NAP who had narrowly missed flying into my Wildcat's tail when we took off from Quantico for our cross-country flight in December, 1941. Kenny's commission had been a long time coming through because he was so much younger than most NAPs. But his incredible success as a combat pilot with VMF-124 had made his elevation to officer status inevitable. In fact, he was on his way home to be awarded a Medal of Honor for having destroyed 20 Japanese warplanes between April 1 and August 30, 1943. Nearly all of Kenny's victories had been multiple kills; he had bagged four Japanese aircraft on one mission and had scored three kills on each of three separate missions. Only one or two Marine pilots equalled or bettered Kenny's record in the entire Pacific War.

We made our way very slowly back to San Francisco, arriving some time in early October. I do not think that ship ever made more than 20 knots the whole way back. I was really chomping at the bit to get back, but I resigned myself to the interminable journey by thinking about how fortunate I had become; the shower water aboard the ship was on the cool side and the food was fair.

★

The slow entry into San Francisco Bay beneath the Golden Gate Bridge took my breath away. The bridge had become the Pacific warrior's symbol of home. Like millions of other Americans of my generation, I felt that I was truly home as soon I saw its twin spires loom up out of the chilly gray sea.

It was mid afternoon when we docked. About a dozen returning pilots made straight for Fisherman's Wharf for a good American meal and drinks. We were treated with extraordinary courtesy, for, as we learned, we were among a very small number of combat veterans who had thus far returned to the States. The city was packed with servicemen, but only a few of us were wearing combat ribbons. It made all the difference in the world. Everyone wanted to know about the war.

After dinner, we all took a cab to the Marine Corps receiving station to report and drop off our orders. This was merely a formality; I was essentially on my own. My new orders were waiting for me; I was to report to a similar station in San Diego for official reassignment to an aviation command somewhere in the continental United States.

After dispensing with the formalities, one of our group asked about transportation to Los Angeles and San Diego. The officer on duty shrugged his shoulders. "Fellahs, I doubt that you'll be able to find anything, but I'll try to get you booked onto The Lark," which was then *the* passenger train plying between the major West Coast cities. He seemed so doubtful of the prospects that we took his advice to have a good time at the Top of the Mark, which was *the* night spot in San Francisco. If anything came through, he promised he would phone us there.

We were well into our alcohol therapy by eleven o'clock that night when I was paged to the phone. I had no idea what the trouble could be; I had not bothered to call home because I had no idea when or how I would be getting there.

The receiving officer was on the line; he told me that he had managed to get all of us tickets aboard The Lark. All we had to do was get to the station on time.

I have no idea where any of us had thought we were going to spend the night. We had not booked ourselves into a hotel; all our gear was stacked in the cloakroom at the Top of the Mark.

All of us with family in Southern California called home. Then we all piled into the elevators with our bags and grabbed several cabs at the taxi stand in front of the Mark Hopkins Hotel.

Our tickets, which were given to us by a Marine runner at the station, entitled us to sleeping accommodations, but we all passed that up (we had slept ourselves out on the long boat ride back from Noumea) in favor of occupying the club car.

I was not nearly the drinker most of my companions were, but I had imbibed a great deal by the time the train pulled out of the station. One or two of my companions were falling-down drunk, and all the rest of us were silly drunk. But why not? Not one of us was over 25 years old, and most of us had already killed people.

We quickly attracted several civilian businessmen who asked us endless questions about the war, in return for which they bought endless rounds of drinks.

When the call for the last round came at two or three in the morning, one of the civilians called the porter over. "We'll have a last order. Get us twenty-five scotch and sodas, thirty bourbon and ginger ales, and fifteen martinis."

The porter did as he was told, and we did our part. Every one of those glasses was empty by sunrise.

★

I was greeted by my parents during our brief layover at Union Station in Los Angeles. (We still had to report at San Diego before actually being granted leave.) It was a pleasant reunion, but I could not help wondering where my bride was.

As soon as Mother and Father had calmed down, I asked Mother where my wife was. She was rather cool when she told me that that reunion would take place in San Diego. That made sense; I was on my way to San Diego anyway. However, I was puzzled and hurt by her failure to greet me in Los Angeles.

★

We reported to the receiving station in San Diego, where my orders were awaiting me. I had been reassigned to the new Marine Corps Air Station at El Toro, in Orange County, near Santa Ana. I had to stop and think about that for a moment, for there had been no base at El Toro when I left home in February, 1942.

I shook hands all around with my traveling companions and headed straight for the hotel at which I had booked a room by phone for my reunion with my wife.

She met me in the lobby and we went to the bar for a few drinks. The conversation was superficial, but I credited that to nerves and our long separation.

My wife, who was a classic blonde beauty of the period, had not exactly been at the top of my mind for the twenty months I had been overseas. But that was understandable, at least to me. Most combat pilots were able to put their family lives behind them when they were away from home; I suppose it was a survival mechanism.

I had regularly written to her, and she had dutifully written back. I was not much given to intimate language in my letters, and I gathered she was not, either. I was also a big enough boy to know that our entire relationship was on the superficial side. Our romance and marriage had been undertaken during the whirlwind weeks when I was preparing to go to war. We had not had enough time together for anything more than the physical aspects of married life.

Still, I thought I had the basis of a good marriage.

We went up to the room, and, before I had an opportunity to embrace her, she told me straight out that our marriage was as good as over.

I blinked at the news, not really sure I had gotten the message straight. I was speechless.

She calmly explained that she had come to realize that I was not, after all, the man for her. She was fond of me, but she was definitely not in love with me. She told me that she supposed I had had relations with other women during my time away, but that it was okay with her; she had been seeing other men. However, she emphasized that there was no "other man," that she had made her decision solely on the basis of our relationship.

Given the circumstances, she was quite gentle. I was more shocked and hurt by her infidelity than by the news that she did not love me. But, then, I was a man of my time. I had had no qualms about shacking up with Samoan lovelies, and neither had I held back an ounce of desire during my madcap leave in Sydney.

My momentum carried me right over the bad news. I was saved from causing a scene by how utterly tired and hung over I was when she broke the news. I am not even certain that it sank all the way into my sleep-starved, liquor-sodden mind. I do remember how determined she looked, and how she went to great pains to explain that she had scrupulously banked every penny of the $200 monthly allotment I had had sent to her from my pay. She even handed me a bank book, which was in my name only, with exaggerated care.

I'm not sure how it happened, or why, but she stayed the night. Eventually, my sleep-starved body fell into a stupor. By then, I had agreed to the annulment, which she emphasized she would pay for herself.

In my heart, I knew that she was right. I had had inklings during my many months overseas that she had fallen for the dashing aviator in his dashing uniform and that I had fallen for her considerable charms and sophistication.

She left in the morning and I never saw her again.

★

I remained in a bit of a fog for a day or two, at least in part because it took that long for the alcohol to leave my system. When I was ready to face the world again, I joined up with Jeff Poindexter, who was winding up a few weeks on the town with his wife before returning home to Montana.

After Jeff left, I moped around for a few more days and half-heartedly allowed myself to be drawn into the activities of scores of combat pilots who were making San Diego their leave headquarters. When I had had enough revelry, I headed back to Los Angeles to spend time with Mother and Father. I tried looking up old high school and college friends, but every one of them was gone to the war.

The best reunion I had in Los Angeles was with my cherry-red 1941 Ford convertible. My soon-to-be-former wife had given me the keys in our hotel room in San Diego.

I had not seen it since I flew out of New Bern, North Carolina, on my way to Quantico and the West Coast. The plane captain to whom I had given the keys as I was climbing into my Wildcat's cockpit that December morning had used the car for as long as he was on the East Coast. He then passed it along to the wife of my squadronmate, Lieutenant Jack Lyons (VMF-111's first fatality in Samoa), and she drove it to San Diego when she moved there to await Jack's return. She in turn had passed it along to my wife, who drove it straight to Los Angeles to store in my parents' garage. A local mechanic had taken care of all the details for storing it safely and had even left written directions for reinstating it to active duty. I swear that, despite the many thousands of miles it had on the odometer, that Ford ran better in 1943 than it had when I bought it new in 1941.

I drove back to San Francisco to work out the car's kinks as well as to work off some of my restiveness. But I only wound up killing time in bars with fellow fighter pilots.

★

I had a difficult time getting used to the wartime economy. The rationing drove me straight up the wall. I refused to accept the shortages, and I took gasoline rationing as a government effort to curtail my good time. I frankly bought gasoline on the black market, as much to twit the rationing board as to get around in my convertible. I also used my combat ribbons, skinny body, and yellow complexion (a side-effect of antimalaria drugs) to get the choicest foods from local markets.

Before I knew it, my leave was up. By then, I was glad to be heading back to work.

23

As soon as I reported in at El Toro at the conclusion of my leave in November, 1943, I was assigned to the new Combat Fighter Training Command, a finishing school for newly commissioned fighter pilots on their way to operational squadrons in the Pacific.

The group adjutant quickly read through my orders and told me to report immediately to the group operations officer. I did as I was told and soon found myself standing at attention in front of Major Bob Fraser, my old roommate and dear friend from my New Bern days before the start of the war.

I had just missed meeting up with Bob at Guadalcanal. The squadron he commanded—VMF-112, known as the Wolf Pack—was rotated to Turtle Bay the very day we reported in at Henderson Field. (Sam Logan, whose foot had been chopped off by a Zero, was flying with Bob's squadron.) But we had briefly crossed paths at Knucklehead when he arrived to command VMF-122 toward the end of my tour there.

My friend smiled his broad, handsome smile and greeted me with his normal level of enthusiasm. "B-b-bruce! W-w-welcome ab-b-board! How're you d-doing?"

He offered me a seat, and we killed most of the rest of the morning telling each other war stories. Bob had six kills to his credit, all with VMF-112. He had also been shot down once. As soon as Bob had landed safely in the water, the Zero pilot who had done him in had passed so low overhead that "he alm-most p-parted my hair, r-right d-down the m-middle!"

In between the war stories (air combat in the Solomons and ground combat in Sydney), Bob managed to fill me in on the mission of the Combat Fighter Training Command. Simply put, older pilots (I was 23 years old) with combat experience were teaching inexperienced pilots the subtle, up-to-date tricks of the trade so the younger pilots would have an opportunity to survive the war. Even though the quality of the Zero pilots deployed on land bases in the Solomons and Bismarcks had been steadily declining, there remained a hard core of proven killers to be faced out there.

I also learned that Lieutenant Colonel Sad Sam Moore, the former MAG-12 executive officer, was working at El Toro as the Combat Fighter Training Command executive officer. And the group commander was Lieutenant Colonel Paul Fontana, who had been Bob's predecessor as skipper of the Wolf Pack and with whom I had occasionally flown during the Red-and-Blue combined services exercises in late 1941. I had also run into him on numerous occasions around Turtle Bay, where every senior air officer wound up at one time or another.

As the reunion was winding down, Bob suddenly sat up in his chair and pointed his right forefinger at me. "S-say, B-bruce, w-why d-don't you t-take another thirty d-days l-leave? W-we can sp-pare you f-for that l-long."

"Major, old buddy, if I take just one more day's leave, I'll wind up a complete alcoholic. I haven't been in a cockpit in two whole months. I need some stick time or I'll die!"

★

My job was to run six fresh-caught second lieutenants through a not-too-grueling six-week training syllabus. In that time, I would have to cram all the knowledge about fighting and evasion tactics that I had learned and relearned during my ten months in Samoa. I was to hone their skills in gunnery, dogfighting, formation flying, cross-country and over-water navigation, and evasion in the Corsair.

It was strange to have six men roughly my age report to me. I was just about to make major, and they were all second lieutenants. In our world, my rank and my standing as the clear victor in at least three one-on-one dogfights placed me so far ahead of them that I easily thought of and referred to them as "kids."

My first task was to see for myself what kind of pilots they were. I was immediately struck by their uniformly high skill levels. Their record books showed that each of the six already had about three times as many hours in the air as I had had when I shipped out to the war in February, 1942. They were all just plain good pilots.

Unlike Marine cadets of my day (was it only two years ago?), who all went through fighter training at Opa-Locka, these kids had been specially selected from a large pool of trainees to become fighter pilots because they had marked aptitudes and predatory instincts. Other types of measurable aptitudes would have seen them assigned to bombing or even transport squadrons. In my salad days, everyone wanted to be a fighter pilot, and the bombing and transport units were all manned by men who had been dragged kicking and screaming from Opa-Locka's front gate.

So, the raw material was there—in abundance. All I had to do was form it.

Before me lay one of the most pleasurable tours of my flying career. I just loved getting up in the morning to work with those new fighter jocks. I could actually see them refining their skills.

We worked an easy schedule. The Pacific was filled to brimming with fighter pilots, so we had all the time in the world to get our students ready. We had most evenings off, and I never saw an airplane on a weekend during my tour. In fact, the program was entirely in my hands. If I wanted to take a day off in midweek, I did. My superiors had complete confidence in my abilities—and my honor—and they left me completely alone. My only real guide was my conscience. I knew I had to teach those kids how to stay alive. Despite the easy atmosphere, my six fledglings kept me in the air; they wanted all the flight time they could tuck away.

★

It was during one of those easy days that I came the closest to losing my life at the controls of a fighter.

All seven of us were up over the ocean, and I was demonstrating in the role of a Zero while two of the kids tried to trap me. I simply got too big for my britches and pulled far too many G's as I twisted out of their clutches.

I distinctly felt my mind close down, and I knew that I was facing a long trip into the water. Just before the lights went out, however, I managed to roll the trim tab with my thumb and the last of my conscious energy.

There is no telling how long I was out. I came around to the sound of frantic chatter in my earphones. I heard all my trainees' voices yelling my name. I milled about in confusion for a few moments, trying to learn where I was. Then I snapped right out of it. I was suddenly aware enough to feel the hair on the back of my neck stand on end.

The F4U was bobbing through the air. It needed guidance, but it was not going to fall into the blue Pacific after all. All that had kept me aloft was that last conscious act where I rolled the trim tab. I had miraculously set the controls more or less on automatic.

As soon as I recovered full control of the airplane, I ordered everyone back to base. My landing was about as shaky an effort as I had put in during the past two years, and my legs were unsteady when they hit the hardstand. I had a pounding headache, the worst of my young life. Boy, was I glad have a headache instead of the pain I would have had if I not not instinctively rolled that trim tab.

In the end, my brush with death became one of the best object lessons I was able to get across to my six new fighter pilots. I simply would not have survived had my mind and body not been in total concert with one another and my airplane.

My parting lecture to my six tyros was delivered word for word from Bob Fraser's standard brief: "Fighter pilots should be patient and not fall into silly traps. Your chance will come soon enough, and you will get back home and eat more Spam. Don't rush it. They're still making Zeros in Tokyo, so there will always be plenty to go around."

★

My tour with Combat Fighter Training Command would normally have lasted a year, and I would have been happy for that. But Captain Wally Sigler, whom I had met in the Pacific and with whom I palled around during my first weeks at El Toro (we soon roomed together) heard through the grapevine that the Marine Corps was getting ready to activate its first operational night-fighter group and would soon be looking for skilled, experienced day-fighter pilots who wanted to transition to night fighters.

I was galvanized by the news. My mind immediately went back to my first night at Henderson Field with VMF-121, when I had seen a Japanese night intruder swatted from the ether by an Air Corps P-38 fighter. I also realized that there would be the chance of rapid promotion and certainly a clear road back to combat. Those two factors motivated me to put my name in early, along with Wally; some of my exact contemporaries, including Jeff Poindexter and Jack Amende, were already in line to command newly-formed fighter squadrons, and I was determined to become an ace, in which case I needed a way to score two more confirmed kills.

Perhaps of equal importance in my decision was the persistent rumor that Marine night-fighter pilots would be trained by the Royal Air Force in Britain and that I would be paid a per diem on top of the $500 per month base salary and flight pay I was then receiving. I was no idiot; I would take London over Turtle Bay any day of the week.

Wally and I and several of our buddies signed up as soon as the Marine Corps tendered its offer.

★

At the conclusion of my six-week training tour, I was assigned to a war bond tour. In fact, I became the temporary pilot of an F4F Wildcat that had been flown by Captain Joe Foss during VMF-121's second combat tour at Guadalcanal. This was one of the F4Fs Joe had flown on his way to downing 26 enemy warplanes and earning a Medal of Honor. I spent about two hell-raising weeks with Wally Sigler on the tour of West Coast cities and then returned to El Toro to check out of the Combat Fighter Training Command.

On my last day at El Toro, I made a point of saying good-bye to Bob Fraser, and then I headed East with Wally Sigler.

It was a last good-bye. On June 18, 1945—two months before the end of the war—Bob, who was by then a carrier air squadron commander, was on a routine training flight out of Santa Barbara when his F4U inexplicably pointed its nose down and flew straight into the sea. Pilots who were there later agreed that the rubber raft Bob wore in a seat pack beneath his parachute pack must have accidentally inflated so quickly that Bob was wedged in the cockpit, unable to regain control of his fighter or even bail out.

I lost more friends in the war than I care to remember. Bob Fraser's was the only loss I cried over.

24

The Marine Corps night-fighter program had been launched in 1941 when several Marine aviators were sent to Britain to study RAF night-fighter operations. The senior Marine pilot on the tour was Major Frank Schwable, who spent nearly four months working and living with British night-fighter pilots as well as attending the RAF fighter-direction school at Stanmore.

During Schwable's time in Great Britain, he learned of the importance of close cooperation between the ground-based fighter director and the aircrewmen aboard the night fighter. Without powerful ground radar to guide him, the night-fighter pilot would have to rely entirely on luck to find an enemy airplane within the very small range of his own airborne radar.

When Major Schwable returned to Washington, he brought back operating information about the somewhat outmoded British Mark IV Aircraft Interception (AI) radar.

Except for the aids brought back by Major Schwable and his team, the Marine Corps's experimental night-fighter program began from scratch immediately after Pearl Harbor. But the program was nearly stillborn, for there was some question in very high places as to the necessity and desirability of even launching a Marine Corps night-fighter effort.

Both the Army and Navy had been groping in the dark—literally—for some time before the Marine Corps got started. They, too, had copied the successful British model. The Massachusetts Institute of Technology Radiation Laboratory had built fifteen experimental AI radar sets in 1941. About half of these had been turned over to the Army Air Corps, which placed them aboard converted A-20 light attack bombers (redesignated P-70) and P-38 twin-engine long-range fighters. The Army also built several Northrup P-61 Black Widow prototypes, the first airplane in the world to be designed from scratch as a night fighter.

The Navy was tinkering with F4F conversions at the time of Pearl Harbor, but it had no operational night fighters at the time. It immediately took a close look at the nearly operational F4U as well and soon settled on it, pending receipt of the first Grumman F6F Hellcat production models in mid or late 1943.

In January, 1942, Captain Ralph Davison, of the Navy's Bureau of Aeronautics, committed the Marine Corps to a night-fighter program by writing, "The job of the Marines is to seize a beachhead and hold it until replaced by the Army. To do this, night fighters will be an absolute necessity."

When the internal authorization for the night-fighter program emerged from the office of the Commandant of the Marine Corps in January, 1942, night-fighter enthusiasts felt as if they had been shot down. The Commandant's office approved the creation of eight 12-plane squadrons for the period from January 1 to June 30, 1945!

The rapid deflation of the program was seen in the end as a practical solution to the Marine Corps's rapid wartime expansion. There were simply too many good ideas from which to choose, and night fighters did not then seem high on the list of necessities.

As the Marine Corps exerted more and more control over its burgeoning expansion programs, a rosier picture was painted. In June, 1942, the Commandant's office approved the formation of a single experimental night-fighter squadron for the period January 1 to June 30, 1943.

★

Marine Corps Aviation immediately started looking for an adequate airplane model on which to base its program. The first obvious attention went to the superb Air Corps P-61, which was due to become operational in mid 1943, right on time for the Marine Corps program. However, only a limited number were to be built, and all were earmarked for the Air Corps. The Marine Corps then looked into the A-20 conversions as well as a promising program built around the swift B-26 twin-engine bomber. Neither of these conversions fulfilled their requirements, so the program chiefs moved on to British night fighters: Beaufighters and Mosquitos. The Mosquito was a superb night-fighter gunnery platform, but someone higher up wanted an American-built model. The Navy's new SB2C Curtis Helldiver dive-bomber was briefly considered but given up as too slow. The F4U Corsair seemed to be the perfect model because the Marine Corps had so many of them, but it too was rejected for arcane reasons.

In the end, the Marine Corps settled on equipping its first operational night-fighter squadron, VMF(N)-531, with the Lockheed PV-1 Ventura medium patrol plane. This was a very strange choice, but necessary in light of the weapons-building capacity of the wartime aircraft industry. The search for a more suitable airplane would continue, but it was politically expedient at the time to get VMF(N)-531 operational as soon as possible.

As it turned out, the PV-1 conversion was not a bad choice for the experimental program. Like the Beaufighter, the RAF's first night-fighter conversion, the Lockheed was a twin-engine airplane with plenty of room for the radar set, the radar operator, and extra communications equipment. Also like the Beaufighter, the PV-1 was a stable gun platform, which was crucial. Its stringers were located in a man-operated overhead turret. Its main flaws were its relatively slow speed and its 15,000-foot battle ceiling; most British night intercepts were taking place at 25,000 feet and above.

★

On November 15, 1942, VMF(N)-531 was commissioned at Cherry Point, North Carolina (which had been under construction when I was flying out of nearby New Bern). The first squadron commander was, fittingly, Lieutenant Colonel Frank Schwable, and the exec was Major John Harshberger, an early night-fighter enthusiast.

From the outset, the new squadron was plagued by a shortage of radar test equipment, spare parts for the airplanes and the radar sets, and spare Vegas. Nearly all the pilots assigned to the squadron were right out of flight school, and every one of them needed every sort of advanced training.

Despite the problems, VMF(N)-531 was split in two to form VMF(N)-532 on April 1, 1943. Also formed on that date were Marine Night Fighter Group 53, a group headquarters squadron and a group service squadron. The entire group was placed under Lieutenant Colonel Schwable. John Harshberger took over 531.

Grueling months of work ensued, in which VMF(N)-531 was prepared for its first deployment. In early July, Lieutenant Colonel Schwable turned MAG-53 over to a replacement and voluntarily reverted to command of VMF(N)-531. The squadron was transferred to the new airbase at El Centro, in Southern California, for a last round of training. Then only six of the PV-1s were hoisted aboard light carrier *Long Island*, which sailed for Hawaii.

In the meantime, VMF(N)-532 began experimenting with radar-equipped F4Us, as did a Navy squadron, VF(N)-75.

VMF(N)-531's forward flight echelon arrived at Turtle Bay on August 25, 1943—during my last week with VMF-121—and conducted its final round of preparations. The six PV-1s then flew to Knucklehead on September 11. On that date, VMF(N)-531 became the first naval service night-fighter squadron to arrive in the war zone; it had beaten the Navy F4U night fighters of VF(N)-75 by several weeks. However, it was months behind the Air Corps P-70s. (The P-70 program came to nothing because the converted, heavily laden A-20s could never match altitude with the Japanese raiders. The pilots of the radar-equipped Air Corps night fighters eventually switched over to A-20s guided by ground-based searchlight batteries. It was one of these that I had seen score a kill on VMF-121's first night at Henderson Field.)

The Marine night fighters immediately undertook night patrols over the Russells and up The Slot as far as Vella Lavella. But these were catch-as-catch-can affairs because the essential Ground Control Intercept (GCI) teams had not yet arrived with their powerful ground-based radars.

On the night of October 31, 1943, a VF(N)-75 pilot flying a converted F4U scored the naval service's first night kill—and America's first radar-guided night kill—in the Pacific. The tracking was done by VMF(N)-531's GCI equipment, which was located on Vella Lavella. The control officer was Major Thomas Hicks, one of six Marine pilots who had been thoroughly trained in night-fighter ground-intercept techniques by the RAF earlier in the year.

VMF(N)-531's first kill was scored by Captain Duane Jenkins at 0420, November 13, 1943. Ironically, however, Jenkins was not under GCI, nor did he use his radar. He found a Betty bomber in the moonlight as it and five other Bettys were attacking naval targets off our two-week-old beachhead at Bougainville.

It was not until December 6, 1943, that a VMF(N)-531 Lockheed teamed up with VMF(N)-531 GCI radar to score a kill. Fittingly, the pilot was Major John Harshberger, who got a single-engine amphibian over Bougainville.

VMF(N)-531 served in the Pacific until August, 1944. It was then brought back to Cherry Point and disbanded. By then, technological advances had passed it by.

25

It was February, 1944, by the time I headed east to begin night-fighter training. I had finished my training duties well before Christmas and then had to pass the time as a senior captain assigned to several boards that were convened at El Toro and other Southern California bases. I had the impression, also, that there were not yet any billets for me in the newly forming night-fighter squadrons. I was more than ready to shove off when my orders finally arrived.

I had been talked into selling my cherry red Ford convertible to another pilot at an enormous profit soon after joining the Combat Fighter Training Command in October, so I was totally dependent on my roommate and fellow night-fighter hopeful, Captain Wally Sigler, for getting me to Cherry Point, North Carolina, from California. Wally was having a romance with a Canadian girl who had gone back to Montreal, and he insisted on taking leave so he could drive up to see her on our way to our new station. I figured I could use the time off, so I literally went along for the ride.

We managed to get a flat tire dead in the middle of the New Mexico nowhere, and the winter chill nearly froze our California-acclimated blood. We survived until a tow truck found us and hauled us into Albuquerque, where I had my next run-in with the rationing authorities.

Here we were, two decorated Marine combat pilots on our way to an important new assignment. We had blown a tire because the rationing system had prevented Wally from purchasing a new set before setting out on what was then an arduous cross-country trip. We were on the road because of military orders.

Do you suppose that had any influence on the minds of the cowpokes manning the fully convened rationing board that had to pass judgment on this "extraordinary" requisition?

The request was denied.

We ambled back to the garage to tell the mechanic the good news. His face broadened into a knowing smile, and he wrote something on a small slip of paper. "Them cowboys must be gettin' even with the guvment fer somethin'. Here." And he handed Wally the paper. "Jus' walk on down there an' buy yourselves a good black-market tire." We bought four.

The rest of the trip was cold but thankfully uneventful. We crossed the Canadian border in uniform (which earned us snappy salutes from the Canadian border guards) and finished up in Montreal.

Wally had a fine reunion with his fiancee, Micheline, who was a ballet dancer, and my time was well spent with one of her gorgeous girlfriends. Then we drove straight through to Scarsdale, New York, to visit with Wally's family. We wound up at Lakehurst, New Jersey, where we spent a day with one of Wally's Dartmouth College chums who was flying blimps out over the Atlantic in search of German U-boats.

★

As soon as Wally and I arrived at our destination, we were assigned to one of the new night groups then being formed at Cherry Point. The new group commanding officer was Colonel Edward Montgomery, one of my senior instructors at Pensacola who had led the first group of Marine pilots to England for GCI training aimed at supporting VMF(N)-531 in the Pacific. He was especially happy to see us as, very few fighter pilots with solid combat experience had as yet volunteered for night-fighter duty.

Wally was immediately assigned to VMF(N)-542 as flight officer, and I went to VMF(N)-544 as the squadron executive officer. However, we no sooner checked in than we received orders to Vero Beach, Florida, for up to six weeks of night-fighter training.

Wally and I arrived at Vero Beach aboard his well-traveled junker and immediately found adjacent rooms in one of the nicest bachelor officers quarters I ever saw. We reported for duty on March 18 and were assigned to a class mainly composed of young second lieutenants right out of fighter school.

★

After I had been at Vero Beach for only a few hours, I was ordered to report to the base's senior Marine aviator. I had no idea who the man was or what he wanted of me. Before going, I took the precaution of asking who he was, and I was pleasantly surprised to learn that he was Lieutenant Colonel Hugh Brewster, the same officer who had stolen Roy Margrave and me from the Navy back in 1939.

We had a very pleasant reunion, in which he revealed that I had somehow really impressed him as a comer during our brief association a world war ago. He had watched my career and had been gratified to learn only that morning that our paths had crossed again—as inevitably they must in a community as small as the Marine Corps aviation family. I was a bit sad to realize that my mentor had not fared as well as many of his contemporaries; I'm not sure why, but he had never been given command of an operational air unit.

Lieutenant Colonel Brewster finally came to the point. "Porter, I understand that you've been selected for major. I happen to have a slot for a major that needs filling, and I'd like to keep you here at Vero Beach as a senior instructor. I see from your record that you've had a good tour as an instructor, and I can sure use someone with your knowledge and experience. What I'm really looking for, and what I think you can handle, is for someone to eventually take over the reins here for me."

The man dazzled me for the second time in our two meetings, and I agreed to the proposed transfer. He immediately wrote up orders for my permanent change of duty and sent them to Washington by teletype. We parted with instructions for me to report back directly to him the next morning.

I no sooner reported myself present the next day than a clerk handed Lieutenant Colonel Brewster a teletype hot off the wires from Headquarters, Marine Corps. It was a response to the message of the previous afternoon. I could read the key word from across the desk and upside down: CANCELLED. I was destined for a night-fighter squadron after all.

★

There were only four experienced pilots in our class of twelve. In addition to Wally and me, there was Major Jim Maguire and Captain Norman Mitchell. Jim was to be my new commanding officer once we got back to Cherry Point. He had been in TBF torpedo bombers in the Pacific and had worked at the advanced-training base at El Toro as an torpedo-bombing instructor at the same time I was working at the fighter school. Jim had always wanted to fly fighters, and the night-fighter program was his only entre. Norm Mitchell had served with me in VMF-111 in Samoa. Unfortunately for Norm, he had remained in VMF-441 and had gone with it for an unexciting tour at Funafuti.

At least four of the lieutenants in my class were earmarked for duty with VMF(N)-544. I found it a bit unsettling to be training with the squadron CO and so many future subordinate members of our command. Jim Maguire and I had to work extra hard to establish and maintain our credibility.

Our class went straight to work on developing our instrument qualifications, which is what flying night fighters is all about. This meant endless hours of "ground" flying in Link trainers, which are automated training aids, and even more hours in the air and under the hood aboard SNJs. Early on, we also got time to familiarize ourselves with the Grumman F6F Hellcat night fighter, a Navy model on which the Marine Corps, like the Navy, had finally settled as the basis of its night-fighter program.

In the end, we did an enormous amount of flying at Vero Beach. As the course progressed, more and more of it was at night under the control of GCI officers. Several people washed out of the course, which was a given. But the rest of us became quite proficient not only at flying at night but at allowing ourselves to be guided onto the tails of target aircraft by low voices in our earphones. We older pilots (several of the second lieutenants were actually older than I!) had to break a lot of old habits to achieve night-fighting proficiency, but our superior flying skills more than made up for the relative flexibility enjoyed by our less experienced classmates.

Throughout the training, it was impressed upon us that we were the elite of an elite community.

I was promoted to major in late April, 1944, shortly before the conclusion of the night-fighter course.

★

I faced a personal dilemma while I was at Vero Beach.

While serving as flight officer of VMF-121, I had been left with the onerous duty of informing the next of kin of pilots killed or missing in action. This was really the job of the commanding officer, but it had fallen to me because, frankly, our skipper was squeamish. I was, too, but I toughed it out.

One of the letters I had had to write was to the family of my old and dear friend, Louis Gordon, who was a native of Miami. I had briefly met members of Louis's family when Louis and I had served together as cadets at Opa-Locka.

It came as no great surprise that the family learned of my return to Florida, and I soon received indirect hints that my presence was desired in Miami to tell them about Louis's last days.

Louis had probably been shot and killed while descending in his parachute near Munda Field during the big fighter battle on June 30, 1943, the day of the Rendova landings. I had written the required letter to accompany his personal effects, but I had left out specific information, both about the way I believe Louis had died and about the fact that I had actually seen his body in the surf beside Munda Point. There was no need for the family to know.

I do not know precisely why I reacted so badly to an invitation from the family that eventually made its way to Vero Beach. I simply could not face them knowing what I knew. After days of torment, I finally declined. I knew I could not look any of Louis's relatives in the eye and simply lie. Nor could I tell them the truth.

In the end, I could not bring myself to face that sort of pain. Theirs or mine.

★

The F6F night fighter was similar to the F4U I had been flying for about a year. Its speed (360 miles per hour at 18,000 feet) and rate of climb (3,100 feet per minute) were nearly identical to the Corsair's, but the Hellcat was a much easier airplane to land. I have no doubt that this was a key factor in its adoption for Marine Corps night operations. In fact, the F4U had been washed out of Navy carrier operations because of its landing characteristics. (Perversely, the Marine Corps took the F4U aboard carriers when the new Marine carrier air groups went operational in 1944.) Most experienced pilots also considered the F6F a more stable gun platform than the F4U, but I personally could not favor one over the other in this important regard.

The night-configured Hellcat could be identified by two unique characteristics. All of them were painted nonreflective matte black and featured a bulbous pod beneath the starboard wing.

The pod housed the new APS-6 radar, which weighed only 70 pounds but allowed the pilot to "see" across a search radius of from five to five-and-a-half miles. Unfortunately, the APS-6's blind-fire control was considered unreliable, and its use was proscribed in many operational Navy and Marine squadrons. Combined with larger, farther-reaching ground-or ship-based GCI radars, the APS-6 was more than adequate for getting a night fighter to within sighting distance of an enemy intruder; it worked extremely well to within 400 or 500 feet of a target and could detect a large ship at 20 miles.

One important innovation found in the APS-6 that had been lacking in the early AI sets was a double-dot display. Besides reflecting a true "blip" returning from the target, the system painted a ghost blip on the pilot's cockpit screen just to the right of the true bogey. The ghost image gave height readings relative to the F6F, so the night-fighter pilot could tell if the target was above or below his direct line of sight. The bearing reading from the true image and the relative altitude reading from the ghost thus provided the pilot with a three-dimensional view of the battlefield.

The APS-6 was very easy to operate. It had only six dials or knobs plus a simple on-off switch. It was thus extremely popular among pilots, who invariably found night flying to be a very busy enterprise.

Other necessary innovations found in the F6F-3E model we flew then were low-intensity cockpit lighting and red instrument-panel lights, which protected our night vision and stood less chance of being seen from afar. Our airplanes were also provided with flat windscreens to help reduce glare. In time, we acquired modern APS-13 radars, which provided 60 percent coverage *behind* the fighter out to ranges of 800 feet.

By the end of the training cycle at Vero Beach, we had total confidence in our airplanes and, indeed, in the entire interdependent air-ground night-fighting system.

26

Major Jim Maguire and I returned to Cherry Point with our young tyros and immediately commissioned VMF(N)-544 on May 1, 1944. Before us lay months of exhausting flight training and the absorption of a full complement of even newer pilots.

A great deal of the responsibility for getting the new squadron fell on my shoulders. As the squadron exec, I had to take on numerous administrative duties I had never before faced. And I had to log as many flying hours as everyone else in the squadron. My administrative skills were pretty basic, but I was driven by the knowledge that a good rating as a squadron exec could propel me toward a coveted command of my own.

★

We acquired our Hellcats very slowly. In fact, they came through more slowly than new pilots, if that can be believed. And nearly all of them were standard production models that were pulled from the Navy's stock of replacement carrier fighters; they all had to be fitted out with radars, extra radios, and all the other specialized gear that we would need in the air at night.

I finally got away on May 17 to fly my own personal Hellcat to Brown Field, at Quantico, where all the night-fighter conversions were being handled.

I knew that the job would take at least four or five days, so I arranged to stay at the Roosevelt Hotel, which had a great reputation among fighter pilots. I had been assured by my friend, Major Joe Foss, our first 26-kill ace in the war, that the place practically featured hot-and-cold running women. I quickly learned where Joe got his ideas; the Roosevelt hosted two full floors of Woman Marines, who were actually *billeted* there. Their presence, along with the presence of no end of Waves (lady sailors), made for a very wild time.

The sybaritic holiday was shattered when Jim Maguire called from Cherry Point to tell me that Colonel Montgomery, the group commander, had been inquiring about what was taking me so long. Jim agreed to fob off the old man with a story about technical difficulties while I reversed engines and applied pressure to get the job completed. (Of course, on arrival, I had told the engineers to take their time.)

I headed straight back to Brown Field and found that the Hellcat conversion had been completed the previous afternoon. I figured I had better push it in order to impress the group commander, but I was brought up short by the sudden onset of some really foul weather conditions.

The base operations officer was an old flying buddy from the South Pacific, so I was able to work on him to give me clearance to take off despite the weather. As a night-fighter pilot, I argued, I had more than the usual instrument training and would thus be okay. In fact, I viewed this as just another form of flat-hatting—showing off my superior flying skills.

★

I took off straight into the murk and gloom. I was on full instruments by the time I topped 100 feet.

I continued on up to 12,000 feet and came down with the first case of outright vertigo I had ever suffered in my life. I suddenly felt that my instruments were wrong (and my inner ear was right). I *knew* that I was flying upside down and backwards.

By that time, I had about 250 hours in Hellcats, and a good 200 of those were on instruments. I had long since passed the point where reading the gauges had become second nature, an absolute must for night work. More to the point, I had long ago learned to ignore my personal senses and rely exclusively on my console readings.

An echo from my earliest flying days cried out to me, a form of self-preservation from the darkest depths of the fears I suppose every pilot secretly harbors. I heard my first flight instructor's voice, which sounded tinny and distant, as if it were arriving through an ancient gosport. "Needle-ball airspeed, Porter. Goddamnit! Needle-ball airspeed!" the voice berated. And I straightened myself right out.

My newly cleared mind saw that I was hurtling straight down at an amazing 300 knots. So I pulled back on the throttle and eased back on the joystick. Instantly, I flew out of the haze and bellied in directly over the Potomac very close to Brown Field, my starting point. I saw that I was heading north, back toward Washington, which was in the opposite direction of my objective in North Carolina.

I took a moment's breather to decide if I wanted to land and settle myself, but I decided to fly on home.

The Hellcat eased back into the clouds, I went right back on instruments, and I climbed to about 27,000 feet, where I broke out of the weather. That was one dense storm!

After flying south for a while, I began picking up air controllers talking commercial airliners into Richmond. I was still stricken by my near calamity, so I decided to follow the beam into Richmond and pull myself together before flying on. Besides, except for the civilian chatter, I had no way of knowing exactly where I was in relation to the unseen land below.

I cut into the civilian channel and requested permission to land at West Point Field, an Air Corps airstrip near Richmond. My request to land was approved as soon as I checked in with the Air Corps controller. I began flying down through the weather, being very careful to believe my instruments.

The Hellcat popped through the overcast at about 300 feet and screamed down along an unfamiliar narrow river. I had no idea where I was in relation to my immediate objective; I was lost. I tentatively circled a few times, widening my search area each time around. Finally, after four or five circuits, I saw the vague outline of a tiny runway some way off. It was a minuscule civilian field adjacent to a nondescript little town. I made a beeline for the flat place, threw down the landing gear, and landed.

As I taxied to the end of the field in search of another living soul, I saw that a whole bunch of civilian automobiles were coming out to the field to head me off. Fearful that some fool would drive into my propeller, I stood on the brakes and lurched to a stop. By that time, the lead car had resolved itself into a police or sheriff's car, complete with blinking lights and wailing siren—the whole works.

As the lawman's car skidded to a halt beside the starboard wing, I threw back the canopy and began unbuckling my harness. All the while, I was thinking about the great service these southern townies were doing for their countryman in uniform.

Well, needless to say, the sheriff saw things a mite differently than I. By the time I climbed down to greet the officer of the law, I was staring at the working end of a huge hogleg .45-caliber revolver.

This character was something right out of the movies. He had on the peaked, flat-brimmed hat, jodphurs and leather puttees. He had more leather belts and harnesses and braid on than any general I had ever seen. And there was that pistol!

He was looking at me like I was a creature from Mars. I could hear him *thinking* that.

I suddenly realized that my freshly-painted matte-black F6F had no markings on it, none whatsoever. It could have been a Martian fighter for all the sheriff knew. Or a German raider!

"Hi, there!" I bluffed. "I'm Major Porter, United States Marine Corps. I kinda got lost in that bad weather and I barely made it into your field here. I woulda crashed if I hadn't found you." I had learned a thing or two in my four years in the service about maintaining my composure under pressure.

The puzzled look gave way to one of concern and the revolver quickly disappeared into its sparkling leather holster. Then he pulled in his huge belly and . . . threw me a salute!

Following up on my advantage, I asked if I could use a phone to call Quantico to tell them that I had gotten down safely; I was by then well overdue from my expected arrival at West Point.

The sheriff snapped to attention again and brayed, "Yes, Sir!" (This was getting to be as bit much. I had an extremely hard time preventing my inner mirth from producing uncontrollable laughter of the falling-down variety.)

Then, in a cross between a masterful stroke and real concern, I explained that my strangely painted fighter had to be guarded "with your life" as it had top-secret equipment aboard.

That fat old sheriff shot straight back to attention and said, "I'll guard it myself, Major. Ain't no one gonna get closer to that airplane than I am right now."

"I'd offer you a seat in the cockpit, Sheriff," I told him in my warmest voice, "But there's a lot of top-secret gear up there, so I have to lock it up." With that, I climbed back up onto the wing and did indeed lock the canopy shut.

By the time I returned to the sheriff's side, he had called over one of the numerous townies who had gathered into a half-circle around us and ordered me driven to the nearest telephone. I was just climbing into the car when the sheriff yelled, "Now don't you worry, Major-Sir! I'll guard it with my life!"

Who could worry in the presence of such selfless dedication?

My civilian driver no sooner pulled away than the weather front dropped in, and great gusts of storm wind carried sheets of rainwater across the tiny country road. I cringed as I thought of that old man I had left guarding my Hellcat; I could just see his priceless uniform going literally down the drain.

We got into town within minutes. I ran out to the pay phone and placed a collect call to the operations center at Brown Field. Minutes were consumed while my friend, the operations officer, was located. No word had come in about my being overdue, but he thanked me for calling just the same and urged me to call again "if" I reached West Point.

Then I dashed back through the storm to my transportation, and we drove straight back to the field through the teeming rain. I expected to find the sheriff little more than a uniformed puddle, but that sly old country fox was safely and dryly ensconced in his spiffy patrol car. I was wetter than he was by the time I climbed into the passenger seat.

I wasn't going anywhere, at least until the rain abated, so I shot the breeze with the old man. He was a good ole boy, a type I had not encountered before. I will say this, he was a vigilant protector of his community. He shared a bit of his philosophy with me and was soon transformed from a laughable parody to an image of respect.

When the rain slackened to a drizzle, I left the patrol car to check the surface of the field. I could manage a takeoff, and the wind was right. I trotted back to offer thanks and say good-bye and wound up signing a receipt for the return of "one black fighter airplane."

"Oh, by the way, Sheriff, which way is it to Richmond?"

He broke into a creased grin. "Jus' follah them rayroad tracks that way, Major. They'll getcha right inta the city."

And that's what I did. I landed at West Point in water so deep I barely needed my brakes, and in weather so thick I could not see fifty feet at ground level. I had rolled to a complete stop and was looking around to find the taxiway when a military jeep loomed out of the murk. It had a big sign attached to the rear fender. I strained my eyes to read "FOLLOW ME," which I did. The jeep led me right to a hardstand beside the operations office, and I checked in with the Air Corps duty officer. In response to his inquiries, I snowed him with a brief tale of my instrument-flying prowess.

I was given quarters in the BOQ. After changing out of my flight suit, I found my way to the Officers' Club. Word of my flying prowess had preceded me, and I was stood to round after round of drinks by Air Corps pilots eager to hear how I had gotten through the biggest storm of the year when even their multiengine airplanes had been grounded from Philadelphia all the way down to Savannah.

★

It was back to the grindstone for the next few months. My life became so routine that I took the trouble to figure out how many hours of training I had devoted to how many hours of combat flying. I no longer have the figures, but the training hours outnumbered the combat hours by several hundred to one, and the balance kept shifting farther and farther toward the training hours. Still, we were getting a pretty good squadron for the trouble we were going to.

About the only excitement during that spring and early summer came in the form of several hurricane alerts. When that happened, Cherry Point flew everyone and everything flyable out of range of the wicked storms. Only one or two hurricanes actually blew over the air station, but they did a terrific amount of damage. It was like nothing I had ever seen in California.

We also enjoyed a liberal leave schedule. I often flew to Quantico alone aboard a night fighter or ferried younger pilots or old friends north aboard the squadron's own Beechcraft SNB transport-trainer. Somehow, I always managed to book myself into the Roosevelt Hotel in Washington or the Commodore Hotel in New York.

I had a few casual affairs during this period, but I was still rocky from the dissolution of my marriage, so I kept myself from getting seriously involved with anyone.

★

On August 1, 1944, we were asked to ferry one of our night fighters to North Island, San Diego, where VMF(N)-541 was preparing to head out to the war zone. They were one Hellcat short, and we were ordered to provide it. I wanted to get back home for a while and I found a double incentive to visit San Diego since my old friend Major Norm Mitchell was the exec of the departing unit. Jim Maguire endorsed my request, and I was on my way within two hours.

Transcontinental navigation aids had been much improved since my last coast-to-coast flight in December, 1941. So had the ranges of our operational fighters. With only a few stops for refueling and with the use of minimal night-flying expertise, I rode the beacons all the way to El Paso, Texas, by the early evening. If all went well, I would be in San Diego by the next afternoon, August 2.

As soon as I awoke and showered and dressed, I headed to the operations center to get a weather briefing. The incoming reports were bad. There was heavy cloud cover to the west, and many intermediate strips were grounding all flights because of storms and disturbances.

I pooh-poohed the reports and fell back on my trusty instrument training. The Navy operations officer asked twice if I really wanted to go, and I told him twice that I did. He shook his head, but he told me I was on my own.

Shortly after takeoff, I entered the heavy cloud cover and took a magnetic heading for Yuma, Arizona, which was as good a place as any to top off my fuel tanks. I climbed through the storm to a safe altitude and headed out over the pass. No sooner done, however, than my compass went out on me.

The options were minimal. I had learned my lesson in May. I was less than thirty minutes out of El Paso, so I banked around and began descending through the weather. I spent many long minutes feeling my way through the solid mass of clouds in search of a break from which I could see the ground. The break eventually came, but by then I was a tad disoriented.

I spiralled down through the clear area and saw that I was directly over a highway—a first-class good sign. As I flew yet lower, I saw that a road crew was out with heavy equipment. I lowered my wheels and flaps and made a pass over the work area to determine if there was enough room for me to get down to ask directions.

The roadway was very narrow, but it looked like I would have about 2,500 feet of useable runway. This would be a piece of cake, so

I lined up and touched down for a perfect landing.

Recalling my run-in with my sheriff friend in May, I cranked back my canopy, flashed a huge grin, and began waving at the gathered, astounded road crew long before I rolled to a complete stop well short of the nearest earthmover.

I climbed down from the cockpit and hailed the foreman, a big red-faced Irishman who was striding purposefully toward me as I dropped to the ground. We introduced ourselves and I briefly explained my predicament. The big man nodded and offered me a cup of hot coffee from a huge thermos jug.

As I sipped the wonderful coffee, I unfolded my map on the hood of the foreman's truck and asked the question my sheriff friend had taught me: "Where's the nearest railroad?" The Irishman smiled and pointed out over the nearby hills, then showed me just where I was on the map.

The road crew backed up some of its equipment to give me a little extra takeoff room, though I protested that I had more than enough. Then I roared down the smooth, newly laid highway surface, climbed to 200 feet, and headed over the hills toward the nearest town. I easily found the railroad tracks and followed them back to El Paso. I landed within 30 minutes of lifting off from the road.

The weather cleared the following morning, and a very chastened Major Porter completed a routine flight to North Island, with brief stopovers in Yuma and El Centro.

I dropped the Hellcat off at VMF(N)-541's flight line, had a brief reunion with Norm Mitchell, and left to find a flight to El Toro for a one-day reunion with some other old buddies.

★

I was just striding onto the tarmac leading toward the base flight line when I heard my name called from afar. My ears tracked the oncoming sound and I soon saw that it was emanating from a flight-suited figure hobbling toward me on an obviously game leg.

The figure's face soon resolved itself into the broad-smiling countenance of Captain Sam Logan, my old "half-a-caste" wingman from my Samoa and Funafuti days. But wait a minute! Hadn't Sam had a foot chopped off by a Zero just a year before, in June, 1943?

But it was Sam all right! He overtook me on that game leg and wrapped both arms around me. I had a tear in my eye as I returned the embrace.

Sam explained that he had just plain refused to be separated from the service following his recuperation in the States. Moreover, he had simply refused all efforts to have him placed on nonflying status. Except for the replacement of his real foot with an artificial one, he was perfectly fit to fly. So he was allowed to requalify on multiengine airplanes and had been plying the skies over the West Coast ever since, flying equipment between bases and hauling bigwigs wherever they wanted to go.

In the course of our stand-up reunion, I told Sam that I was expected in El Toro, and he immediately volunteered to fly me there. He checked out a twin-engine Beechcraft and offered me the co-pilot's seat. "On these runs, Major, I'm the command pilot." To which I heartily assented.

"It's not like flying fighters, Bruce. But it *is* flying."

27

The entire squadron, bag and baggage, left Cherry Point on November 1, 1944, and arrived at Marine Corps Air Station, El Centro, California, on November 3. Our understanding was that we would complete the final months of training and eventually deploy to the Pacific. I was eager by then to get back into the fray because pilots from night-fighter squadrons already in the war zone were racking up kills; I had every reason to believe that I could score the two confirmed kills I needed to become an ace. All I had to do in the meantime was endure some more of what already seemed like a lifetime of preparation.

El Centro featured a small simulated carrier flight deck so that we could all practice carrier landings and takeoffs. Despite my relatively many years in Navy-model fighters, I had yet to work off of a carrier. The last time I had practiced carrier landings was at Kearny Mesa in very early 1942. The course came complete with a Landing Signal Officer, a carrier-qualified Marine aviator who controlled the last moments of flight by means of signals passed from a pair of outstretched hand-held luminous paddles. We all had to suffer through no end of simulated carrier landings, which consists of a controlled stall and a sudden stop when the fighter's tailhook connects with lines of arresting cables. It did not occur to me then that anyone might be thinking of operating night fighters from carriers.

El Centro is in the desert on the far side of the coastal hills that hem San Diego to the sea. It was then rough desert country. Some sick souls in the carrier training group discovered that killing rattlesnakes was a fun pastime. We always had a crash truck and an ambulance beside the flight deck because crashes among tyros were quite common. Whenever a rattlesnake got too close, someone would get a carbon-dioxide fire extinguisher from the crash truck and, while someone else lifted the snake on a stick (if possible), would spray the critter with the freezing solution. The result would be a twisted, frozen, dead rattlesnake, which then would be cracked to bits. I suppose that this was all in the way of honing predatory skills.

★

I am not altogether sure that the Marine Corps was fully committed to its night-fighter program, despite all the hoopla and material expenditures. The essence of night-fighter work is honing *individual* skills, for night stalking is invariably a solo enterprise. All the group work that serves as the basis for a well-trained fighter pilot was supposed to have been handled before new pilots reported in to the night squadrons. However, we faced seemingly endless daytime training in formation flying and other group skills. So, despite the need to turn out competent lone wolves of the air, we inevitably served as a finishing school with duties similar to those of the Fighter Combat Training Command at El Toro.

We had to run numerous cross-country hops, and most of them were just plain boring. One, however, was more interesting than I would have liked it to be.

A number of our new second lieutenants approached me one day to ask if I would be interested in leading a cross-country hop to Reno, Nevada. I gathered that they had heard about the night life there from fellow pilots and that they wanted a crack at some of the fun and games. We had been training hard to that point, so I agreed to the proposition.

I led five of the lieutenants aloft from El Centro early on the morning on November 20, 1944. It was a bright, beautiful day, until we arrived over the mountain town of Bishop, which was one hundred percent socked in by a weather pattern over the high Sierra Nevada mountain range. We were at 20,000 feet and just approaching the weather front when I radioed Reno to ask for some advice.

The ground controller suggested that we return to El Centro. However, we had passed the point of no return; we had to press on.

I led the flight up to 25,000 feet (the crest of the mountain range was up around 14,000 feet at that point) and headed straight up the spine of mountains toward our objective. Fortunately, the weather was not affecting the navigational signal beacons we were by then riding, so I assumed that we would have a relatively easy run through the weather.

The approach was no problem; the navigational beam held up all the way to Reno. The problem arose when we wanted to get down. This was by far the most vicious rainstorm in which I ever flew. I felt my way down through the utterly black, windy storm, riding the beam all the way in. It was absolutely teeming. I got us all into the field, but something was just not right.

I taxied to the first building I could discern, leading five other matte black Hellcats. My objective was a big civilian airfield that shared facilities with the Army Air Corps. The place I had found was a civilian field, but it was very small. I saw no signs of a military presence. It was obvious that I had led my flight into the wrong airfield.

Since I was responsible for the screw-up, I told my subordinates to remain in their dry cockpits, then I cracked my canopy and stepped out into the vortex of the storm. I was blown halfway to the tiny shack by which I had parked, and then I was blown through the door into a cozy little operations center.

The civilian air controller on duty bid me welcome and asked me if he could help. It was almost like walking into a lonely gas station in the middle of nowhere to ask directions.

First, I asked where I was, and he pointed us out on the map. Then I told him where I wanted to be, and he pointed that out on the map. Then I asked where the railroad tracks were and if they were going my way. He found them on the map, running right beside the Truckee River. Wow! Two landmarks! The civilian wished me luck and then stood in the window to watch as I wrestled the headwind back to my night fighter.

The trouble began as we taxied out. The wind was ferocious, and the propwash from each big high-performance radial engine blew up a little storm of its own. One of the lieutenants must have needed some extra power because he cranked his engine up so high he literally blew a little civilian airliner far back into its hangar bay, causing some damage. We had no way of knowing about this at the time, but we sure heard about it later on.

That was Strike One.

We felt our way over to the larger airport by following the river and the tracks and set down safely. When I checked in at the operations center, I found it manned by a cast of incredulous Army types. "How in the hell did you get in here? Who sent you? Don't you know that this field is totally restricted?"

It turned out that B-29 heavy bombers, which were on their way to China bases, were weathered in. Because the new Superfortress were still a very top secret, the base was closed to all other aircraft.

Our reception was partly based on our perceived skill as airmen. Even the B-29s, which were manned by crews of ten, including co-pilots and navigators, had been grounded because of the severity of the storm, which made navigation impossible.

We traded our secret for theirs. When they told us about the B-29s, we told them we were night fighters. That seemed to explain our flying skills and why we were crazy enough to brave the weather. The fact that we were Marines seemed to add to the devil-may-care aura perceived by our hosts.

Landing at the restricted field was Strike Two.

We spent a wild night in wide-open Reno. Hung over and tired, we took off the next morning, totally on instruments, through an incredible mountain fog. There were peaks higher than the airfield, so we all climbed with our radars on to help us avoid hitting them.

The Hellcats were breaking through 10,000 feet (only about 3,500 feet above the field) when one of my irrepressible lieutenants blurted into the radio net, "Hey, let's take a pass at the field."

I got caught up in the craziness (we were on full instruments!) and wound up leading my flight back down through the fog. We ran a line-astern group split-S, roared down the length of the runway, and disappeared back into the fog.

That had to be Strike Three.

We followed the spine of the Sierra Nevada back to Bishop, where the weather cleared, then overflew the length of the gorgeous Owens Valley, peeled out over the high desert, and let down with no further strain at El Centro.

★

I no sooner dropped to the hardstand than Major Jim Maguire, the squadron commander, strode up with a pained expression on his face. "Bruce, your ass is on a hot rock."

"Huh? What happened?" For a second there, I could not imagine what could be wrong.

"You know about the pass you made over that Army field, *don't you*? Someone raised holy hell about it. Prepare to meet your maker."

I told Jim that I had made absolutely certain that there was nothing in the traffic pattern and that I had closely monitored the entire evolution. I admitted that it was a wild stunt, but I excused myself with an old saw about frisky young fighter pilots.

"Don't make a damn bit of difference to me, Bruce. I'm not the one who's doing the bitching. What you did was strictly against regulations. A new base commander checked in while you were gone, and he wants your ass."

I left my flying helmet and gloves with Jim and walked straight over to the commanding officer's office. I announced myself to the adjutant and was ushered into the inner sanctum within about five seconds.

Sitting behind the big polished wood desk was none other than Lieutenant Colonel Hugh Brewster, the Marine aviator who had sworn me into the Marine Corps and who had offered to train me as his replacement at Vero Beach just the past March.

"Close the door, Porter." Which I did. Then Brewster proceeded to chew me up one side and down the other without taking time to spit out the gristle and bone. The harangue lasted a good ten minutes, by which time I was numb.

Suddenly, he paused and lowered his pitch. "Do you know what the hell you did, Porter?"

"Sir, I really had no idea it was this serious."

"It was. I had to take flak from an Army general about your flat-hatting over their base. I took a call from someone pretty high up in the War Department about your breaching security— though I admit you had no way of knowing that. And I just got a call from some joker at the Civil Aeronautics Board about the damage you caused that civilian airliner." (The last was still news to me, but I refrained from requesting details; this was clearly not the time.)

He went on without a pause, but in a more even tone. "Ordinarily, this would all add up to two or three court martials, but I've decided to pass along the word that I have issued a severe reprimand, and I will recommend against formal proceedings. Your record is unusually clean up to this point, and that warrants some consideration. I'll get off a telegram to that effect right away. But

don't you ever wind up in front of this desk again unless it's for an
official visit or a friendly chat. Never again, Porter! Hear me?"

I snapped to attention. "Aye aye, Sir."

"Now, get the hell back to work."

"Sir!" And I was out of there.

28

Shortly after my triple-threat run-in with all the authorities, I was approached by several senior officers I knew and asked to form a nine-plane night-fighter detachment that was scheduled to operate as part of an experimental mixed day-night fighter squadron. The new hybrid was to begin training for around-the-clock *carrier* operations.

The Marine Corps had built up its air establishment by mid 1944 to over 10,000 qualified Marine pilots operating in five Marine Aircraft Wings comprising 128 operational squadrons. Marine airmen had helped to destroy so many Japanese warplanes, particularly in the Solomons and Bismarcks, that senior Marines were concerned that the Marine Corps might play a limited role in future aerial operations. We were victims of our success.

As a result of the sterling successes in the Solomons, the Marine Corps was able to force itself into the job of staffing "jeep" escort carriers (CVEs), which the Navy was by then producing in excess. The move to carrier-based operations was a perfectly natural evolution for the Marine Corps in two regards. First, Marine pilots were basically naval aviators; we all received some form of carrier training. Second, and more important, a key task of Marine aviation was to provide integrated, on-call, close air support to Marine ground units operating on a hostile beachhead. The way the war was going in the Central Pacific, it was clear that new landing operations would continue to take place beyond the range of land-based fighter support. So, if Marine aviators were to support Marines in action on the ground, we literally had to man carriers so that we could get close enough to actually run the support.

The logic of the last argument, and the almost embarrassing plenty of pilots we then enjoyed, mitigated in favor of a rapid shift in priorities toward a fairly large carrier-borne Marine air strike force.

It took only four or five months to perfect the notion, find the men and planes, and secure several ships. While the procurement of material and manpower was going on, planners high up in Marine Corps Aviation circles perfected the so-called Marine Corps carrier air groups on paper. The two came together in October, 1944. At that time, Colonel Albert Cooley, Henderson Field's first fighter-operations chief, established two new air groups that were eventually designated Marine Air Support Groups (MASG) 48 and 51. Each of the MASGs were built to oversee four carrier air groups (designated MCVG; the CV is the standard designation of an aircraft carrier). In turn, each MCVG consisted of one 18-plane Corsair squadron and a squadron of 12 Grumman TBF or Martin TBM torpedo bombers (which were essentially the same airplane).

Theory held that the entire MASG of four carrier-borne MCVGs would operate together and in the company of two additional CVEs manned by Navy groups. The Marine CVEs would support landing operations, while the Navy CVEs would launch antisubmarine and combat-air patrols to guard all six carriers and a bevy of surface warships attached to the escort-carrier task group (known, confusingly, as "divisions").

While the day groups were being organized, it seemed a logical step to form and train carrier-based night-fighter squadrons. Once again, the logic was overwhelming.

New beachheads had consistently become the focus of retaliatory airstrikes from Japanese bases within striking distance. From the earliest days of the war, the Japanese had favored night harassment raids as a means of rattling—and killing—American infantrymen within the new beachhead. If daytime close air support operations required the presence of Marine warplanes aboard carriers in proximity to the beachhead, it was logical that Marine night fighters might just as well be launched to interdict incoming night raiders.

As soon as this concept dawned on the planners, an experimental model was authorized. For reasons I cannot begin to fathom, the task of organizing the first carrier night-fighter detachment was offered to me.

★

I had always been particularly afraid of landing on a carrier deck at sea. Somehow, the opportunity to overcome the fear had eluded me, for I was never assigned to a carrier, not even to get from one place to another. I was frankly growing bored and restless with my administrative duties and particularly with the endlessly repetitive training schedule that VMF(N)-544 was maintaining. I needed some new challenges, so I immediately accepted the offer.

The best part of the deal was that I was given the opportunity to personally select the other eight Hellcat pilots from among a large number of volunteers pooled from all the night squadrons based at El Centro. And the pilots and I got to select a strong core group of groundcrewmen. The priority we received was so high that everything got done within a matter of days.

For the duration of the experiment, I and my demi-squadron would remain administratively attached to VMF(N)-544. If the experiment failed, I would return to my job as the squadron exec; if it was successful, I would very likely win a squadron command of my own. (That was overdue. By the end of December, 1944, my old buddy and Opa Locka classmate Jack Amende was skipper of VMF-217, a Marshall Islands-based Corsair squadron preparing for carrier duty, and Jeff Poindexter was also in the Marshalls commanding VMF-224.)

I was ordered to draw airplanes, and, while the ground echelon drove up from El Centro, I was given a flight plan that included a brief stopover at North Island, in San Diego, followed by a straight-through flight to our new base at Goleta, just north of Santa Barbara.

★

The flight to North Island was literally a hop; it could not have been more than 30 miles. But there is a line of hills between there and El Centro, and on the day we took off there was some weather stacked up over the hills and on down to the coastal plain. The result was that my flight of nine F6Fs had to let down through a thick fog.

I received clearance via radio to land, but the ground controller did not bother to mention that the overcast at lower altitudes was mixed with rain. The visibility was meager.

We sailed in over Point Loma and made the usual sweeping turn over San Diego. As always, our flight path paralleled the approaches to Lindbergh Field, the city's civilian airport. I had no idea where the civilian traffic might be, and the weather prevented me from seeing any of it.

As usual, I entered the landing circle with my full powers of concentration focused on getting myself down; all my pilots were big boys fully capable of getting themselves down. I made a normal approach and landing. As I taxied up to the dispersal area, a jeep pulled up beside my fighter. The officer-driver jumped to the ground and waited for me to secure my fighter.

"Are you Major Porter?"

"Yes, I am."

"Sir, Colonel Moore wants to see you right away."

I immediately assumed he was referring to Sad Sam Moore, my old Knucklehead strike commander. I had heard that he had just gotten to San Diego from a previous assignment at El Toro. Well, it sure was nice of old Sam to send a jeep out so I wouldn't have to walk back in the rain.

But Sad Sam Moore was not being a nice guy. I found him in his office gargling on his rage. I had never seen him in such a state.

He saw the confusion painted on my face and broke off what must have been a stream of thoughts aimed at venting his anger at me. "Do you have any idea what happened?"

"Happened, Sir? No, Sir!" I had no idea.

"One of your fighters flew so wide over Lindbergh Field that he forced an American Airlines DC-3 out of the landing pattern. I just got a very irate call. The way I have it, your pilot was so close to the airliner's cockpit that the civilian pilot could see your guy's face. The airline pilot got rattled—and no wonder!— and pulled up. Several passengers were jarred out of their seats. The DC-3 had to abort its landing and go around again."

I just took it all in. I was the senior officer; I was responsible. I saw my career enter a screaming, uncontrollable nosedive.

"I have no idea what I'm supposed to do with you, Bruce. Report back to me in the morning."

I spent a very miserable night in the bachelor officers quarters and the North Island Officers' Club and I made all the pilots in my group at least as miserable. When I reported back to Colonel Moore's office at 0800 with a pulsing hangover, I fully expected to meet the defense counsel Sad Sam had surely appointed by then to defend me at my court martial.

But Sam was calm. If not quite back to the affable personality I knew, he was downright friendly in comparison with our last meeting. He even offered me a chair.

After reviewing every detail he had learned since the previous afternoon, he said, "Well, I think we've got this cleared up. We made a passle of excuses, and the civilians have agreed not to file any notice on you or the squadron at this time. I think it will all blow over, so you're in the clear. But, Bruce, for Christ's sake, keep your pilots in line. And never do it again!"

"Sir!"

29

We were nominally assigned to the new escort carrier, *Block Island II*, which was fitting out for her first cruise at San Diego. However, since the ship was in port and we were not fully trained for carrier operations, we entered a period of intensive simulated carrier operations. In fact, all of our initial work consisted of simulated carrier landings at various airfields: Goleta, Mines Field, El Centro, and even others. I have no idea why we moved around so much. In the end, I'm sure we did more simulated carrier landings than any other Marine fighter pilots of the period. That was because we would eventually be landing on small carrier decks at night; we had to get the preliminaries exactly right. We also spent some time keeping up our night-flying skills, but the real emphasis was overwhelmingly on simulated carrier landings, including progressively more difficult night landings, and catapult takeoffs at Mines Field.

I took ten days leave at Christmas to see my parents and get set for New Year's Eve. I frankly needed a little time away from my Hellcat and the cares and woes of training. To get home, I simply signed out an SNB and flew myself and several passengers to El Toro. There, I checked out a car and driver for the 50-mile drive to Los Angeles.

On the morning of December 26, I checked into the Ambassador Hotel on Wilshire Boulevard. That was the place to bump into Marine pilots. Thus, that very morning, I received a message to call

Captain Ed Dunnigan, who had trained with VMF(N)-544 at Cherry Point but who had been detached before we flew out to the West Coast.

Ed was a wild sort of a guy whom I had had a hand in keeping out of trouble when he was serving under me at Cherry Point. So, when a young-sounding female answered the phone, I assumed she was Ed's live-in lover. I made a ribald comment, but Ed came back so fast with a protest that I immediately believed that she was indeed "just someone I know."

Ed and I talked on the phone for a while, then we agreed to meet at the Ambassador Bar that afternoon.

I was a little late for the date, so when I arrived I found Ed at a little side table with a stunning brunette he introduced as Patricia Leimert, the girl who had answered the phone. I became convinced again that Ed and Pat had something going.

Somewhere after the preliminaries, Ed sort of dropped out of the conversation, and I focused all my attention on Pat. I found out that she was nineteen, which seemed a million years younger than I could remember ever being, and that she was a college sophomore studying anthropology at UCLA. From that news arose some light banter based on the old crosstown rivalry between her school and mine, USC.

I found myself totally captivated by this young woman.

Pat was, of course, under the legal drinking age, and the waiter proved to be stodgy in that regard. Ed and I drank up and agreed to move across Wilshire Boulevard to the Brown Derby, which I was pretty sure would look the other way in Pat's behalf. I was right; the party went on, and my affinity with Pat seemed to grow by the minute.

At first, I was leery of making a move on Pat because she had arrived with Ed Dunnigan. Soon, however, it became clear that there really was nothing going on in that quarter; Ed was a friend of a friend who just happened to be staying over at Pat's mother's house in Beverly Hills. Pat was just showing Ed around town for the day. That seemed to be the last roadblock.

Since we were both Los Angeles kids, Pat and I began playing "who do you know." We came up with a lot of mutual acquaintances. One, Jack Armitage, had been a year behind me at Los Angeles High. Pat told me that Jack, who was a top city football player, had joined the Marine Corps and was an infantry lieutenant serving with a rifle company. It also turned out that Pat's brother, Tim, was a war correspondent, and her mother, Lucille, was the gossip columnist for the *Los Angeles Times*.

★

I saw a great deal of Pat during the rest of the week, and I even met her mother, a very active, attractive lady with whom I became fast friends at the first meeting.

Pat and I spent December 31, 1944, at the Beach Club in Santa Monica. With us were my good friend Major Bob Baker, the VMF-121 ace who had insulted Generals Vandegrift and Geiger in the shower at Knucklehead, and his wife, Dorothy.

The afternoon was winding off toward dinnertime when Bill Summers, a Seabee and an old friend of Pat's, joined us for a drink. Bill, who knew all the movie people, asked us where we were headed to celebrate New Year's Eve. Pat told him we planned to hit a few of the night spots but that we had nothing special planned.

"Well," Bill offered, "I just spoke with Constance Bennett, who is having a little get-together at Darryl Zanuck's house, out at the Malibu colony. I know that she would love to have you come by. Why don't you tell me when you're ready to leave, and I'll call Constance back to tell her you'll be coming over."

I was a little taken aback by this, and Bake and Dorothy were simply aghast. Darryl Zanuck? Constance Bennett? Malibu?

I was a Los Angeles native and thus used to hearing about such things, but this was still a bit much for me. A squadron of Zeros could not have kept me away from the "get-together" at the Zanuck bungalow.

We finished our drinks, thanked Bill Summers for making the call, and headed up the coast to the Malibu colony, which is about ten miles north of Santa Monica, just off Highway 1.

Bill was as good as his word. The colony gatekeeper expected us and gave us detailed directions to the Zanuck bungalow. And when we arrived, a beaming Constance Bennett answered the door and ushered us into the den. We were introduced to Gregory Ratoff, the actor and producer, with whom Constance had been playing cards when we arrived. Ratoff, who was feeling no pain, lurched over to shake hands with Bake and me, and to embrace Pat and Dorothy. By that time, Constance was back with a full, unopened Haig and Haig "Pinch" bottle, one of 1944's rarest commodities.

Bake and I were fixing a round of drinks when our host, Darryl Zanuck, appeared. He was wearing a bathrobe and slippers, which I later found out was his typical uniform of the day away from the studio.

It was a thoroughly charming evening, and we were warmly accepted—I am sure for Lucille Leimert's sake—into this very top echelon of movie people.

We guests were at a loss when someone brought up the subject of how we were going to spend the remainder of our time that night. But Constance had the solution. "Jack Benny is having a big party at his home in Beverly Hills. Why don't you all go there? I know you'll be welcome; just tell them that I sent you. It will be pretty formal, but Bruce and Bob are in uniform."

Bake and I were indeed dressed in our Marine green uniforms, complete with Wings of Gold and award ribbons. This was considered formal attire during the war.

And so we headed back to Beverly Hills.

★

For all of Jack Benny's public displays of crying poor, the house in Beverly Hills was something far more than opulent. And it was filled with formally attired revelers helping themselves from a lavish spread.

When we entered, our host was speaking with several people beside the door, but he nodded a friendly hello and motioned the butler, who took our overseas caps.

We stood in the foyer for a moment, trying to recognize anyone we knew in the sea of faces. My glance fell upon a man in the uniform of a Marine Corps first lieutenant. I saw the Wings of Gold before I recognized the face. It was Tyrone Power, whom I had met earlier in the year at Cherry Point, where he was flying transports. We had formed a friendship and had even gone out on a few double dates. (Needless to say, Tyrone's only problem with women was selecting only one at a time from crowds of admirers.)

My eyes tracked around the table at which Tyrone was seated. Next to him was Captain Clark Gable of the Army Air Forces. He was in uniform, complete with combat ribbons. And next to him was Caesar Romero, who was wearing the uniform of a Merchant Marine officer.

I guided Pat toward Tyrone, and Bake and Dorothy followed. As soon as Tyrone recognized me, he threw his arm around my shoulder, shook hands with Bake, and introduced us around to Gable and Romero. The conversation turned immediately to air combat. Bake and I dazzled them with tales of our heroic exploits, and Clark Gable told us, in very modest terms, about his duty as an intelligence officer with a B-17 group in England. However, he did not tell us that he had flown as a volunteer aerial gunner on several dangerous bombing missions, which was well outside anything expected of an overage group intelligence officer. It also turned out that Caesar Romero had seen duty aboard Merchant Marine transports in the Pacific. He had even been at Tarawa in late 1943. I was thoroughly impressed by the stars' low-key presentation of the facts surrounding their wartime service.

We were easing our way into an extremely good time when a large man in a blue serge suit suddenly loomed over the table. Beside him was Mary Livingston, Jack Benny's wife. I was really taken aback when the big man—a security guard—ordered us to leave. I explained that Darryl Zanuck and Constance Bennett had urged us to attend the party, but Mary Livingston launched into a tirade about Constance and firmly held out the fact that she had not invited us into her home. At that point, Clark Gable and Tyrone Power jumped in. But I had had enough. I was still a kid of 24, but I had learned a bit about dignity in the service. I held up my hand in the way I am sure only a Marine officer can command total attention. The immediate arena became instantly quiet, and I calmly thanked Mary Livingston for allowing us to stay for as long she had.

"I'm sorry if we put much of a dent in your liquor supply, Ma'am. I'll be happy to pay for what we consumed."

By that time, a visibly horrified Jack Benny had shouldered through the crowd. He heard what I had to say and turned on his wife to ask that she change her mind. But she stood her ground. And it was *her* ground, so Dorothy, Pat, Bake, and I shook hands with our new friends and left.

We finished the evening with John Russell, an actor who had enlisted in the Marine Corps at the start of the war but who had been discharged because of severe wounds he had received at Guadalcanal. Pat and I and John and his date celebrated the arrival of 1945 at a small club Pat knew would let her in. In the end, we had a pretty good time of it.

When we arrived home in the morning, Pat told her mother about our run-in with Mary Livingston. This gave Lucille a pretty good laugh. She had been a top ballerina in the late 1920s and had worked with Mary Livingston.

I had no part in it beyond filling in some of the details on New Year's morning, but Lucille launched a brief campaign against Mary Livingston. First, she called her good friend, Hedda Hopper, who conducted a 15-minute national radio program and wrote a syndicated column devoted to Hollywood goings-on. Hedda really blasted our wouldn't-be hostess.

Lucille wrote in her "Confidentially" column in the *Los Angeles Times* of January 14, 1945:

"*Faux Pas*—Do a certain widely known couple, whose war activities are frequently mentioned in the press, know that they turned out of their home a war hero and his girl friend? It happened that this young pair were guests of a colonel (retired) and his wife, who assumed that you usually can bring almost anyone to a Hollywood party, and so invited the youngsters to accompany them to this home where several hundred guests were lavishly provided for.

"*Strange Welcome*—The young man, a 24-year-old major, was being greeted by his friend, Clark Gable, when a man in a blue serge suit tapped him on the shoulder and showed him the front door. The hostess, following, said to the plainclothes man, "I told you to be careful who comes in here. Our friends don't look like THAT!" "I hope we didn't put a dent in your refreshments," said the major on leaving. The major, recently back from the South Pacific, had 10 Jap planes to his credit and owns two rows of decoration ribbons, which he never wears. But how could the hostess know? The nearest she ever came to a hero was to have her picture taken with one!"

Thank goodness Lucille kept my name out of that!

★

Pat Leimert and I became engaged in late January, 1945. I would have married her then, but I still harbored some bad feelings from my earlier rush to marital bliss. I knew that I was going back to fight, so I postponed the wedding until my safe return.

30

My half-squadron of night fighters reassembled at El Centro a few days into the new year to resume our boring routine of simulated carrier landings. I was by then quite concerned that we were overdoing our training; I had seen trainees get cocky from too much practice before the real thing, and I knew that the upcoming "real thing" had to be undertaken at peak awareness.

I made my feelings known, but nothing happened. I soon learned that the extra training had been laid on simply because our carrier was not yet ready to undertake flight operations; we were just marking time. So, as soon as we all reported in, we went back to work on simulated carrier landings. The whole month of January passed in this manner. The only break in the routine came in the form of several night missions designed to rehone our night interception skills, or perhaps to pacify me.

Finally, on February 1, 1945, our landing signal officer announced—long overdue, I thought—that we were all ready to try an actual landing aboard our escort carrier, *Block Island II*.

On February 2, my half of VMF(N)-544 was redesignated and made a part of VMF-511, the half-squadron of Corsairs with which we would be sharing the carrier. I found myself very sad to be officially leaving VMF(N)-544, which I had helped form and mold. I actually found myself immersed in self-doubt over my earlier decision to form the carrier-based night-fighter contingent, but my reasons were selfish. I was sure that 544 would soon be in the war and

that I would be stranded on the West Coast making practice landings for the rest of the war. As it turned out, VMF(N)-544 was still
in the States when the war ended.

Added to my ill feelings was a profound disappointment. I was
designated executive officer of VMF-511 and night-fighter flight
leader. The squadron skipper, whom I had met at early briefings,
was Major Bob Maze, a former ground officer who had converted to
fighters well after the start of the war. The group commander
aboard *Block Island II* was Lieutenant Colonel John Dobbin, a
highly respected fighter pilot who had served his first combat tours
at Midway and Guadalcanal. Rounding out our carrier air group
was a contingent of nine TBM Avenger torpedo bombers under
Major Bob Vaupell, another Guadalcanal veteran who had graduated from Pensacola two classes behind me.

★

The big event was scheduled for February 5, 1945. On that date,
the ship, which was then berthed at North Island, would sail up the
coast and meet us about 60 miles off Santa Barbara. As we would
henceforth be permanently stationed aboard the carrier, we packed
our gear and sent it off to North Island with our ground echelon.
Then we flew to North Island on the afternoon of February 4 to join
the air group. We also put our Hellcats through final maintenance
checks.

We launched from North Island late the next morning, well
after the TBMs and F4Us had flown off. I led the Hellcats aloft,
circled the base once, and flew out on a straight-line compass heading to meet *Block Island II*, which had left the harbor the previous
evening.

It was apparent from 10,000 feet that the sea was quite rough
that day. For all the countless approaches and landings we had conducted over the past boring months, every one of us well knew that
we had been landing on solid, unmoving ground. We had been prepared, as much as possible, for the reality that a carrier deck moves
up and down and from side to side even in the calmest seas. The
extent to which it moves is governed in part by ship handling, but
for the most part movement is in direct proportion to the roughness
of the waters in which the ship is traveling.

I had no doubt about my flying skills; I was one helluva of a
pilot. And so were my squadronmates. But despite my success at

every flying chore I had ever taken on, I still harbored a feeling that carrier landings would wind up killing me. I thus approached the rendezvous with an outsized feeling of trepidation.

I began the approach at 10,000 feet as soon as I visually acquired the carrier and reported my presence to the air boss, a Navy commander. My mind immediately went into overdrive. My first clear thought was that the flight deck looked to be about the size of a postage stamp. As I got lower it got bigger, but never bigger than a mere cork bobbing in a huge swell. Then I was prematurely terrorized by the entire notion of landing on such a small deck at night, but I stifled that notion as utterly premature; I reasoned that I had to live through day landings before I would be given an opportunity to kill myself in a night landing.

As I spiraled lower and led my two divisions into the traffic circle, I ruthlessly thrust all irrelevant thoughts from my mind. I relied on my training and placed my life in the hands of the Landing Signal Officer, Captain Marshall "Stork" Tutton, a 6'4"-tall Guadalcanal veteran and Corsair pilot who happened to be the younger brother of my old friend and cadet classmate, Stan Tutton.

★

In its essence, a carrier landing consists of a sequence of the following phases: while the carrier sails at top speed into the wind, the airplane lowers its tail hook and approaches the carrier flight deck from dead astern; guided by the LSO, the pilot lines up on the flight deck at just the right altitude and speed and enters what can only be described as a controlled stall; if the LSO is satisfied that the airplane is in the correct position vis a vis the deck, he signals the pilot to land; if the airplane is not in the correct position and cannot be guided into "the groove" in the time remaining, the LSO will wave it off for another try; if the pilot is allowed to land, he drops quickly to the deck with the intention of catching the extended tail hook on any of the five stout cables running the width of the deck; if the tail hook catches a cable, the cable gives a bit while the airplane is forced to a rapid stop; if the tail hook misses all the cables, and if the deck is clear, the pilot simply guns the engine and takes off for another try; if the tail hook misses the cable and the deck is obstructed, the nose of the plane is arrested by a flexible barrier, which will usually ruin the propeller but will prevent a flaming collision between the airplane and whatever obstructions lie ahead.

On the day of our first carrier landings, each night fighter would begin its final approach only if the deck was completely clear from the previous landing. We anticipated a fair number of wave-offs and missed cables; we had plenty of fuel and plenty of time. It was heartening to know that all the TBMs and F4Us had landed without casualties or serious mishap.

Only the LSO could determine when an approaching pilot was ready for the carrier. Stork Tutton, himself a qualified pilot, had been working with us for many weeks. In that time, he had learned to anticipate each approaching pilot's typical response to any signal he gave with his two outstretched luminous paddles.

I licked my lips and went over part of the litany again: A one-second delay in cutting the throttle makes the difference between a normal cable-arrested landing and a crash on the flight deck. Never touch the throttle until safely on the deck. If you miss the cables, immediately push the throttle forward to acquire lift-off speed. If the airplane is properly arrested, cut power to the absolute minimum and taxi off as soon as the hook and the cable have been separated by a deck crewman.

★

My stomach was doing flipflops.

I had been an active competitive athlete at USC, on both the swimming and water polo teams. I had weathered numerous competitions, and I had long ago learned the signs of a parasympathetic nervous reaction—anxiety, tightness in the stomach, perspiring hands, dry throat, shortness of breath, pounding heart, momentary lightheadedness. And that is precisely what I felt as I put myself in position to become the first of the night-fighter pilots to land on tiny, bobbing, pitching *Block Island II*.

I well realized that there was no way I could take a wave-off and retain my hitherto unassailable reputation as the red-hot combat fighter pilot.

I concentrated everything I had on altitude, attitude, propeller pitch, throttle setting, landing gear, flaps, tail hook, the rapidly approaching LSO, and the tossing, twisting postage-stamp-sized flight deck.

I saw Stork standing tall in front of his protective windscreen on the right aft corner of the flight deck. I had once naively asked him what the screen was for and had received a sarcastic answer that the ship would be doing 18-20 knots, which, combined with a wind-speed factor of anywhere from zero miles per hour to infinity, usually created enough of a breeze to pitch a sturdy LSO into the drink. I was also told that the dark-colored screen aids the pilot in finding and following the motions of the LSO, who was invariably clad in light-colored clothing.

On the far side of the screen was the LSO's assistant. It was his job to see if my tail hook, landing gear, and flaps were down. If so, he would yell above the wind, right into Stork's ear, "All clear." Then he would turn to watch the deck as I hurtled past the LSO platform into the cable.

Unlike many other LSOs, who waved their paddles with a great deal of energetic flair, Stork passed the standard thirteen landing signals in a straightforward manner (which utterly belied the warped if lovable personality he displayed when not doing his job). Ten of the signals told the pilot of some specific error in technique or procedure—wrong height, wings not level, approach speed too fast or too slow, even that the tail hook was not deployed or the main landing gear was not down. The remaining three signals were "Roger", "Cut," and "Wave-off."

I wanted a Roger on the first pass. If I was correctly lined up, Stork would hold his paddles straight out from his shoulders to signify that I was "in the groove," that the approach was satisfactory.

I got the desired Roger and blurted "Hot dog!" into the open radio channel.

As my Hellcat hovered in several feet over the fantail, Stork abruptly slashed his right paddle across his throat and dropped his left arm to his side. That was Cut.

I immediately chopped back my throttle and held the stick rock steady. The Hellcat was now in a perfect three-point landing attitude, which meant that all three wheels would strike the deck at the same instant.

I nearly panicked in the second between the final maneuver and the thud of my landing gear on the solid wooden deck. It was all I could do to keep myself from pouring on the coals and getting back in the air, where I *knew* I was safer.

Things happened fast from that point, as my mind came out of hyperdrive. There was literally nothing for me to do; the laws of physics were running the show.

I felt the tail hook grab hold of the wire. It was the first wire, so the landing was perfect! My shoulder straps took all the strain of my own forward momentum as the mass of the Hellcat rapidly decelerated and came to an abrupt no-brakes near stop. Immediately, the tension on the arresting cable eased, and the Hellcat's remaining momentum pulled it forward about 40 feet with the hook still attached. This brought the fighter to a slow, controlled stop. At that point, I came under the direction of the deck crew and plane handlers.

No more than five seconds had passed from Stork's Cut to the rolling stop.

Once the pressure was off the hook, I and my Hellcat became the center of furious activity. A quick glance into my rearview mirror revealed a deck crewman in a bright-colored jersey ducking beneath the tail to release the hook from the cable. At almost the same instant, another deck crewman in a jersey of another color took charge of my taxi routine by passing up his unique set of signals. First, on signal, I retracted the tail hook. Then I had to get lined up with the centerline of the deck to get into taxi position. The vertical barrier, which looks like a large tennis net and is raised for all landings, had been dropped as soon as my hook caught the cable. The instant my tail wheel was clear of the barrier, it was raised again in preparation for the next landing.

I knew that, as soon as I was clear of the barrier, the LSO's assistant, who was by then standing with his back to Stork, would turn aft and yell "All clear" into Stork's ear.

If the recovery operation is perfect, the succeeding airplane will be in position to take the Cut just as the previous airplane clears the deck barrier. We were not trying for perfection this time, so the intervals between the landings were longer than standard.

The Wave-off had to be passed to two or three of my boys as the Hellcats felt their way into the groove one after another. To pass this signal, Stork simply waved both paddles over his head. The wave-off has the force of absolute law. Even if the pilot is in fact right in the groove and lined up for a perfect landing, he must obey the wave-off signal, as there might be an emergency beyond the pilot's knowledge or range of senses—such as an imminent enemy attack.

★

Once all the night fighters were safely aboard, we all took a break while our airplanes were refueled. In order to become "carrier qualified," we each had to complete five landings.

There was no way I was going to allow myself and my pilots to undertake night carrier landings until we were all one hundred percent proficient in day operations. I was tired of simulated operations, but this was not a simulation.

Since we were the last group element aboard, my night fighters went to the front of the line, and we all quickly qualified with our five landings. As soon as I was relieved of flight duties, I went up to the LSO's platform on the fantail to stand beside Stork Tutton and watch first the unqualified Corsair pilots and then the unqualified TBM pilots run their landings.

Between landings, Stork pointed out his—and my—only avenue of escape in the event an incoming plane looked as though it were going to crash on the fantail. A large net hung out over the wake of the ship ten feet below the level of the flight deck. If Stork felt the need to clear out, he could only go into the net, or overboard, depending on his aim.

The humdrum of the day's routine was heightened considerably by the plight of one of Major Bob Vaupell's Avenger pilots. The kid had managed to get aboard okay on his first-ever carrier landing that morning, but he had also managed to let his imagination work him into a state of terror by the time he came around for his second landing of the day, his second ever.

The youngster was having a bad time getting into the groove. On his first approach, he came in too steep and looked from my vantagepoint beside Stork to be diving on the ship. Stork could not correct the kid in time, so he waved him off. Several TBMs got in safely, and then the young pilot with the problem lined up for his second approach.

Stork had to wave him off again. As the big, lumbering TBM passed only a few feet from the LSO platform, both Stork and I chanced to see the face of the radioman—one of three men aboard the airplane. The young enlisted Marine was peering out of a porthole with a very sad expression on his face.

The air officer then told Stork to belay landing the last TBM while the other eight torpedo bombers flew off to undertake their third qualification landings.

Following the launch and rendezvous, the TBMs approached one by one. Most made it in; one or two had to be waved off. Then Stork faced the third approach of the kid who had already been waved off twice.

I am sure the combination of bad dreams and two consecutive wave-offs had totally destroyed that youngster's confidence. The next approach—and four or five after it—was totally erratic. The boy overcorrected at every subtle motion of Stork's paddles. He kept getting worse. His radioman's expression of concern deepened, and his skin grew increasingly pallid.

My ribald comments, and Stork's, gave way to expressions of concern each time that particular TBM hove into view over the ship's wake. As the hours passed, he wound up being the only member of the entire air group who had not yet qualified. Indeed, he had not completed his second landing. We were by then less concerned about qualifying him than we were about getting him and his crew down alive.

It was beginning to get dark when a young seaman came down from the air officer's perch on the carrier's superstructure with a written message. Stork looked at it and passed it to me. It read, "Get the son of a bitch aboard right now!"

I looked at Stork and Stork looked at me. Then, in unspoken agreement, we looked down at the escape net to gauge our chances of hitting it on our one and only try. Together. I should have left then, but I felt I had to stay to lend my moral support.

The TBM appeared over the ship's wake and slowly dropped into the groove. The distant approach was wobbly and, if anything, less certain than all the ones that had gone before. I tried to imagine myself at the controls, and I forced my mind to send clear messages aloft to the suffering pilot. The near approach was a bit more settled than any up to that point, but he was a bit high, and one of his wings was lower than the other. Stork had to make an instant decision. He knew the kid was tired and anxious, and I think Stork was, too. The approach was on the high side of marginal, but it was as close to perfect as the young pilot had gotten that day.

I felt rather than saw Stork hold both paddles straight out. Roger! The TBM began to straighten out, but it was still high and it had run out of space. Then I felt Stork's emphatic Cut.

The huge single-engine bomber, capable of carrying three crewmen in spacious luxury and four 500-lb bombs or one huge aerial torpedo in its internal bomb bay, fell out of the sky. Stork and I both leaned over the edge of the deck in the direction of the safety net. I cannot speak for Stork, but the only thing that held my fearful body on the platform was curiosity. I had to see how it turned out.

The pilot overcorrected at the last possible millisecond and liter-ally bounced that big airplane over the first four arresting cables. I was there. I saw it all. I can think of no reason why the tail hook indeed plucked the last of the stout cables and abruptly came to rest.

The big airplane had not even cleared the barrier when a hatch flew open and the radioman popped out onto the flight deck. His legs had started windmilling while he was still in midair, and he was going, going, gone the instant his feet gained traction on the wooden deck.

I have no doubts that the story about the radioman's refusal ever to fly again were true. I had made five perfect landings that day, and I doubted if *I* ever wanted to fly again after seeing what I had seen.

★

The next eight days—with no time off—were spent in intensive carrier flight operations. We flew routine day patrols—no night work yet!—and worked out formation procedures with the F4Us and TBMs. In general, we tried everything we would normally be expected to undertake on our upcoming war cruise.

February 14, 1945—Valentine's Day—was to be a sort of gradua-tion day. The entire group was to mount two mock airstrikes against Channel Island, a small outcropping off Santa Barbara. We would make the first strike in the morning, land for refueling and rearming, and head out again as soon as the warplanes were ready to go. This was as much a test of the ship's air department as it was of the Marine carrier air group.

Nine each of our group's Corsairs, Avengers and Hellcats—every operational airplane aboard—got airborne without a hitch and ren-dezvoused near the carrier to form up into an attack wing. The flight was made through worsening weather, but the strike, com-plete with live bombing and strafing passes, went off precisely as planned.

We had had a weather brief before launching; there was no indi-cation then that we would be facing bad weather, so we did not pay too much attention to it until we started back for the carrier. By then, the sky was slate gray and filled with rapidly moving storm clouds. And the flying conditions continued to deteriorate.

Visibility deteriorated to the point where the 27 Marine warplanes formed into line astern—an extended, staggered formation in
which all the aircraft flew off the wings of the airplanes on either
side. The aim was to visually cover as much ocean as possible. The
only rule was that every pilot remain in visual contact with the
airplanes on his left and right. The first man to spot the carrier
could be counted on to sing out over the net to let everyone know.

As the weather continued to deteriorate, we droned on for what
seemed like an inordinate period. Finally, the carrier was spotted
and we lined up to land. Stork smoothly reeled us all in without
delay or loss.

I had originally planned to head directly for the ready room to
brief for the second strike, but I could not imagine flying into the
murk again. I headed for my compartment to change out of my
flight suit.

I had just pulled the long front zipper down when I heard my
name blared out over the shipboard speaker system. I was to report
to the Combat Intelligence Center on the operations deck of the
tower.

The group commander, Lieutenant Colonel John Dobbin, col-
lared me as soon as I entered the CIC compartment. "Bruce, I need
your opinion. You're the senior night-fighter pilot aboard; can you
lead the second strike on instruments? What do you think about the
weather?"

I told the CO exactly what I thought of the notion of flying in
such weather if there was not an absolute need. Weather such as
this, in tandem with my former cockiness, had nearly killed me at
least three times in less than a year.

Dobbin agreed with me and led me to the bridge so he could tell
the captain of the ship, Captain Massey Hughes, that he recommended aborting the training mission. Hughes was an oldtime
naval aviator who had flown a PBY patrol bomber out of Midway
during the big battle in June, 1942. He had a good reputation. He
listened to the group commander and patiently heard me out as
well. I told him that the weather seemed to be coming from inland
and had deteriorated with awesome speed. I pointed out through
the bridge weather screen and observed aloud that it was twice as
bad out there as when I had landed minutes earlier.

The captain told John Dobbin and me to return to the CIC compartment while he sought an updated meteorological report. I was
stunned when word arrived that the second strike would go off as
planned.

The airplanes were quickly refueled and rearmed, and all pilots were ordered to the ready rooms for final briefings. Then the loudspeakers blared the familiar, "All pilots, man your planes."

I climbed into my cockpit and strapped in. Then I ran the engine up and distractedly checked the magnetos. There was a fault. My Hellcat had to be scrubbed from the mission. We had a spare Hellcat stored below deck, but the flight and hangar decks were overcrowded and the spare was in no condition to fly. I would have to sit this one out. I cut the engine and allowed the plane handlers to scoot me out of the way.

As it happened, only 18 of our 27 warplanes got airborne, an odd mixture of TBMs, F6Fs and F4Us. Even Bob Maze, the VMF-511 skipper, had had to shut down because of an engine malfunction. The senior pilot aloft was Major Bob Vaupell, the TBM commander.

Bob Maze and I joined John Dobbin in the CIC compartment to follow the progress of the raid. Normally, I would have been angered by the magneto problem that had left me deckbound. But not this day. My keenly felt trepidation over the safety of my fellow aviators was more than recompensed by my personal relief.

Soon, reports from the strike group revealed that the weather over the target was far, far worse than my direst predictions. Several F4U and TBM pilots reported that they had become separated from the group and asked for a heading to the ship. The weather over us was so bad by then that it was difficult to offer a good radar fix.

At last, Captain Hughes ordered the strike group to abort and return to the ship or head for Goleta or whatever airfields on the coast they could get in to.

A great hand reached down and squeezed my soul. I knew that we would be losing some friends today. Bob Maze and John Dobbin registered similar feelings of dismay; it was graven on their ashen faces and obvious in their sagging shoulders.

All of the night fighters got down safely; they were as much in their element in bad weather as they were in the dark. Several even managed to find the carrier.

Of the 18 airplanes aloft that terrible Wednesday afternoon, a total of eleven landed safely, on the carrier or at bases on the coast.

That left two F4Us and five TBMs carrying a total of 17 Marine pilots and crewmen. One by one, they or others reported in. First, two F4U pilots were killed when their planes collided as they attempted to make simultaneous emergency landings on Channel Island. Then a TBM pilot killed himself and his two crewmen when his emergency water landing near Channel Island went awry. A second TBM cracked up during a blind approach on a coastal airbase, but the pilot and crewmen were rescued despite their injuries. Then two TBMs made bumpy water landings; all six crewmen were injured, but all were soon rescued. Soon, all but one of the strike planes, the last TBM, were accounted for. The tally so far was five killed and nine injured.

The last TBM, with Major Bob Vaupell at the controls, flew inland through the bad weather until its fuel gave out. Bob must have had no idea where we was, for he crashed into the ground, killing himself and his crewmen, near the desert farming town of Bakersfield.

Thus, eight Marines were killed and nine were hospitalized.

As soon as I awoke the next morning, I gave in to a compulsion and ran up to the flight deck to see about the weather. It was one the finest mornings I have ever experienced—absolutely perfect flying weather. I was physically ill.

An immediate board of inquiry totally absolved Captain Hughes and laid all of the deaths and injuries to pilot error.

The air group was so badly depleted that all the survivors were immediately reassigned to Goleta to train replacements.

★

Compounding my cycle of grief was news about a week later describing the loss of my dear friend and flight-training classmate, Jack Amende, then commander of VMF-217, which was stationed aboard the carrier *Wasp*. Jack's F4U had been shot up by a Zero on February 16 following a raid on a Japanese airbase near Tokyo in support of the Iwo Jima landings, 800 miles to the south. His smoking fighter had left formation and was never seen again. Though Jack was officially listed as Missing in Action, the unofficial word on the pilots' grapevine was that he must have crashed into the sea.

No one ever saw Jack Amende again.

PART V

Ace!

31

Our carrier air group, MCVG-1, operated out of Goleta until March 16, 1945, when we were ordered back to North Island to board *Block Island II* for a wartime cruise to Hawaii and points unknown.

I was very anxious to get back into the Pacific. The war against Japan was going exceedingly well. Our ground forces had captured Iwo Jima in the Volcano Islands, and our air forces were already at work bombing the Japanese home islands. While everyone was certain that the eventual invasion of Japan would drag all available hands into the war, there was always the chance that the Japanese military leaders might capitulate early. I had set a personal goal of at least five confirmed kills—thus elevating me to "ace" status. I well realized that I might never even *see* the two remaining Japanese airplanes I needed to destroy, but that was beyond my control. I felt to the core of my being that I would score the two kills if only I could lay my gunsights on the two required targets.

As things turned out, that is exactly what happened. But it took no end of work and worry to get to that point.

★

The carrier finally pulled out of San Diego harbor on March 22, 1945, and shaped course for Hawaii.

As the ship was preparing to leave the dock late in the morning, I joined Major Bob Maze topside for a last look at San Diego. I was absently watching a destroyer escort race across the harbor when Bob finally broke a long mutual silence. "Hey, Bruce, I just realized that the last time you pulled out of here was around this time in 1942. Right?"

"Sure was, Bob. February, 1942. I was just thinking about that." I had indeed just flashed on those terrifying early war days. "I guess a lot of water has passed over the dam since then. I've lost a few good friends who were on that trip." I vividly saw Jack Amende's smiling face. And Louis Gordon's. Together with Jeff Poindexter and me, we had been the Fearsome Foursome. Now, only Jeff and I were left. And both of us faced new perils in the Pacific, I in night fighters and Jeff as skipper of a day-fighter squadron.

Bob and I looked out over the flight deck and to the blue Pacific as far out as the horizon. Beneath us, the tugboats were gathering strength to boost us out on our own. I heard one of them pipe a call on its steam whistle; to me, at that moment, it sounded like a lament.

★

As with all carrier air groups at sea, even in 1945, we all flew routine combat air and antisubmarine patrols throughout the voyage. However, there were no night landings or takeoffs. No one in the squadron was yet qualified to undertake night carrier operations.

As we were nearing Hawaii, our group commander, Lieutenant Colonel John Dobbin, called me to his office for a briefing. At that time, I learned that the entire group would be temporarily attached to the combat training unit at Barber's Point for a final course before we shipped out to join the "division" of four escort carriers to which we had been operationally assigned. The first question I blurted out naturally had to do with our overdue night carrier qualifications. The group commander held up his hand and calmly got to the point.

My night fighters would be attached to the newly activated Night Fighter Combat Training Unit, a joint Navy-Marine Corps venture. There, we would be taken under the wing of VF(N)-41, a blooded all-Navy unit commanded by Commander Turner Caldwell. Dobbin explained that he knew Caldwell from their days together at Guadalcanal—the dark, early days when air operations had been menacing to everyone involved. At that time—late August through early October, 1942—Dobbin had been exec of VMF-224, and Caldwell had commanded a detachment of eleven *Enterprise* SBD Dauntless dive-bombers, which had been marooned during the carrier battle in the Eastern Solomons.

VF(N)-79 had had a marvelous cruise as part of light carrier *Independence*'s Air Group 41 between September, 1944, and January, 1945. In ample air action over the Philippines and Formosa, the night-fighter squadron had scored kills and, more important to me, had ironed out an adequate doctrine to govern carrier-based night-fighter operations.

At our very first meeting during my first hours at Barbers Point, I was struck by one rather telling point a steward's mate managed to get in. He described carrier night-fighter operations as "a new experiment in suicide." Much later, he told an interviewer, "Man was never made to fly, no how. And if he was made to fly, he was never made to fly off a ship. And if he was made to fly off a ship, he was never made to fly off a ship at night." I never felt any different.

★

As *Block Island II* neared Hawaii on the morning of March 27, 1945, the air group assembled in the ready room for prelaunch instructions. We were to launch in 30 minutes and, as was the long-standing custom, fly directly to our ground base while the carrier tied up empty of her air complement.

With that, the announcement "Pilots, man your planes" came over the loudspeaker, and we raced to the flight deck. Within minutes, the carrier turned her bows into the wind, and we launched. I spiralled up to 10,000 feet and orbited there while my eight Hellcats joined up in their two divisions. The Corsairs were above us by a few thousand feet, and the TBMs were beneath our wings. As soon as the Corsairs peeled out, I took my heading to Barbers Point and followed them in.

It took us all of 90 minutes to sight our objective and another 30 minutes to fly across Diamond Head and Waikiki and get down. As soon as I landed and taxied to the dispersal area, I was picked up by a jeep and taken to meet Navy Captain John Griffin, the CO of our night-fighter "finishing" school. I had already been briefed on Griffin. He was one of the Navy's earliest radar officers and had served as an ad hoc fighter direction officer aboard *Enterprise* during some of the critical early battles off Guadalcanal.

Our schedule allowed us only the briefest stay at Barbers Point. Following a lecture by Captain Griffin and a meeting with Commander Caldwell, we were given the day and evening off. The next morning, we would reman our Hellcats and fly out to the escort carrier *Tripoli*. Our final training phase would begin in earnest as soon as we were aboard *Tripoli*. The news made the hair on the back of my neck stand on end. Did I hear correctly? Did he say we were going to conduct night operations from a strange carrier with a strange Landing Signal Officer? I was a Marine major and he was a Navy captain, so I bit back my feelings and uttered a formula response.

★

We launched on schedule, rendezvoused at 8,000 feet, and flew out on the supplied bearing toward the big island of Hawaii, where *Tripoli* was sailing in circles waiting for us. I managed to circle over Pearl Harbor, trying to imagine the scenes of destruction that had greeted the eyes of the first carrier pilots to fly in on the afternoon of December 7, 1941. A clear image of that bustling base lying in ruin was beyond my imagination.

We headed straight up our bearing for a full hour, at which point I spotted the flight deck we were seeking. I switched on my VHF transmitter, tuned in the correct channel, and requested permission to land.

We wheeled overhead in the by-then familiar oblong "racetrack" pattern with 40-second intervals between the nine Hellcats. As was the case for all nine of us, I ran through my prelanding checklist: Canopy back and locked (for quick escape in the event I somehow hit the water), shoulder harness tight (to keep my face from colliding with the instrument panel in the event of a too-abrupt stop on deck or on the waves), fuel on rich mixture (for immediate added power if I suddenly needed to fly away from the groove), fuel coming in from the fullest internal tank (so my engine would not suddenly die from fuel starvation while my mind was on other matters), cowl flaps partly open (to keep the engine cool), prop in low pitch at 2400 RPM (so I could bite the maximum amount of air at the low landing speed).

I was ready to land.

As the flight leader, I was to go in first. I reached across my body with my left hand, found the required lever, and dropped the tail hook. I had by then slowed my Hellcat to an indicated air speed of 120 knots. Next, I lowered my landing gear and landing flaps; the latter caused a slight downward pitching motion. As I came up *Tripoli*'s wake, right in the groove, my air speed indicator registered the desired 90 knots, and the fighter was in a perfect nose-high attitude. As with all my carrier landings to date, I marvelled at the Hellcat's stability and ease of handling; it was the perfect carrier fighter, at least with respect to its handling characteristics during the critical landing phase. I was able to fly by feel alone, which totally freed my eyes to follow the motions of, to me, the most important man in the world, my LSO.

My doubts about being landed aboard a new ship by an LSO I had never met were left in the slipstream as my mind and body went on full automatic. I sighted the outstretched colored paddles and noted that they were being held straight out from each shoulder. Roger! That confirmed what my senses already knew: I was right in the groove. If I had felt what I felt then but seen a different signal from the paddles, I would have instantly obeyed the paddles, so great was the ingrained, acquired reliance upon the LSO's judgment.

Just as I sensed that my Hellcat's nose was over the carrier deck, the LSO's right arm lifted and the right paddle slashed across his throat. Cut!

I chopped back my throttle and held the joystick rock steady. I felt the shock of the landing gear hit the solid deck, then felt myself lurched forward into the harness as the tail hook grabbed the number-one cable.

My plane captain motioned me forward, out of the way, as soon as my tail hook was cleared from the cable. After rolling to a dead stop, I unbuckled my seat and shoulder harnesses and stood up in the cockpit to watch all my night fighters get aboard. To my satisfaction, there were no wave-offs.

Protocol demanded that I report to the captain of the ship, so I dropped to the deck and strode over to the hatchway in the side of the carrier's island. A spiffy Marine sentry snapped to attention as I entered the bridge, then he motioned me through to the outer bridge, where the captain was waiting. We both saluted and muttered the formula litany, then the captain got down to business. The Hellcats would be checked over by pilots and maintenance crews for the rest of the daylight hours. Then we would all be launched one at a time beginning at 2000 hours to begin our night qualifications.

As soon as the captain finished speaking, he motioned over two young lieutenants, whom he introduced as combat-experienced night-qualified pilots on loan from VF(N)-79. I had already met briefly with the squadron skipper, Turner Caldwell, so I had expected the two to be aboard.

The squadron assembled in the ready room, and there we spent the rest of the day going over and over the last-minute pointers brought up by our experienced brethren. My group was a pretty wild and woolly bunch, even by the crazy standard of the day. Many of them had often appeared to be beyond the listening stage in their flying careers. But everyone hung on every word and gesture by those two blooded Navy lieutenants.

First on our evening's agenda was a short demonstration hop by the two VF(N)-79 pilots, just to prove it could be done. While I watched from the Air Ops bridge and my pilots crowded around the LSO platform, the two Navy Hellcats were catapulted out over the bows. Then, with landing lights on to mark their flight paths, the two joined up and entered the racetrack separated by a 40-second interval.

The feeling that crept over me was about as eerie as any I have ever had. All I could hear were two high-performance engines. All I could see were two sets of landing lights. There was absolutely no moon to light the wake of the ship or to give a hint of the ship's whereabouts. There was a slight breeze coming in over the bows.

Suddenly, one set of lights was out over the wake. The approach was textbook perfect, right up the wake at precisely the correct speed, attitude, and altitude. I heard the engine drone lower as the pilot took the Cut, and I watched the outline of the night fighter arrest on the first or second wire. As the first Hellcat taxied forward to just beneath my perch, the second one set down in another textbook landing.

For all the hours of training and instruction I had received, I had not really believed it possible before seeing it with my own eyes.

My Marines gathered around the two Navy veterans and asked a rapid-fire set of nervous final questions. Then someone with a bullhorn blared the dreaded message from Fly-One: "Marines, man your airplanes."

★

We had decided that only one of us would launch and recover at a time until everyone had completed one landing. I was the only major in the group, the "old pro," so I volunteered to be the first. I did my best to hide my terror, but I think the only reason I was not found out was that everyone else was too deeply involved in masking their own terror to be aware of mine.

My flight gear was still in the cockpit of my Grumman, so I climbed aboard and quickly snapped snaps and pulled straps. I flashed on my first real moment of truth in an airplane, my qualifying solo at elimination base at Long Beach. Wow! To have come so far! I had been eager to fly then and had remained eager as I passed every milestone to this moment. I found myself unforgivably apprehensive for the first time in my flying career. The prospect of first combat had not come as close to terrorizing me as this flight.

I turned up the engine and allowed myself to be guided to the catapult.

A catapult launch is never a pleasant experience; it goes too quickly, and the pilot takes control of his airplane only after he and it have been hurtled out into space. A catapult launch this night was like adding injury to insult.

Before giving the catapult officer the "Ready" signal—a salute to the chin—I nervously checked and rechecked my harnesses, pulling on each one last time for good measure. Then I ran through my preflight checklist—and screw the men in the island who were moaning about how long I was taking: Canopy back and locked; engine at full RPM; prop at full pitch; flaps all the way down for maximum lift; right foot hovering above right rudder pedal, ready to kick out to overcome the left torque of the spinning prop; stick held loosely in my right hand; throttle grasped loosely in my left hand; head resting against the headrest to take up the shock of the catapult.

I looked to my left and saluted to my chin. Ready! In response, a dimly perceived deckhand standing over the catapult crew's catwalk whirled a flashlight: Go! I turned my eyes front, loosened my grip on my joystick, set my jaw, and leaned back into my seat.

WHACK!

My conscious mind was eons behind my senses—as it had been on all previous catapult launches. I had a very busy couple of seconds as I kicked the right rudder pedal and yanked the joystick all the way into the pit of my stomach. I had no time to dwell on how dark it was out there.

When my equanimity returned, the Hellcat was climbing away to the left. I got the wheels and flaps up almost in one motion. I had that familiar short sinking sensation in the pit of my stomach as the flaps went up and the Hellcat dropped slightly. Then my mind hollered, "Needle-ball airspeed, you dumb cluck!"

A destroyer passed beneath my low left wing; I had just enough time to notice two blinking navigational lights before the inky black of the perfectly dark night enfolded me.

All my training and experience saw me through a climb to 3,000 feet. While my mind reeled off a thousand facts about my flying, my voice talked to the ship in calm tones, reporting on routine matters the Air Officer would want to hear about. I was neither here nor there.

I was cleared to land, which was of some relief and some concern. I wanted to get down, but first I had to *find* the carrier.

I coaxed my Hellcat into one full circuit of the area in which I was pretty sure I had left *Tripoli* and her escorts. Yes! I saw the two navigational lights on the forward guard destroyer I had zoomed over on my way aloft. Then I saw two more aboard what had to be the plane-guard destroyer, which was deployed a few thousand yards directly to the rear of the carrier to pick up downed zoomies, as we carrier pilots were known.

Now I knew exactly where the flight deck lay. I also knew that, in the event of extreme danger, the carrier's flight deck lights would be flicked on to help me find a safe roost. But that would mean failure. And there were too many people watching for that.

After reassuring myself that I was flying on a heading opposite that of the carrier, I flew down the carrier's port side and approached the plane guard from ahead, keeping it just off my port wing. I could not help ruminating about how useless a night search for a bilged aviator must be.

Next, I flicked on my radio altimeter, a brand new instrument that had been installed in my cockpit just before we left San Diego. I had set it for 150 feet. If I flew above that altitude, I'd get a white signal light. If I flew below 150 feet, I'd get a red—danger!—light. If I was flying right at 150 feet, I'd get a comforting green light. The light was green when I turned the altimeter on.

I flew upwind the length of the tiny destroyer and sighted her tiny deck lights, which could only be seen from the air. This was the only concession to a pilot's natural aptitude for becoming disoriented across even the briefest interval of night space.

I had been timing my flight ever since passing the carrier and picking up the plane guard's lights. At what I judged to be the best moment, I turned 90 degrees left, dropped wheels and flaps, enriched the fuel mixture, partly opened cowl flaps, put the prop in low pitch, and turned another 90 degrees to the left to arrive at a downwind position dead astern of the carrier.

My night vision was by then as good as it would ever become. I had spent a full year training myself to find dim objects with my peripheral vision, which was the preferred method. Thus, I was able to dimly perceive the huge bulk of the totally darkened carrier as I floated up her wake.

Then I was committed to the approach; all my attention was aimed at visually acquiring the LSO's luminous paddles.

I momentarily panicked and said, or thought I might have said, "Where the hell are you?"

First I sensed the colored paddles, then I knew I saw them. Both of the LSO's arms were straight out. Roger! My ragged confidence was totally restored, though I yet remained a good deal less than cocky. I checked my airspeed, which was down to the required 90 knots. Before I knew it, I saw the Cut! Then, bango, my tail hook caught a wire and I was stopped on a dime.

I taxied up past the barrier, came to rest beside the island, and cut my engine. As had been the case after my first live combat mission, my flight suit was reeking of sweat.

During the rest of the night, all nine of us each made one night landing. My subordinates accounted for more than a few wave-offs, but that was partly my doing; I had asked the LSO to be particularly unforgiving of minor gaffes. We all knew how important it was to get this exercise 100 percent perfect.

★

We left *Tripoli* late on the afternoon of March 29, after we had all managed to get a few hours' sleep. We flew out along a heading supplied to me just before takeoff, and in 90 minutes I was in the landing circle over Barbers Point. We got the night off (most of us slept) and took off early the next morning, March 30, to find *Block Island II* cruising 60 miles off Hawaii—in much the same area that we had left *Tripoli*.

That very evening saw the beginning of intensive night carrier air operations from *Block Island II* and *Shipley*, another jeep carrier that sailed in our company. We became steadily more effective, and the ships soon featured two fully trained day-night air groups. We even had time to run night intercepts with the aid of carrier-based GCI officers. Everything checked out perfectly. By April 11, I had 43 carrier landings to my credit, about half of them at night. I still had a basic fear of carrier landings, and particularly of night carrier landings, but I felt I was as good as any night-qualified carrier pilot in the fleet.

Late on the last day of training, April 11, 1945, we flew off to Barbers Point while *Block Island II* tied up in Pearl Harbor to provision for her first war cruise.

★

The next day, April 12, 1945—the day President Franklin Roosevelt died in Warm Springs, Georgia—I was called to the Naval Air Base operations office and ordered to pack my gear and report as soon as possible for reassignment to Colonel Sam Jack at the Marine Corps Air Station at Ewa.

I was poleaxed by the news. I asked for details, but the Navy officer had zero information beyond the coldly worded order. I noted that all my gear was still aboard *Block Island II* and asked if I could delay my departure until the ship docked. A quick phone call bought me the needed time, but no new details were forthcoming. I left to join my squadron and tell John Dobbin and Bob Maze what had happened.

I just knew some well-meaning buddy was doing me a favor I didn't want or need. I just knew I would miss the rest of the war!

A jeep was provided as soon as I reported back to the Barbers Point operations center with my gear, and I was driven straight to Colonel Jack's office.

I had not seen Sam Jack since I had left VMF-121 in early 1941. He looked fit, if a little grayer. He had had a good war so far as a group commander, and now he was pretty high up on the staff overseeing Marine air units throughout the Pacific. He was his usual affable self, and he quickly quelled my unstated ire with his typically gentlemanly small talk.

Then he came to the point of our forced meeting. "Well, Bruce, what do you think of your night-fighter role aboard the carrier?"

"Well, Sir, it certainly was a challenge. To put it mildly."

"Do you know Lieutenant Colonel Marion Magruder?"

"I never had the pleasure, Sir."

"Well, he's CO of VMF(N)-533, which is out at Engebi, in the Marshalls. Mac's been CO since 533 was formed in October, '43, and he's been out with it in the war zone since mid April last year. He's way overdue for some relief.

"Frankly, Bruce, I'd like to get you reassigned as Mac's executive officer so you can take over for him."

I was honored, dismayed, and relieved—all at the same time. I told the colonel that I felt overdue for a squadron command, but I added that I completely identified with VMF-511 and that I hated to leave it just before it sailed into combat. I did not tell him—nor did I have to—that I considered an assignment at Engebi to be about a half-step away from giving up on ever seeing combat again. My dismay, however, lay at a deeper level. I had hated working for *Block Island II*'s Captain Hughes ever since his St. Valentine's Day Massacre of our air group off Santa Barbara. I held the ship's captain responsible for every one of those absolutely needless deaths, and, while I had been at pains to mask my true feelings, there had been friction between us. It did not occur to me until much later that Captain Hughes might have requested that I be transferred. I was glad to get out of his grasp, but I was also sad to see my boys left to his brand of leadership.

Colonel Jack brought no overt pressure to bear, but he quickly talked me into agreeing to take the new assignment. Well, if I was going to miss combat, I was going to miss combat. I was a Regular officer, I planned to stay in the Marine Corps for a full career, and a command was a command.

With great reluctance, I asked, "When do I leave, Sir?"

I should have had more faith in my old skipper.

★

Major Bob Maze was shot down and lost on a rocket attack flown from *Block Island II* against an island off Okinawa on May 27, 1945.

32

I left for Engebi on the night of April 23, 1945, aboard a Martin PBM Mariner long-range patrol bomber. We left Oahu without incident at seven or eight o'clock in the evening and headed directly to Midway, where the pilot misjudged his approach altitude and we made the biggest "drop in" landing I have ever heard about. I am sure we put up enough of a tidal wave to bilge every small boat on that side of the island. I headed for a mess hall to recuperate while the plane was refueled (and, I am sure, checked for structural damage). As I sipped my scalding coffee, I overheard two officers talking about a PBM that, two nights earlier, had struck a log while landing and had sunk to the bottom of the lagoon with all hands. The sour landing and the further good news confirmed all my beliefs against placing my life in the hands of another pilot.

Our next stop was Eniwetok in the Marshalls. I was met there by a pilot and an SNJ two-seat trainer thoughtfully provided by my new CO, Lieutenant Colonel Marion "Black Jack Mac" Magruder. We made the short hop out to Engebi without further incident, and I reported aboard VMF(N)-533.

As soon as I left the CO's office to find my sleeping quarters, I was accosted by Captain Sam Folsom, one of the night-fighter pilots who had been aboard VMF(N)-544 when Jim Maguire and I formed it at Cherry Point a year earlier. So, I had one old flying buddy who could tell me all I needed to know about the squadron. As it turned out, Sam was the squadron flight officer, third in command after Black Jack Mac and me.

The only personal belongings I had were everything I had been able to fit into a small overnight bag. All my other gear was to follow by "available transport," which is to say that I had to anticipate living out of the overnight bag for an interminable period. I had gotten pretty good at that sort of living, but I hated it.

The best news I received upon reporting in was about the squadron's future status. Sam Jack had failed to mention that VMF(N)-533 was slated to move to Okinawa soon. The big island, with its three air bases, had been invaded by several Army and Marine divisions on April 1, and there already were several Army and Marine night-fighter squadrons there. Okinawa was being built up as an advance air base from which the expected autumn invasion of Japan would be supported. The news was that VMF(N)-533 would be the next to go.

I had to brush up a bit on the F6F-5N night fighter with which VMF(N)-533 was equipped. I had been flying a similar model with VMF-511 when I was pulled out of carrier duty. There were some minor differences that I mastered in only a few hours of practice flying. Then, in addition to my administrative duties (which I had not missed while I was with VMF-511), I drew the usual night and day patrols. As yet, the squadron had not scored a single kill.

My stay in Engebi was blessedly brief. I had been aboard only a few days when Black Jack Mac called everyone together in the ready room and announced that we had orders to proceed to Okinawa as soon as we could mount out.

Nearly all of the equipment and ground personnel would leave Engebi aboard ship while we pilots flew the Hellcats via several intermediate islands. VMR-252, a transport squadron, was to provide several Curtiss R5C (C-46) guide planes to shepherd us along and carry emergency spare parts and one scratch ground crew apiece to service the Hellcats and our radar along the way. The CO next pointed out that we would be undertaking the longest overwater flights thus far assigned to single-engine aircraft in the war. We would be flying first to Saipan, in the Marianas, then to Iwo Jima, and then on to Okinawa. In the event of problems, we were given the radio call signs and emergency frequencies of three destroyers and two fleet submarines that would be plying the waters near our flight path between Engebi and Saipan.

★

The three R5Cs—which were commanded by Captain Bob Thayer, a former Corsair pilot—took off fully loaded at 0800, May 7, 1945, and the Hellcats launched shortly thereafter. We rendez-voused with the multiengine aircraft at 10,000 feet and formed up into several fairly tight elements; one each under the CO, the exec, and the flight officer. As soon as we had formed up, all hands leaned our fuel mixtures to eke out extra miles.

We were airborne for six and a half hours. It goes without say-ing that everyone's butt was especially sore, and there was the old bladder-and-bowels problem to contend with. However, there were zero problems on the first leg, and all hands landed safely at Saipan in the early afternoon. Most of the lieutenants took off to tour the former battlefields around Saipan, then everyone met by invitation at the VMR-252 officers' mess for dinner.

I had just entered the tent when I was pulled aside by, of all people, 1st Lieutenant Tyrone Power. The movie actor greeted me formally as major, but we knew one another well enough to dispense with that, so I insisted that he call me Bruce.

Tyrone saw to getting me a drink, and, as soon as we sat down, apologized profusely and at agonizing length for the New Year's Eve flap at Jack Benny's home. He said that we should have stayed and that he and Clark Gable had given Mary Livingston plenty of heat for the rest of the evening. I just passed it off and told him to forget it; the memory of the whole affair was reward enough. After that, the talk shifted to flying stories, including news of takeoff problems being encountered by the recently committed B-29s flying out of neighboring Tinian.

We all made a short evening of it as we had to fly out the next morning.

I joined our CO and the R5C pilots for a flight-plan briefing after dinner. Black Jack Mac revealed that the meteorological fore-casts indicated a possible deterioration of the weather along our flight path. This gave me intimations of doom; the St. Valentine's Day Massacre was still vivid in my mind. We would be airborne for five hours if the weather favored us; we could stretch our air time to just under eight hours if we had to fly around a storm or if we got "a little lost."

★

We met the R5Cs at 8,000 feet and settled into our formation of three elements. Our point of no return arrived at the tail end of four hours; we could no longer return to Saipan but would have to forge ahead to Iwo Jima, no matter what. We encountered the forecasted heavy weather 30 minutes after that.

There was no choice; we had to bore into the towering clouds. Visibility closed down around us as we advanced into the murk. Each fighter element closed up really tight on the transports, which began a slow ascent to 12,000 feet in the hope of finding smoother air. At length, the escort commander said that he was sure there was no top to the weather that we could reach. We were really being buffetted around by then, so it was agreed to descend back to an even 10,000 feet, where it was marginally calmer.

As the leader of my own element, I was closest to my own R5C; I was *really* parked on that guy's wing. It was all I could do to handle my controls, so I was stunned when I saw the multiengine airplane's co-pilot looking out from the flight deck with a cup of coffee in his hand. I am sure I cursed him, and I am not sure but that the curse was broadcast to the squadron.

We droned on for a bit beyond the really heavy weather front, and then I quickly glanced over my shoulder to see how my two wingmen were doing.

They were gone!

I was certain they had succumbed to vertigo and spun into the sea. I was mortified at the notion and angry with whomever had sanctioned this fools' flight into bad weather. Two more good pilots gone for no good reason.

There was nothing I could do, so I ordered the remainder of my flight to close up and returned my full concentration to keeping the R5C in view. I continued to pass the time looking into the interior-lighted transport. I saw through the portholes in the fuselage that the passengers were comfortably eating sandwiches and drinking hot coffee from metal cups—and they were staring out at me! It made my stomach growl as I had not had a bite or a swallow since downing a monumentally lousy breakfast on the flight line at Saipan. My discomfort was reaching epic proportions because of the cramped quarters and the raw, clammy air that was penetrating my cockpit from the storm outside. My head ached from constant monitoring of my instruments, for we were on full instruments despite the guides. I had been squeezing fighter joysticks for so many years that I had muscle spasms from time to time—including for hours this day.

We very slowly felt our way down through the almost total cloud cover and found Iwo Jima from a height of only 200 feet. Below that was a misty fog all the way down to the surface of the water. I was scared to death of flying into Mount Suribachi, which I had heard about in connection with the Flag Raising photo that had instilled so much national and Marine pride when it had appeared a few months earlier.

Sure enough, the R5C on whose wing I had been flying turned out and circled right over Suribachi. The improved captured Japanese airstrip that was our destination was literally in the shadow of the peak. As I lowered my landing gear and entered the landing pattern, I could easily see that crews of Seabees were still working on the verges of the runway.

I came in right behind the R5C and rolled out to a safe stop. As the guide jeep rolled by with its "Follow Me!" sign, I turned into the dispersal area. By then, I had time aplenty to really lament the loss of my two wingmen. I was determined to run over to the base operations hut to see if anyone had picked up a call on our prearranged distress frequency.

After rolling into the dispersal revetment, I cut my Hellcat's engine and shrugged out of my seat belt and shoulder harness. I no sooner looked up to orient myself than I saw two familiar F6Fs parked in revetments exactly on the opposite side of the taxiway. My two lost sheep!

I jumped to the ground, waited while another Hellcat taxied past, and legged it over to the two grinning Marines standing between the two night fighters.

After shaking hands and thumping their backs, I asked the natural question, "What the hell happened to you two? How'd you get here alive?"

As I had suspected, they had become disoriented while passing through total clouds. One had spun out and the other had followed him down. Somehow, they had talked one another into obeying their instruments. As soon as they had righted themselves, they had realized that there was no way they were ever going to find the squadron formation again. They flew several circles trying to figure out what to do and how to proceed. One remembered to tune in the emergency distress frequency. As it happened, there had been a large B-29 strike against Japan some hours earlier. Iwo Jima was the designated emergency destination of disabled bombers that could not get back to Tinian. As soon as my lost birdmen tuned into the emergency frequency, their ears were filled with an enormous amount of chatter emanating from the B-29s and the island's bomber field. At that point, it became a simple matter of riding the beams in. They arrived dead on target and had landed only a minute or two before the rest of us topped Suribachi

★

Our original plan had been to spend the night on Iwo Jima and then fly on to Okinawa. However, the continued bad weather and our rather ragged condition necessitated a longer rest. We were given the next day off to pull ourselves together.

After I had stowed my gear in the puny little puptent to which I was assigned, I headed through the squadron bivouac to see if everyone had found a spot. I was just finishing up when one of my pilots, 1st Lieutenant Robert Wilhide, approached me. "Say, Major, I just borrowed a jeep from an Air Corps squadron for the rest of the day. How'd you like to take a ride around the island with me?"

I was tired but very curious to see the battlefields, so I jumped into the passenger's seat for my unguided tour.

My knowledge of the battle for Iwo Jima was minimal, just what I had read in the newspapers or heard on the radio while dealing with the details of my own war in the wake of the St. Valentine's Day Massacre. As I later learned, Iwo had been assaulted by elements of two Marine divisions (and would eventually use up most of a third) on February 19, 1945. The importance of the island—which claimed 5,453 Marine lives and resulted in injuries to about 20,000 other Americans—was that it lay only 700 miles from the Japanese home islands. It had several runways already built, and at least one of these could be (and was) quickly lengthened and strengthened to land the numerous shot-up or malfunctioning B-29s (and other aircraft) engaged in the massive bombing raids against Japanese cities and military targets. (We did not know it then, of course, but by war's end, over 2,200 B-29s with over 24,000 crewmen made emergency landings at Iwo. There is no telling how many of those warplanes and crewmen would have fallen into the sea in the absence of the haven at Iwo Jima.)

Wilhide and I drove around the airbase a little, then headed right up to Mount Suribachi, which dominates the entire island. On the way, we passed the gigantic Marine cemetery. I cannot begin to describe the overpowering feelings generated by the rows upon rows of gleaming new white crosses and Stars of David. They seemed to be laid out in rows that stretched for miles.

Personalizing the sense of loss and waste was recent news from Pat that her friend and my former schoolmate, Lieutenant Jack Armitage, was among the many thousands of dead Marines buried on that island. Jack had commanded a rifle company in the first assault waves until struck down by the massive fire the defenders had placed on the crowded beaches.

It was all I could do to fight back the overwhelming torrent of tears.

We eventually had to abandon the jeep in our quest for Suribachi's crest. After blundering around for a bit, we asked our way to the site of the Flag Raising. I did not then know the story behind the Flag Raising, but I had been caught up with virtually all my countrymen in the outpouring of feeling the publication of Joe Rosenthal's timeless photo had evoked. Without quite realizing why, I was again overcome by tears and emotion as I stood upon that truly hallowed ground and stared up at our beautiful Stars and Stripes as it snapped in the breeze. I was beyond words during those moments, and so was Bob Wilhide. We silently thought our thoughts for a few moments, then turned in unison to begin our descent. Beneath us lay the landing beaches; they were starkly delineated by a jumble of wrecked landing craft and shell craters. The signs of the battle lay everywhere.

We drove back to our bivouac in total silence, each of us unable to muster the banter that young warriors typically broadcast to cover honest emotion. As we entered the bivouac, however, I finally piped up, "We better get the jeep back to its owners."

★

Our hosts were members of the Air Corps' 531st Fighter Squadron, a unit equipped with P-51 Mustangs. After returning the jeep, Wilhide and I got to talking with one of their pilots, a captain. He explained that the long-legged P-51s were undertaking escort missions, guarding the B-29s as they entered and left Japanese air space and strafing Japanese airfields.

We talked shop for awhile, then got ready to part company. As we were leaving, the captain cautioned, "Be careful tonight. There's still plenty of Japs hiding out underground, and they come up at night to scrounge food or kill Americans."

That sort of stopped me in my tracks.

Undoubtedly prodded by the look on my face, the captain glee-fully continued. "About two months ago, on March 26, the squadron was overrun by Jap suicide troops. That was five weeks after D-Day, and this whole area was supposed to be secure. We were operating out of Airfield Two, and we had a normal bivouac set up—tents, flight line, the usual. All of a sudden, hundreds of 'em just up and charged out of the black night. They overran us and a Marine shore party battalion, the 5th Pioneers. They cut right through the tents and slashed up a bunch of our people before they could get out of their cots. Grenades were going off all over the place, and there was no end of screaming.

"I was in one of the tents farthest from where the action started. It took me a minute to pull myself together and figure out what I was hearing. I couldn't find my shoulder holster and pistol, so I rolled out of my rack and pulled my cot down over me to pretend that I was dead or wouldn't do any harm to anyone.

"Later, we found that many of the dead Japs were carrying American weapons they must have taken off of dead Marines.

"The fighting in the dark was confused and terrible. Some of 'em penetrated all the way down to the 38th Field Hospital and killed a bunch of people there. They tore out phone lines, slashed up the hospital tents, and machine-gunned ambulances bringing wounded in from the rest of the fight.

"Anybody who could get his hands on a weapon joined in. I eventually found my pistol, and I started shooting at targets in the night. The Seabees joined in and launched a little counterattack through our bivouac. Army medics from my squadron were blowing people away in between helping the wounded. And the Marine pio-neers came through to pry them out.

"We didn't really get much of a counterattack going until it was light enough to see, but we held 'em. Finally, well after first light, the Army 147th Infantry swept through here in a really organized attack. That was four hours after the start of the fight, around eight o'clock. By that time, the battle was pretty much over, but there was still plenty of shooting.

"The squadron lost 44 killed and about 88 wounded. And the Marine pioneers lost something like nine killed and 31 wounded. I don't know how many Seabees or soldiers were hurt or how many people were killed or injured at the hospital. They buried 262 Japs and took about 18 prisoners."

Wilhide and I returned to our tents after this eyeball-popping story. The very first thing I did after I crawled into my tiny tent was lay out my .45-caliber automatic and an extra magazine of bullets. I easily overcame whatever notions I had that I was overreacting to two-month-old news. I hardly slept.

★

The weather the next day was as bad as it had been when we arrived, so we were all given another day off. Most of us spent our time checking out our Hellcats and watching the P-51s take off and land. Some of our guys even got to swap war stories with temporarily marooned B-29 pilots and aircrewmen, but I have no idea what our tyro night-fighter warriors had to tell blooded bomber crewmen that was worth hearing.

33

The weather lifted enough on May 10 to allow us to see our way between Iwo Jima and Okinawa. We joined up on our R5C pathfinders for the five and a half hour final leg of our record-breaking redeployment. It was, by our standards, an easy hop.

We entered the war zone—for the battle for Okinawa was still raging—and flew along the west coast to our destination, Yontan Airfield. Our new base was located only 325 air miles from southern Kyushu, the southernmost of the main Japanese home islands. As we neared the base, our future home, we broke away from the R5Cs and formed up in a full squadron formation. Black Jack Mac Magruder announced our arrival and requested permission to land.

As soon as we had seen to our airplanes, which were temporarily in the hands of a scratch ground organization directed by the groundcrewmen who had flown aboard the R5Cs, we drove to our campsite. The rest of the day was spent setting up housekeeping on a steep hillside overlooking Yontan. It was quite a walk from the aircraft revetments.

Though we were slated to join MAG-22 (commanded by my old VMF-111 skipper, Colonel Dan Torrey), we temporarily became part of MAG-31 the following day, May 11. On that day, also, VMF(N)-533 drew its first scheduled night patrols, which were to commence that very evening. A squadron brief at Group Operations provided us with all the essential details.

The area around Yontan was divided into four night-fighter sectors. VMF(N)-533 was to share the northwest and southwest sectors with VMF(N)-542, also based at Yontan. The only other Marine night-fighter squadron on Okinawa at the time was VMF(N)-543, which was based on the east coast at Awase; it covered the southern areas, which were still in Japanese hands and which were farthest from bases in Japan. Each squadron regularly put up four teams (eight aircraft in four two-plane relays) each night.

Yontan's runways were configured as a large triangle, but the main runway ran east-west. Numerous others squadrons were already operating from the field, and many others were slated for arrival over the succeeding weeks. Together with squadrons operating out of the other principal Okinawan base, Kadena, we were part of a huge assembly known as the Tactical Air Force. Together with Navy and Marine carrier squadrons, we were by far the largest assemblage of tactical air power ever to operate under one command in the Pacific. Our primary job was to support the Marine and Army infantry fighting ashore and, secondarily, to support tactical and strategic airstrikes against Japan.

Our squadron's main reference point was a tip of land northwest of Yontan that had been dubbed Point Bolo. All of the early warning picket ships arrayed around Okinawa referenced their sightings as if from commonly known points, such as Bolo, Tare, Nan, Mike, and others, depending on the patrol sector they and their night fighters were covering. Our Ground Control Intercept (GCI) radars set up on Okinawa or nearby Ie Shima used the same common reference points.

For the time being, the primary mission of night fighters based at Yontan was to protect friendly vessels anchored or operating near Okinawan shores. Japanese kamikazes—suicide aircraft—had struck many vessels early in the campaign, and they just kept right on coming, despite the fact that nearly all of them were downed before even getting an opportunity to dive on our surface ships. In addition to our own night prowlers, which were just getting into the scoring business, the Navy covered the fleet at nearly all hours with smoke screens. Since the prevailing wind was from the China coast, landing craft equipped with smoke generators constantly plied the waters to the west of the anchorages. Unfortunately, the smoke also masked the approaches of kamikazes from the view of our vigilant day-fighter pilots, and it caused problems for our night squadrons as well.

Daily, MAG-31's Corsair day fighters roved the skies over and around Okinawa from just before sun-up until, at that time of the year, 1630 or 1700 hours. At that interval, in the late afternoon, our first night teams launched and took up position overhead, just before the day fighters headed for the barn. Because of Yontan's position on the west coast, the weather, and the smoke screen, our first teams of night fighters usually faced zero-visibility launches. That was no problem, however, because of our radar and instrument training. The end of our strip also featured a 300-foot drop-off into the ocean. This, I pointed out to my fellow night stalkers, was something like ten times the distance between a carrier flight deck and the ocean—and Okinawa did not pitch and roll quite as much as a carrier.

★

My first operational night launch was on May 12, 1945.

I took off with the second team—the graveyard shift—in utter darkness. As I left the smoke behind and entered a clear, moonlit canopy, I found that I had to make an immediate tight right turn to evade fire put out by jumpy antiaircraft gunners aboard transports and warships just beyond the smoke. I was lucky, but one or two of the Hellcats following me aloft were hit, though none had to abort.

As I climbed to patrol altitude on total instruments, I reported to my assigned picket ship and told him my current heading so he could locate me on his radar. As soon as he had me, my controller vectored me to a 30-degree turn and ordered me to climb to 10,000 feet. When I arrived at the correct altitude, he told me to orbit and report to a controller based on Ie Shima who would take over my patrol. I reported "Over and out" to the picket ship and climbed to the designated altitude. I reported my position to my ground-based controller, a member of Air Warning Squadron 1 (AWS-1). He told me that the weather over China was deteriorating and that the storm front would eventually strike Okinawa. With that cheery news, he parked me in a constant orbit. I would remain there until further notice or until it was time to land.

The storm that overtook me was terrible. The rain was terrible and the lightning was terrible. For all my eagerness to be on my first real night mission, I could not sustain enough enthusiasm to remain aloft for essentially no reason. At length, I called my controller and asked permission to fly home. The reply, which came a few minutes later, was a negative. I queried that, and the GCI told me that the fleet wanted all friendly airplanes to remain clear of the island for a while. That did not sound right, but I let it pass. A minute or two later, the GCI told me that I had been the last night fighter to ask for permission to land. All the others had received permission, but the fleet commander had insisted that at least one friendly night fighter remain aloft. Just lucky, I guess.

I continued to cut circles in the storm for about another hour. It was extremely hard to maintain or properly monitor my position on instruments as my Hellcat was really getting jerked around up there. I thought I knew where I was, but in the course of time I became completely lost.

After an hour, I sensed that enough was really enough. I was willing to face an admiral's wrath if need be, but I would do so on the ground, or even aboard ship.

I placed a call to my AWS-1 GCI on Ie Shima, but the radio waves were about blotted out by electrical disturbances. I got no answer beyond a wheezing crackle. I was on my own. Undecided and fearful that I might be off course, I tried the back-up ground control station at Iwoshima.

"Handyman from Muscles Two," I kept saying into my mike. But Handyman did not answer. My sense of being lost grew and grew, and so did my sense of despair. What a dumb way to go!

Then, literally right out of the blue, a picket ship chimed in loud and clear. "Muscles Two, this is your friend, a picket ship. We have you on radar. We will vector you on course 90 [due east]. Do you read me? Over and out."

"Friendly picket ship from Muscles Two. Yes, I read you. Give me my vector. Over and out."

"Muscles Two from friendly picket ship. We give you 90. Maintain your same angels [altitude]. Over and out."

Shortly after this, I was handed off to the next radar picket ship on patrol duty. "Muscles Two, this is radar picket ship two. Would you please circle." I did this to help establish my identity for the radarman. "Muscles Two. Maintain your altitude and continue circling." Come on! Then, at last, "Muscles Two. We have you on our screen. Muscles Two from picket ship two, angels 10 [10,000 feet] and take a heading of 98. Drop down to angels 4. Over and out."

I quickly replied, "Radar picket ship two from Muscles Two. Negative your last order." I was certain their radar had registered a ghost bogey. While waiting for them to find the real me, I pulled out my plotting board and tracked myself. By the time I completed my computations, I was pretty sure I knew which way Yontan lay. According to my figures, dropping to 4,000 feet on the eastward heading I had been given would have flown me straight into Okinawa's central cordillera.

With my plotting board still on my knee, I maintained my altitude of 10,000 feet on Course 90, which brought me all the way across Okinawa. I wound up somewhere over Buckner Bay, the province of Air Warning Squadron 6 (AWS-6), which was based offshore on a tiny island group called Katchin Hanto. I radioed AWS-6, got a response, and listened appreciatively as the voice on the radio told me that they had me on their radar. They brought me smoothly on course and vectored me straight to Yontan. I visually acquired the cliffs on which the runway was built, then called in to say I was approaching the landing pattern from due east on a 270-degree heading. I was immediately cleared to land from my straight-in approach, and I did so with alacrity.

★

I flew again on the nights of May 14, 16, and 18, but I never saw an enemy airplane. However, two of our pilots scored the squadron's first kills of the war on the night of the 16th. The very first of those scorers was 1st Lieutenant Bob Wilhide, who downed a Betty bomber. Tragically, Bob followed up his attack through heavy friendly antiaircraft fire and was never heard from again.

On the night of May 18, 1st Lieutenant Edward LeFaivre of VMF(N)-533 scored an extremely rare double night kill. On the same night, and during the same patrol period, LeFaivre was outdone by 533's 1st Lieutenant Robert Wellwood, who downed three Japanese in under two hours.

34

I was awakened late in the morning of May 22, 1945, an act which got my ire up. I had flown the night before, and I was due to sleep at least until lunchtime. But the word was that I was to report immediately to the squadron commander, Lieutenant Colonel Marion Magruder. I knew that Black Jack Mac would not have disturbed my sleep unless something important was going on.

The news really threw me. I was being detached from VMF(N)-533, effective immediately, to take command of neighboring VMF(N)-542. Mac had no details beyond the fact that I was to report forthwith to the MAG-31 command post to discuss the matter with the group commander, Colonel John "Toby" Munn.

I had never met Colonel Munn before, though I knew of his reputation. A highly regarded pilot, he had served as intelligence officer of 1st Marine Aircraft Wing at Guadalcanal during the dark days, then had spent several years in Washington overseeing important aspects of the dramatic growth of the Marine Corps aviation program.

The colonel was fairly circumspect about the reasons for the sudden command change. I gathered, however, that the squadron was undergoing a traumatic morale problem in some way caused by the performance of the outgoing squadron commander. I also gathered that I had been selected for the command because I was, first, an outsider who could get things straightened out among strangers and, second, because I was the senior and only night-qualified major available on short notice.

The press of events since my arrival on Okinawa had prevented me from visiting 542, so I was not yet certain if any of my friends from Vero Beach and Cherry Point were still with the squadron. I was delighted to hear from Colonel Munn that my close friend and former roommate, Captain Wally Sigler, was now the squadron exec. I was relieved to learn that Wally was in no way involved in the command problem. His continued presence would certainly make my life easier. In fact, Colonel Munn said that Wally would have been given command of the squadron if he had had a little more rank.

Since VMF(N)-533 was slated to become part of MAG-22 as soon as it set up headquarters on Okinawa, I had paid zero attention to who was who in MAG-31 during my week ashore. I asked in passing who the group's day-fighter squadron commanders were, and I was floored to learn that Major Jeff Poindexter had VMF-224, and Major Perry Shuman, with whom I had flown in VMF-111 and VMF-121 in Samoa and the Russells, had VMF-311. Completing the sense of arriving in time for Old Home Week, I learned that the third day squadron attached to the group was VMF-441, in which I had served during my last months in Samoa.

My orders, which were being cut while I was talking with Colonel Munn, were handed to me on my way out the door. I was to assume command of VMF(N)-542 effective the next day, May 23, 1945.

★

I grabbed a jeep ride over to the VMF(N)-542 dispersal area and made my presence known to the duty officer. I, a complete stranger, was welcomed with a beaming smile, which spoke reams about the squadron's morale.

I located my new quarters, high up on one of the many hills hemming in Yontan Airfield. I was particularly pleased to see that my tent—the former CO's abode—was located right next door to an Okinawan burial vault, a fantastic airraid shelter. I was greeted at the portal to my tent by a beaming, grateful Wally Sigler. He threw me a big salute and clearly restrained himself from hugging me.

As I was putting my gear away, Wally began telling me about the problems with the old skipper. I let him talk for just a moment, then held up my hand. "Let's start with a clean slate, Wally. I have a good idea what happened. I'm new meat here. I'll prove myself without my drawing comparisons."

Wally hesitated, then nodded. It was the last of the matter I ever heard from him, for which I was especially grateful.

"You know, Sir, you're one of the youngest majors in the Marine Corps. I'd say you're only two years older than most of our lieutenants. In fact, I'm a year older than you."

"Hell, I already know how old you are, Wally! Are you bucking for promotion or just trying to get me under your thumb? I've been a squadron exec too long to fall for that trick!"

And we collapsed amidst peels of comradely laughter.

All of a sudden, before we quite collected ourselves, I heard a jeep stop on a dime right outside my tent. The flaps were pulled apart and in tromped Jeff Poindexter. "Hey, Bruce," he bellowed without a pause to shake my hand or ask how I was, "We're having a little party down at my bivouac. How about you ridin' back with me and we'll tilt back a few."

I glanced over at Wally to see if he had a signal I needed to see. He smiled. "You're not officially here until tomorrow morning, Sir."

"Sure, Jeff. How you doin'?"

"Oh, you know, Bruce. Same old Jeff."

I introduced Jeff to Wally. "You're welcome, too, Wally."

"Thanks all the same, Sir. I have to fly tonight."

And so we were off. It *was* the same old Jeff, too. We drank into the wee hours, stopping only when Japanese night bombers dropped bombs in random patterns across the airfield and bivouac area. One bomb dropped right outside Jeff's tent but fortunately caused no damage or injuries. This brought no end of disparaging comments from my old classmate, but nothing so outrageous I could not adjust to. It also set Wally up for the bad time I was going to give him over the distractions I had suffered at his hands.

★

Sunrise found me hung over. My enthusiasm for taking over a squadron was dampened by the condition of my throbbing head, but I knew I had to rise to the honor. I pulled myself together and got Jeff to find someone to drive me back to my squadron. Unfortunately, the only ride going my way had to drop me off at the 542 flight line, right out in the open among the groundcrews I was to command.

I looked a sight and knew it. My flight coveralls were not exactly slept in, but I had been wearing them since I was awakened the day before. I needed a shave and a shower. And I smelled like a good-sized distillery.

Immediately, I ran into three of the squadron's enlisted movers and shakers, Technical Sergeant Lew Sweezy, our line chief; Technical Sergeant Chandler Beasley, our engine-change specialist; and Staff Sergeant Ernest "Tut" Runyon, one of our leading radar specialists. I later learned the gist of the comments they exchanged among themselves.

Beas asked the others as I approached, "Who in the hell is this guy? No cover and a damned old pair of beat-up flight coveralls. Looks like a reprobate to me."

The others were forming surmises, but they all had to clam up as I approached to within earshot.

I introduced myself and asked to see the Hellcat I would be flying—the only reason I could think of on short notice for being on the flight line. As soon as I learned that I was assigned to the same F6F-5N Hellcat flown by the previous skipper, Number 76, I pulled myself together to give the best impression (and impersonation of an officer) I could. As the three noncoms wordlessly looked on, I conducted a minute inspection of the airplane and muttered just loud enough to be heard, "The ground crew has done a damn fine job." In fact, I was very pleased with what I found. In addition to a gorgeously maintained airplane, I saw that I would be handling a mixed armory of four .50-caliber machine guns and two 20mm cannon. (I soon learned that 76 was the only Hellcat in the squadron armed with the cannon.)

I ended my inspection by looking up onto the matte black engine cowling to see what had been painted there. "What in the hell is *that*?" There was a big red heart overpainted with a white "Millie Lou." "Get that goddamned 'Millie Lou' off my airplane. I want my own painting on the nacelle. Have a big fifth of Schenley's put on with the caption 'Black Death.' "

To top off my great impersonation of a Marine officer, I told the three noncoms that I did not want my personal plane taken out of commission for the job. "I expect to fly tonight, and I better be flying 76 or it's your asses."

And then I left them standing there to mull me over.

"Goddamn!" Beas muttered, "Did you smell that man? I mean the booze, not the B.O. He musta really been partying."

To which Sweez replied, "Oh, he was snockered to hell all right. But I think he'll do. Hell, he owns our asses!"

Beas's Georgia drawl shaped the last part of the conversation, "Gawd! That sure was the raunchiest bastard I ever seen in my life."

In the end, they risked my wrath by pulling 76 out of service for an "oil leak." They pulled off the whole cowling and hauled it over to a neighboring Air Corps unit that was known to have a great artist aboard. In exchange for a bottle or two (I'm pretty sure), he painted the fifth of Schenley's emblazoned with "Black Death," precisely as ordered.

For my own part, I cleaned myself up well enough, but I decided to put off my planned informal walk-around squadron inspection until the next day. I had to get some sleep. I wanted to fly my first night mission as soon as possible, but Wally forcefully insisted that I put that off in order to catch up on some paperwork that had been hanging around since the old CO had left and could not be put off a moment longer. So I spent the afternoon with the squadron's nonflying adjutant and the office staff. I also made a special point that evening to look in on the squadron's leading chief, Master Technical Sergeant Wilbur "Bud" Stuckey. Bud and I had served together in VMF-121 at New Bern and Quantico before and right after the start of the war. I greeted him warmly and was welcomed with a display of great affection.

Next day, May 24, I spruced myself up and made an official courtesy call on Colonel Munn to officially report myself as being in command of VMF(N)-542.

I wanted to fly that night, but Wally pointed out that I had been worked into the regular schedule for the following night. He insisted that I visit the troops. I could see which way the wind blew in 542. Old and dear friend that he was, Wally was not the CO. I told him that I would run my too-long-deferred walking inspection through the entire squadron area, meet with all the pilots at an afternoon pilots' call, and fly my first mission as part of the first shift.

I made a point of meeting everyone who was working on the line and in the command post. I realized that there was no way I would remember everyone's name or job so soon, but I could see that it was important to all hands that I was making the effort. I found, to my satisfaction, that the groundcrews were considerably stiffened by an impressive contingent of experienced noncommissioned officers who had already served in the Pacific war zone prior to this tour. Some of my enlisted technicians were very senior, like Bud Stuckey, and had many peacetime cruises under their belts. However, most of my enlisted men were youngsters who were there only for the war. It was a good mix.

The same was true for most of my 27 night-fighter pilots. Except for me, Wally Sigler was by far the most experienced pilot. In a very important way, he was ahead of me. He had served in the Solomons at about the time I was there and had scored four kills and a proba- ble. Wally had just made Ace status on April 28 by downing a Japa- nese fighter off Okinawa. He was indeed my strong right arm. My Flight Officer, Captain George Gelsten, was a former Royal Cana- dian Air Force pilot, as was the next-senior pilot, Captain Rick Hey. George had had some time in night-fighter control in England before returning to the United States and accepting a Marine Corps commission.

Between its combat debut in mid April and the time I took over, VMF(N)-542 had accounted for eleven Japanese night fighters and night bombers. The squadron had suffered one battle fatality so far; 2nd Lieutenant William Campbell's Hellcat had disappeared from his GCI officer's radarscope on the night of May 16, minutes after claiming his second confirmed kill.

By the standard of the day, my squadron had definitely been pulling its weight. In fact, Marine night fighters generally turned hard contacts into confirmed kills; if we could be guided to within shooting range of a night intruder, we almost always scored.

I ended my first squadron pilots' meeting on the afternoon of May 24 with what I hoped was a rousing crescendo: "Let's try to make this the best damned night-fighter squadron in the Marine Corps. Let's prove it in the air and at night!"

That said, I saddled up for my first "nightcap" (night Combat Air Patrol) as skipper of VMF(N)-542. I knew that all hands were waiting to see how I did.

35

I took off that evening, May 24, as the lead pilot in our squadron's first nightcap. It was an altogether boring evening for me and the other VMF(N)-542 pilots. Our sector to the south of Yontan was simply not where the incoming Japanese intruders were coming from. None of us even picked up a bogey. In general, however, it was a very busy evening for the last day-fighter patrols and for several night fighters.

In the hour before my launch, day fighters accounted for nine Japanese airplanes bent on hitting the fleet. And while I was aloft in a quiet sector, VMF(N)-533's first nightcap picked up a total of five intruders within Yontan's northern and northwestern search sectors. Indeed, all five of 533's first nightcap targets were destroyed. First Lieutenant Albert Dellamano got three of them in 50 minutes, which accounted for 533's second triple night kill of the tour. Later that evening, a VMF(N)-543 pilot working out of Kadena, across the island, got still another night kill.

But the air action elsewhere was beyond my knowledge and concern when I landed and taxied out to our squadron dispersal area. I left my flight gear in the cockpit and drove myself up to my tent. I had crammed too much work into my day, and I was feeling overtired and desperate for a good night's sleep.

I no sooner sat down on my rack to pull off my combat boots than I heard explosions from the field below our hill. Before anything else sank in, the field telephone beside my cot began ringing. I grabbed the handset and shouted, "Major Porter!" A frantic voice I could not place bellowed news that all hell was breaking loose on the airfield and that the Japanese were *landing* planes on our runways. Then I heard only static. Whomever had called had hung up after singing out his dismaying message.

Two or three more calls interrupted the work of getting my combat boots back on. A lot of what I heard from the earpiece clashed with news from other calls. In the first quiet moment, I surmised that from two to fourteen Japanese multiengine bombers or transports had crash landed on all or some of Yontan's three main runways and that the base and group headquarters and various squadron flight lines were under attack. All the calls had been pretty wild.

As my head cleared, I recalled details of the ominous story of the Japanese raid I had heard only two weeks earlier on Iwo Jima. Jeez! There were armed Japs running around the base!

I shrugged into my shoulder holster, made sure my automatic pistol was loaded, and grabbed several extra clips of ammunition. Then I headed for the door to see things for myself. I had already heard several new explosions and could hear small arms popping off from below our hillside bivouac. I hit the door just as a huge light flared into the darkened sky. I was certain that someone had blown up a gasoline dump.

Below my vantage point, I saw that many lines of tracer were flying across the runways and on into flight lines and tent camps on all sides of the airfield. It was totally chaotic down there. It was very evident that I could contribute nothing to events below except the seeds of more confusion. I decided to sit tight, and I ordered everyone within hearing distance to do the same. Within minutes, several coolheaded souls organized all hands to repel boarders, which was just the right thing to do. We all felt that we were ready to make a contribution, while in fact we were prevented from further screwing things up below.

We stayed put until after daylight, following the action as it unfolded. During that interminable wait, I managed to acquire a Thompson submachine gun and several magazines of .45-caliber bullets for it. The last time I had handled a weapon such as that Thompson had been right after our arrival in Samoa, three years earlier, when VMF-111 had been responsible for guarding the beach off Tafuna I was not sure I could reload the weapon, but I knew how to pull the trigger. (I kept thinking, some Marine you turned out to be, Porter!)

While the shooting spree below continued without let-up, we could discern that it became steadily more organized as the raiders were painstakingly hunted down. The scene was pretty well lighted by huge gasoline-dump fires as well as fuel from burning airplanes parked along the edge of the northeast-southwest runway. Also on that runway were parts of one or several of the crashed Japanese airplanes.

I received a number of calls during the dark hours and on into the first daylight hours, but they were not particularly illuminating. It had to wait for the afternoon of May 25 before I received anything like definitive news. It was terrible to be so close to such intense action—to see it unfold in blazing detail—without having a real clue as to what was happening.

★

What had happened was that the Japanese mounted a suicide commando raid against Yontan, the only such airborne assault of the Pacific War.

At about 2000, two R5Cs in the landing circle were shot at by what their crews took to be two Japanese fighters that must have crept in beneath our radar curtain. Next, at 2110, a Japanese bomber dropped six bombs, but they were off target to the northeast of the base. Another bomber bracketed MAG-31 headquarters at 2204 with at least seven bombs. It was during this period that VMF(N)-533 scored four of its five kills.

The fifth VMF(N)-533 night kill—Lieutenant Dellamano's third of the evening—was a Sally twin-engine bomber that was flamed at 2220. Five minutes later, another Sally approached Yontan at very low altitude and was shot down by antiaircraft fire. Five minutes after that, at 2230, three more Sallys flew into the landing pattern and, without question, tried to land on the northeast-southwest runway. All three were downed over or near the runway. (This was about the time I was pulling off my boots. I had landed just after the MAG-31 Command Post was bracketed and just before the first Sally was downed by Lieutenant Dellamano.)

At least two commandos survived the destruction of the knot of three Sallys, and they started fires at two small fuel dumps east of the runways. (One of these fuel fires might have been the one I saw flare up just as I left my tent.)

Another Sally tried to land, but it was badly shot up and veered off the track. It dropped a wing just before striking the ground, and the wing sheared off an antiaircraft mount. The eight Marines manning the mount were buried alive; two suffocated before help arrived to dig them out.

The fifth Sally to make it over the northeast-southwest runway set up a pretty good belly landing, and at least a dozen commandos scattered from the wreckage. These men managed to make it to the nearby flight lines, where they clamped magnetic grenades to all the airplanes they could approach. Almost immediately, fueled airplanes began blowing up in the MAG-31 dispersal area. Three F4Us were totally demolished, along with two large Navy PB4Y flying boats and four transports. One of the destroyed transports was a brand new R5C that had just arrived from Hawaii. This was the personal plane of Major General James "Nuts" Moore (Greg Boyington's sponsor during our Turtle Bay days in mid 1943). Moore was at that moment Commanding General, Fleet Marine Force Air, Pacific.

In addition to the nine airplanes destroyed, 22 F4Us, three F6Fs, two B-24s, and two transports were damaged, mostly by magnetic grenades.

By far the most spectacular loss was the total of 70,000 gallons of aviation gasoline that was set ablaze by the raiders.

Miraculously, only three Americans died in the raid. These were the two suffocated antiaircraft gunners and the control tower duty officer. I learned the next day that the dead officer was Lieutenant Maynard Kelley of VMF(N)-533. It was not known and could not be determined if he was killed by a Japanese bullet or by one of the many thousands of rounds frantic defenders fired across the base during and long after the period of greatest danger. Eighteen enlisted Marines were wounded during the course of events.

The last of a total of 69 Japanese pilots, aircrewmen, and raiders who actually got in over Yontan was killed about an hour after noon on May 25. Most of the Japanese were incinerated when their airplanes crashed. A few of the dead commandos were clearly suicides. No Japanese was taken alive.

Following up on the suicide commando raid (the only so-called *giretsu* raid of the war), the Japanese mounted day-long *kamikaze* strikes. Our day fighters, including a newly landed Air Corps P-47 group, downed a confirmed total of 75 of 165 *kamikazes* and escort airplanes sent to Okinawa that morning. A total of eleven Navy ships were sunk or severely damaged by *kamikazes* and at least one torpedo bomber that penetrated our day-fighter screen.

VMF(N)-542's contribution to staving off the raiders came, surprisingly, on the ground. First Lieutenant Clark Campbell, the squadron's nonflying ordnance officer, was in charge of our standby aircraft on the flight line when the *giretsu* began falling into the runway. Clark and several of our groundcrewmen traded shots with several Japanese who tried to penetrate our flight line. The raiders veered off and left our airplanes alone.

All of the mechanics working on the flight line dived into an Army 40mm gun pit as soon as the attack started. However, a pilot from another squadron ordered one of my technicians, Staff Sergeant Jack Kelly, to help man the outer perimeter. Kelly was heavily armed with a pocket knife and a stubby screwdriver, but he did what he was told. A short time later, the officer who had assigned Kelly to man the line was startled by movement in the flickering light of nearby fires, and he simultaneously screamed "Halt!" and fired his .45-caliber pistol. Jack Kelly had his heel shot off, which earned him a trip home.

Next morning, around 0800, a number of my groundcrewmen ventured out to view the remains of several Japanese who had been killed in the fight and to "ooh" and "aah" over the damage to several of our warplanes. One of the last living raiders happened to be hiding out in the landing-gear well of one of the damaged B-24s when my groundcrewmen stopped off to look. He hurled the last of his hand grenades, and it wounded three of my men. One of my mechanics was blinded in both eyes, another was struck in the thigh, and the last got a nick on his ear. Another one of my mechanics dispatched the raider with his .30-caliber carbine.

Later in the day, as I joined the rubberneckers to view the remains of the crashed Sallys and their scorched occupants, I sincerely hoped that I would see all the Japanese I would ever see in the air, where I could handle them.

My number was coming up for that.

36

The three weeks after the *giretsu* raid of May 25, 1945, were absolutely routine. In that time, VMF(N)-542 pilots flying lone-wolf mission destroyed just three Japanese aircraft with the loss of its second (and last) pilot of the war, 1st Lieutenant Fred Hilliard. On the afternoon of June 20, while on an early patrol, Fred shot down a Japanese warplane right over Okinawa, but he was lost minutes later after reporting that he had spotted and was attacking a second enemy aircraft. We all believed the quarry's rear gunner got Fred.

I flew my share of the lone-wolf missions, but I was never vectored against a target during that three-week period.

★

June 15, 1945, was not a particularly noteworthy day. I received a letter from Pat Leimert, my fiancee, but all she really had to say was that I was approaching my twenty-fifth birthday in August. That only got me to wondering if I would live that long.

Early in the day, my flight officer, Captain George Gelsten, told me that I was slated to fly nightcap from 2000 hours until midnight. This pleased me because half the squadron's kills had been scored during this active period. As I suited up for my patrol, I had an all around good feeling, but I could not decide why. Pat's letter, I supposed.

The night was completely dark; there was no moonlight whatsoever and an extremely thick cloud cover.

I checked my airplane in the darkness, just as I always did before a mission, but that was more customary than practical; I could not see very much. My plane captain, Technical Sergeant G. M. Stanley, helped me on with my harness and told me that my radar and radios were in top working order. He gave me a thumb's up and yelled in my ear, "Good luck, Major!" just before jumping off the wing.

I ran up the engine to check the magnetos. Everything there was fine, so I released the brakes and taxied slowly to the pitch-black runway. I told the tower that I was ready to go, and I was given immediate clearance to take off. I pushed the throttle lever forward and took my feet off the brakes. Within seconds, I was rapidly gaining speed. My feet worked the rudder pedals to keep me on an even keel, and I slowly pulled back on the joystick. I became airborne with plenty of room to spare. As I cleared the abyss at the seaward end of the east-west runway, I retracted *Black Death*'s landing gear and prepared to climb.

Shit!

For no reason I could fathom, nervous antiaircraft gunners aboard several of the numerous transports and warships anchored beyond the cliffs opened up on my night fighter. I had been ready to ease off the power, but I kept the throttle on full power and jinked around to the right in a very tight turn, pulling heavy G's all the way. The tracers did not even come close to my tail as the gunners tried to follow the sound of my engine in the pitch darkness. My heart was hammering in my chest. I thought that I was going to get to 25 the hard way if this nonsense kept up. When I had a moment to spare, I shook my fist at the fleet I was aloft to protect and reoriented myself toward my patrol station.

As I headed out over the empty sea, I listened intently to the sound of *Black Death*'s engine and felt for unusual vibrations through the seat of my pants. Everything sounded and felt fine. Then I fiddled with the instrument lights to set them where they would be most comfortable for my vision in this night's total darkness. I tested each of my radios, primary and spare. All okay there. My radar was perfect, too. I armed my four .50-cals and two 20mm cannon and test-fired them—first the machine guns with one trigger, then the cannon with the other trigger; just a squirt from each to reassure me that they would fire when I needed them. My fuel supply was normal.

As had become my habit, I said a little prayer of thanksgiving for the wonderful, dedicated people who had come into my care and who returned my good feelings and hopes by looking after me.

I reported my position to my GCI officer on Ie Shima, the same Handyman to whom I had reported on my first operational flight in mid May. Procedure dictated that Handyman not respond until he had read my IFF (Identification, Friend or Foe) signal, an automatic emission of changeable radio pulses that were keyed to his master radar set. Anything flying that did not emit a proper IFF signal was considered a bogey, an enemy contact.

"Hello, Topaz One from Handyman. Vector 120, angels 10, and begin CAP [combat air patrol]. Report when at altitude. Roger and out."

I was already in a climb and passing through 6,000 feet when the order arrived. I turned to the new course and continued to climb to my patrol altitude.

"Handyman from Topaz One. Angels 10. Starting CAP. How's business tonight?"

"Topaz One from Handyman. Pretty quiet. I bet it's black up there tonight."

I told him that it was indeed black. On clear nights, I had often been able to see signs of night battles between our ground forces and the island's remaining Japanese defenders. And I had once seen a distant fiery explosion in an adjacent sector when, I suppose, one of our night fighters scored a kill. But on the night of June 15, there was solid cloud between me and the ground, though I was safely above the weather.

I flew lazy circles for the next 45 or 50 minutes. Without help from Handyman, there was little chance of my finding a target. I did remain vigilant in the event the Japanese sneaked one of their night fighters onto my trail.

Suddenly, my GCI officer called excitedly, "Hello, Topaz One from Handyman. I have an unidentified bogey for you. Target range 30 miles at 10 o'clock. Angel 13. He's indicated 170 knots. Handyman out."

Well. That started my adrenalin flowing. The intruder had 3,000 feet on me and was quickly closing. I dropped my belly tank and threw the throttle all the way forward, which added considerable power by engaging the water-injection system. This was good for an extra 15-knot burst of speed in emergencies. I also increased the engine RPM and nosed up into a steep climb. I made sure my guns were armed.

While one part of my mind was attending to putting *Black Death* in a position to score a kill, I reflected on something Jeff Poindexter had observed aloud during a recent get-together. I had failed to note, during my first combat tour at Guadalcanal and the Russells, that I had scored a kill every time I had shared the sky with Japanese aircraft. I had protested to Jeff that that observation hardly rated a response since I had had the honor on only three days. Still, my mind went to Jeff's point as soon as the GCI officer announced the intruder. I found myself muttering "Don't screw up now, Bruce."

The GCI officer reeled off the distances. Fifteen miles, ten miles, six miles.

"Hello, Topaz One from Handyman. Target range three miles at 11 o'clock. Bearing one-one-owe [110 degrees]. Target crossing your screen. Go!"

I changed course and muttered aloud, "Steady, Bruce. This is it."

If Handyman had vectored me correctly, I would be turning right onto the bogey's tail. If not, I was going to be flying up nothing but empty sky.

I flipped on my finder as I came out of the turn. (The radar was on, but we kept the screen off to preserve night vision until we knew a target was out there.) My eyes became riveted to the orange scope on my instrument panel.

Nothing there yet. I was glad to note how cool I was. This was just like a textbook practice mission, of which I had flown hundreds. I was on full instruments and radar. All I needed to do was remain steady and do what my instruments and Handyman told me to do. If I trusted in the system, I would be coaxed into a perfect firing position. If the Hellcat could have flown itself, there would have been no need for me.

I did precisely what I was told, totally without ego.

Bango! My scope indicated a tiny orange blip at the very top. I was dead on target. The bogey was straight ahead. It had been a letter-perfect vector.

"Handyman from Topaz One. Contact!" I winced slightly when I heard my voice crack with excitement. I would rather have shown a better brand professionalism.

I watched as the blip got larger and closer to the center of the radarscope, which represented my position. The bogey remained dead ahead, flying straight and level, as I crept up on its tail.

My ghost blip, which indicated the bogey's altitude relative to me, rapidly clarified itself. It appeared that the bogey was just a little higher than *Black Death*.

I flicked my eyes up to see if the target was as yet in sight. I thought I saw something so, after one more check of the scope, I peered at a slight ripple of movement dead ahead and slightly above my direct line of sight. A second or two later, I knew I was staring at the bogey's exhaust flame.

My long training with similar practice approaches gave me ample reason to believe that the bogey was only about 350 feet ahead of me. He was within *Black Death*'s boresighted firing cone. I flew in a little closer in order to positively identify him as an enemy warplane and to learn precisely what I was facing. I was certain that he was a Ki45 Nick twin-engine night fighter. Thus, there was an outside chance that he would be able to find me before I could open fire.

I climbed slightly to get right over him and then marginally increased my speed to close up. If he did not detect me and did not change course, this was going to be a sure kill.

As I nosed down slightly to bring all my guns to bear, I decided to fire everything in my armory. When I was in the best possible position and only 300 feet from the target, I gently squeezed both triggers. My .50-calibers roared and the 20mm cannon blew off rounds in a surprisingly slow, steady manner: *Bonk*... *Bonk*... *Bonk*.

My initial target was the right engine and right side of the fuselage, where some fuel was bound to be stored. *Black Death*'s outpouring of lead had a literal buzzsaw effect upon the enemy airplane.

I eased off the 20mm because of a limited supply of ammunition, but I kept putting .50-caliber armor-piercing and incendiary rounds into the fuselage. I wanted him to burn so I would know beyond a doubt that I had scored a kill. Licks of flame showed up on the leading edge of the wing. Then a fiery orange tongue swept back over the fuselage. Suddenly, the twin-engined Kawasaki stalled and lurched heavily to the right. My rounds poured into her vitals. I saw tracer strike the canopy. I doubt if the pilot ever knew what hit him.

It was over in about two seconds.

When the Nick nosed over and fell away toward the sea, he was wrapped in flames from nose to tail.

Okay! My fourth confirmed kill.

The GCI officer brought me back. "Hello, Topaz One from Handyman. He's off my scope at 2118. Great work."

I looked at my watch and thought I was taking it calmly.

Handyman brought me back to the center of my patrol sector and left me cutting lazy circles in the sky.

I needed the time to collect myself. As soon as the thoughtful flying was over, as soon as I was parked in orbit, my heart leaped against my ribs. Oh, joy! I had been at bat four times and I had definitely downed four of the enemy. I paused a moment to dedicate this kill to my departed comrade, Jack Amende, who had not once scored in his many combat missions.

Without knowing quite what led me to it, I began thinking about the efficacy of the night-fighter program. I had been steadily training for the kill I had just scored for fourteen months. I knew that some of my fellow night stalkers in 542 and the other squadrons would never score, despite in every case over a year of preparation. Given the resources we had committed to the night-fighter program, we had not scored all that many kills at night. I was not then (and am not now) certain that we had much effect on the outcome of the war. Certainly, we were not effecting the war as much as the very thin day squadrons composed mainly of tyros had in the latter half of 1942. The successful completion of all the missions flown by all the enemy planes we had thus far destroyed over or around Okinawa would not have had an overall negative effect on the outcome of the Okinawa Campaign and, certainly, of the war. We had done good things, I knew then, but I could not help musing on what it took to score even one night kill. Again, given the resources engaged in night work, I had nevertheless just become a member of a minuscule fraternity. As far as I knew, the Marine Corps had yet to produce one exclusive night-fighter ace—that is, a pilot who scored five kills only during night missions. (The Marine Corps' only pure night ace, Captain Bob Baird, of VMF(N)-533, was exactly a week away from his fifth and sixth night kills.)

On the other hand, I also realized that the thrust of the night-fighter program was aimed at putting up 'round-the-clock protection during the projected invasion of Japan, which was set to begin, we were all certain, between late August and late September. Perhaps, I mused, the all-out, 24-hour air assaults we expected to meet in Japan were the justification. Perhaps all the operational night patrols leading to that climax were meant to shake us down, to prepare us for the ultimate confrontation. My own use of a mixed armory incorporating 20mm cannon was an experiment aimed at refining our killing capacity. It was, I realized, still too early to reach conclusions. Early? We were still really infants.

I played tag with my mind that way for about an hour without ever really lowering my vigilance, which was so ingrained that I swear I kept it up on the ground.

★

I heard from Handyman again almost exactly an hour after he had called out the first bogey.

"Hello, Topaz One from Handyman. I've got another bogey for you."

Wow! A double night contact! As far as I knew, this was only the fourth such the squadron had encountered since deploying on Okinawa in mid April. Two of the three double contacts had resulted in dead night stalkers.

"Handyman from Topaz One. Roger that. Out." Damn! My voice had again cracked under its burden of excitement.

"Topaz One from Handyman. Bogey at Angels 14. Indicated 180 knots. Vector 145 at Angels 13."

This guy was coming through high and fast. I would have to race him to the projected contact point.

"Handyman from Topaz One. On my way."

I pushed the throttle forward to get the water injection going, then I hauled back on the stick to rush to the required altitude. Even with luck, I was facing a stern chase. I had the speed advantage, but it would take time to close on him because I had to use most of my power to climb.

As I climbed, I realized that I might face a problem with friendly antiaircraft. Our courses looked like they might converge right near the edge of the fleet's free fire zone. Any airplane overhead was fair game for fleet gunners, except at rigidly designated times (such as during our night changeovers, I grumped, as I vividly recalled my hot reception over the fleet earlier that evening). It was clear from the vector that the bogey was going to try to strike the fleet. This led me to briefly consider that he might be a *kamikaze*, but that was doubtful because suicide missions were rarely launched at night, and even more rarely by lone aircraft. Most likely, he was a bomber, possibly a multiengine bomber with a firm target.

I reached 13,000 feet and leveled off for my approach. Ahead, I could see fingers of light reaching into the black sky— searchlights. Farther on was Okinawa's west coast.

Suddenly, it seemed as if I would not overtake the bogey in time to set up an approach and a good shot before he reached the point where I would be forced to abort my run. Earlier in the month, one of our pilots, 1st Lieutenant Bob Peterson, had locked onto a Nick but had been thrown around when a friendly antiaircraft round had burst beneath his Hellcat. Bob had not been able to reacquire the target; he had been lucky just to survive his encounter with the fleet. There was no way that I was going fly into the fleet's antiaircraft pattern. No way!

But I was not out of the running yet. I flew up to 14,000 feet per Handyman's instructions (he must have thought at the outset that the bomber would drop down once it neared the fleet, but it did not). As I leveled off, I saw that my full power setting had brought my speed up to 260 knots, or 300 miles per hour. As with all tail chases, it seemed to take an eternity to note any relative progress. Handyman kept reading off the closing distances, and I kept monitoring the rapidly approaching pillars of light from the anchorage ahead.

"Topaz One from Handyman. You're closing fast. Range about three quarters of a mile. Target at one o'clock and flying straight ahead. Go!"

I flipped on my finder for the second time that night. The scope flared orange. The bogey was right at the top of the scope and just a little way down toward the one o'clock position.

"Handyman from Topaz One. Contact!"

My closure rate was now too fast. If I kept it up, I would overshoot before being able to line up my gunsight. I eased back on the throttle, but the blip remained too large. Maybe he was throttling back too.

Then I saw flames from the exhaust stacks. He was definitely a twin-engine airplane, but it was still too early to identify the type. The twin flickering exhaust flames seemed about to leap through my windscreen.

The real danger was that he was a bomber with a vigilant rear machine gunner. If there was a stinger, I stood a good chance of being shot out of the sky.

I dropped down a little so the bogey would be silhouetted against the dark canopy overhead. As dark as the sky was, the solid airplane would stand out against it.

My quarry was definitely a Betty medium bomber, a fast, maneuverable thoroughbred. It had a stinger, all right!

Something at the corner of my attention noted that the Betty was carrying an external load on its belly. I thought it might be a so-called Baka bomb, a manned rocket-propelled suicide missile typically hauled to the target by a mother plane—the Betty—and dropped. (The Japanese called it an "Oka" which means cherry blossom, but we called it "Baka," which means stupid.)

There was no time to dwell on the accuracy of my surmise. Someone might see me and the Betty might get away.

I drifted upward a bit to get a good belly shot. By the time I reached a comfortable height, I had closed to within 250 feet. I put the illuminated gunsight pipper right between the body of the aircraft, right beneath the flight deck and the right engine. Then I slowly squeezed both triggers.

For the second time that night, *Black Death*'s .50-calibers roared, and the 20mm cannon slowly spit its flaming popcorn-ball rounds. The tracer and the popcorn balls fell right into the target area.

After only a second or two, the wing fuel tanks ignited in a garish explosion, and the sky in front of my windscreen was filled with an expanding ball of flaming fuel. I instinctively ducked as pieces of the Betty scraped along *Black Death*'s wings and fuselage. Then I dived away as the first fingers of friendly tracer reached up around me from the darkened fleet beneath *Black Death*'s wings. I caught a momentary flash as the Betty's cargo—the Baka bomb—blew up. I supposed, if it was a Baka bomb, that the flames had reached its volatile propellant.

Burning sections of the bomber and the bomb floated down to the surface of the sea, where they were quenched.

"Handyman from Topaz One. Did you get the picture on your scope?"

"Topaz One from Handyman. Roger that. Congratulations. The time is 2226 on confirmation. It's a kill, Topaz One. Resume patrol."

He brought me back to my patrol sector and left me hanging for an hour, until my relief was on the way. I got a heading that would bring me back to Yontan, and a friendly "good night." It was then 2335. I would be on the ground by midnight.

★

I made a routine landing at Yontan, right on time, and taxied up to *Black Death*'s revetment. I was surprised to see that a crowd was gathered just off the flight line.

The first person to greet me was my plane captain, Technical Sergeant Stanley. He shook my hand and patted me on the shoulder. Next up was our flight surgeon, Dr. John Ellis. "Congratulations, Skipper, on your double header. Why don't you come to my tent now? I have a surprise for you."

By then, other pilots and the groundcrewmen on duty that night had crowded around to shake my hand and offer their good wishes. It was all a bit overwhelming.

Once Doc Ellis got me alone and into his tent, he emptied numerous two-ounce medicinal brandy bottles into a pair of tumblers. We clanked glasses, offered one another good health, and swallowed it all down.

Before I got to sleep that night, I heard from the squadron armorers that I had fired a total of 500 rounds of .50-cal and 200 rounds of 20mm for both kills. Since the squadron average was 785 rounds per kill, I was thus the squadron champ for kills per rounds fired—less than half the average. I chalked that up to having the 20mm cannon on board.

What a night! Handyman and I had scored a rare double night kill, and I had fulfilled my fondest ambition as a fighter pilot. I was an Ace!

Epilogue

I never again shared the sky with a Japanese warplane.

I commanded VMF(N)-542 until August 31, 1945. I was on the job when both atomic bombs were dropped and on VJ Day, August 14, 1945. On August 19, I was on the sidelines when two white Betty bombers landed on Ie Shima with the Japanese peace delegation, which was on its way to the Philippines to negotiate peace terms with General Douglas MacArthur.

I left VMF(N)-542 on August 31 to take a job as the MAG-31 supply officer, a long overdue staff assignment that eventually befell every pilot ranked captain and above. At least my turn came after the close of hostilities, just before the formal surrender aboard the battleship *Missouri* in Tokyo Bay.

I flew into the Imperial Navy airbase at Yokosuka on September 3, 1945, with the rest of the MAG-31 headquarters staff. We were among the first operational Marine air units to get onto a Japanese airfield. We oversaw the destruction of the Japanese naval air forces. On September 5, I borrowed a VMF-441 Corsair— the first I had flown in over a year—and fulfilled another longstanding ambition by flying over Fujiyama's snowclad peak. It was a rare thrill of a lifetime to do so. I swung over Nagasaki and Hiroshima on the way back to Yokosuka and was overcome by the devestation I viewed from 1,500 feet.

My long overseas service was rewarded by early detachment from MAG-31 in mid December, 1945. I managed to scrounge a ride home aboard a destroyer escort which was being sent back for an early mothballing near San Francisco.

Pat and I were married during my leave, and then we departed for duty at Cherry Point, where I spent half of 1946 helping to demobilize squadrons and pilots. I had always intended to remain in the Regular Marine Corps, but Pat became pregnant, and I was offered a good job by my father-in-law, a real estate developer who was preparing to sell new homes to the scores of thousands of veterans who would be seeking new post-Depression, postwar opportunities in warm, sunny Los Angeles County. I reluctantly reverted to Reserve status on July 25, 1946, exactly five years after receiving my Wings of Gold and my commission.

I was to spend another 15 years proudly wearing the Wings of Gold I had earned in mid 1941. I finally retired from the Marine Corps Reserve with the rank of colonel in 1960. I would have stayed longer, but a business transfer simply moved me beyond driving range of any active Reserve base, and I could not see the point of holding an inactive commission when there were younger men who might make better use of the rank.

I worked in the oil industry from 1950 to 1975, when I took early retirement to undertake some private business ventures.

One of the warmest experiences of my retirement took place in St. Louis in May, 1977, when many of my VMF(N)-542 comrades held the first of our regular squadron reunions after a 32-year separation.

I have remained an active pilot since my first days at Pensacola. No life I can imagine could have been more fulfilling or any happier than the one I have lived.

Among the proudest of all my possessions are two: my Navy Wings of Gold and my title of Ace.

BIBLIOGRAPHY

Olynyk, Dr. Frank J. *Victory List No. 1: USMC Credits for the Destrucion of Enemy Aircraft in Air-to-Air Combat, World War 2.* Aurora, OH: Frank J. Olynyk, 1982.

Sherrod, Robert. *History of Marine Corps Aviation in World War II.* San Rafael, CA: Presidio Press, 1980.

Tillman, Barrett. *Corsair: The F4U in World War II and Korea.* Annapolis: Naval Institute Press, 1979.

    Hellcat: The F6F in World War II. Annapolis: Naval Institute Press, 1979.

    The Wildcat in WWII. Annapolis: Nautical & Aviation Publishing Company of America, 1983.

The *New York Times* bestselling saga of the proudest profession

BROTHERHOOD OF ☆ WAR ☆

by W.E.B. Griffin

Spanning three decades and four magnificent military careers, the BROTHERHOOD OF WAR is a saga of love, loyalty, victory, and betrayal in the epic tradition of *The Winds of War*. A hit for its spine-tingling adventure, you-are-there realism, and larger-than-life heroes!

____Brotherhood of War I, The Lieutenants   0-515-09021-2/$3.95

____Brotherhood of War II, The Captains   0-515-09138-3/$3.95

____Brotherhood of War III, The Majors   0-515-08995-8/$4.50

____Brotherhood of War IV, The Colonels   0-515-09022-0/$3.95

____Brotherhood of War V, The Berets   0-515-09020-4/$3.95

____Brotherhood of War VI, The Generals   0-515-08455-7/$4.50

WAR BOOKS
FROM JOVE